VISUAL QUICKSTART GUIDE

MICROSOFT®
OFFICE
POWERPOINT®
2003

FOR WINDOWS®

Rebecca Bridges Altman

Revised for this edition by
Rick Altman

 Peachpit Press

Visual QuickStart Guide
Microsoft® Office PowerPoint® 2003 for Windows®
Rebecca Bridges Altman

Peachpit Press

1249 Eighth Street
Berkeley, CA 94710
510/524-2178
800/283-9444
510/524-2221 (fax)

Find us on the World Wide Web at http://www.peachpit.com.
To report errors, send a note to errata@peachpit.com.

Peachpit Press is a division of Pearson Education

Senior Aquisitions Editor: Linda Anne Bump
Tech Editors: Echo Swinford
              Laurie Ulrich
Senior Project Editor: Lori Lyons
Copy Editor: Kelli Brooks
Compositor: Gloria Schurick
Indexer: Julie Bess
Cover Design: The Visual Group
Cover Production: Aren Howell

Notice of rights

Notice of liability

Trademarks

International Standard Book Number: 0-321-19395-4

Library of Congress Catalog Card Number: 2003095734

7 6 5 4 3 2 1

Printed and bound in the United States of America

Dedication

Of all the PowerPoint users we know, our favorite is our self-taught, 10-year-old daughter, Erica, whose latest foray into slide-making was an electronic birthday card for her mother. She even knew to go easy on the checkerboard transitions! We have no doubt that her younger sister Jamie will be working her wipes and fades in no time...

—Rebecca and Rick Altman

Acknowledgments

We suppose that it is too much to salute all 17 million who include themselves in the estimate of daily users of Microsoft PowerPoint. So we'll limit it to the tens of thousands who actively help create community: those who participate in the various online newsgroups, who willingly share backgrounds and templates with one another, who ask of and answer questions from fellow users, and those who are signed up to attend our inaugural PowerPoint Live User Conference in October of 2003.

In addition, we salute the invaluable contributions made by our technical editors, Echo Swinford and Laurie Ulrich, and by the entire Peachpit team: Cliff Colby, Senior Editor; Linda Bump, Senior Acquisitions Editor; Becky Morgan, Editor; Lori Lyons, Senior Project Editor; Julie Bess, Indexer; and Gloria Schurick, Compositor.

Special thanks go to Echo Swinford, who assisted with the text revisions and screen shots during author review.

CONTENTS AT A GLANCE

	Introduction	xiii
Chapter 1	Introducing PowerPoint	1
Chapter 2	A Quick Tour of PowerPoint	13
Chapter 3	Creating Text Slides	33
Chapter 4	Inserting Charts	59
Chapter 5	Formatting Charts	75
Chapter 6	Creating Pie Charts	99
Chapter 7	Using Organization Charts and Diagrams	117
Chapter 8	Creating Tables	133
Chapter 9	Adding Graphical Objects	159
Chapter 10	Importing Graphics	179
Chapter 11	Manipulating Graphical Objects	193
Chapter 12	Making Global Changes	211
Chapter 13	Working in Outline View	229
Chapter 14	Working in Slide Sorter View	243
Chapter 15	Producing a Slide Show	255
Chapter 16	Applying Animation	273
Chapter 17	Using Sound and Video	293
Chapter 18	Taking Your Show on the Road	305
Chapter 19	From Screen to Toner: Printing Your Presentation	321
Chapter 20	Presenting on the Internet	335
	Index	351

TABLE OF CONTENTS

Introduction   **xiii**

Chapter 1:   **Introducing PowerPoint**   **1**

Getting Creative with PowerPoint 2
The PowerPoint 2003 Interface 4
Using PowerPoint Menus 6
Using Toolbars 7
Using Shortcut Menus 8
Using Task Panes 9
Getting Help 10
Using Undo 11

Chapter 2:   **A Quick Tour of PowerPoint**   **13**

Launching PowerPoint 14
Choosing a Template 16
Choosing a Layout 17
Creating a Bulleted List 18
Creating a Chart 19
Choosing a Chart Type 21
Formatting a Chart 22
Navigating a Presentation 23
Saving, Opening, and Closing Presentations 24
Printing a Presentation 26
Using Normal View 27
Using the Outline Pane 28
Using Slide Sorter View 29
Using Transitions and Animation 30
Viewing a Slide Show 31

Chapter 3:   **Creating Text Slides**   **33**

Choosing a Text Layout 34
Entering Text into a Placeholder 35
Creating a Text Box 36
Manipulating Text Placeholders 37
Moving Text 38
Using the Spelling Checker 40
Correcting Mistakes Automatically 41

Working with Smart Tags 42
Changing Case 43
Correcting Style Inconsistencies 44
Numbering a List Automatically 46
Choosing Bullet Shapes 47
Adjusting Bullet Placement 49
Changing the Font 50
Adding Text Effects and Color 51
Aligning Paragraphs 53
Formatting a Text Placeholder 54
Controlling Line and Paragraph Spacing 55
Copying Formatting Attributes 57

Chapter 4: Inserting Charts   59
Launching Graph 60
Chart Terminology 61
Creating a Chart Slide 62
Entering Data 64
Importing Data 65
Linking Data 66
Choosing a Chart Type 67
Inserting Titles 69
Inserting Data Labels 70
Repositioning Data Labels 71
Revising a Chart 72
Creating Two Charts on a Slide 73

Chapter 5: Formatting Charts   75
Formatting Charts 76
Formatting the Legend 77
Repositioning the Legend 78
Changing the Color of a Data Series 79
Filling a Data Series with Textures or Patterns . 80
Filling a Data Series with a Graphics File 82
Formatting Data Markers 84
Inserting/Removing Gridlines 86
Formatting Gridlines 87
Formatting Tick Marks 88
Scaling the Axis 89
Formatting Axis Numbers 91
Formatting Chart Text 92
Adjusting 3D Effects 93
Formatting the Plot Area 95
Choosing a Custom Chart Type 96
Defining a Custom Chart Type 97
Applying a User-Defined Chart Type 98

Chapter 6: Creating Pie Charts 99

Inserting a Pie Chart Slide 100
Entering Pie Data 102
Showing Data Labels 103
Using Leader Lines......................... 104
Formatting Data Labels 105
Exploding a Slice........................... 107
Coloring the Slices 108
Rotating a Pie 109
Formatting 3D Effects...................... 110
Resizing and Repositioning a Pie 112
Creating a Doughnut....................... 113
Creating Linked Pies 114
Entering Data for Linked Pies............... 115

Chapter 7: Using Organization Charts and Diagrams 117

Using an Organization Chart 118
Using the Diagram Objects 120
Editing the Organization Chart
    Diagram Object 121
Creating a Custom Flowchart or Diagram 126
Formatting Box Text 128
Formatting the Boxes 129
Formatting the Connecting Lines 130
Zooming In and Out 131

Chapter 8 Creating Tables 133

Inserting a Table Slide 134
Entering Text into a Table 136
Selecting Cells 137
Adjusting Column Width.................... 138
Adjusting Row Height...................... 139
Inserting Rows and Columns................ 140
Deleting Rows and Columns 141
Formatting Table Text...................... 142
Adding Borders............................ 144
Drawing Table Borders 147
Shading Table Cells........................ 148
Aligning Text within a Cell.................. 150
Inserting a Word Table 152
AutoFormatting a Word Table............... 155
Entering Formulas 157

TABLE OF CONTENTS

Chapter 9: **Adding Graphical Objects** **159**

Drawing Lines 160
Formatting Lines 161
Drawing Arrows 163
Formatting Arrows 164
Adding Connector Lines 165
Drawing Rectangles and Ovals 166
Creating Polygons and Freehand Drawings 167
Using AutoShapes 169
Customizing AutoShapes 170
Filling an Object with Color 171
Filling an Object with a Pattern 172
Filling an Object with a Graphics File 174
Adding a Shadow 175
Adding 3D Effects 177

Chapter 10: **Importing Graphics** **179**

Using the Clip Organizer. 180
Using Clip Art 183
Searching for Clip Art 185
Finding Clip Art on the Web 187
Inserting Graphics Files 188
Inserting Multiple Graphics Files 189
Embedding Graphics 190

Chapter 11: **Manipulating Graphical Objects** **193**

Using Rulers and Guides. 194
Using Grid Snap 195
Snapping to Shapes 196
Zooming In and Out 197
Displaying a Slide Miniature 198
Aligning Objects. 199
Spacing Objects Equally 200
Grouping Objects 201
Copying Object Attributes 202
Recoloring a Picture. 203
Scaling an Object 204
Cropping a Picture 206
Changing the Stacking Order 208
Rotating Objects. 209
Flipping Objects 210

Chapter 12: **Making Global Changes** **211**

Changing the Default Colors 212
Creating a Gradient Background 214
Creating a Two-Color Gradient. 216

Replacing a Font 218
Editing the Slide Master 219
Inserting a Title Master. 220
Using More Than One Master 221
Changing the Default Format for Text 222
Adding Graphics 223
Inserting Footers. 224
Applying a Template 226

Chapter 13: Working in Outline View   **229**
Using Outline View 230
Outlining a Presentation 231
Creating Bulleted Lists 232
Collapsing and Expanding the Outline 233
Rearranging and Deleting Slides 235
Hiding and Displaying Formatting 237
Importing an Outline 238
Creating a Summary Slide 240

Chapter 14: Working in Slide Sorter View   **243**
Using Slide Sorter View. 244
Zooming In and Out 245
Creating a Summary Slide 246
Reordering the Slides. 247
Copying Slides 248
Deleting Slides. 250
Copying Slides Between Presentations 251
Inserting an Entire Presentation. 253

Chapter 15: Producing a Slide Show   **255**
Organizing a Slide Show 256
Displaying a Slide show. 258
Navigating to a Slide 259
Creating Action Buttons. 260
Creating a Return Button 262
Creating Custom Shows 263
Viewing a Custom Show 264
Creating an Agenda Slide 265
Annotating a Slide 267
Creating a Self-Running Slide Show. 269
Rehearsing the Slide Show 270
Taking Notes During a Slide Show. 271

Chapter 16 Applying Animation   **273**
Adding a Transition Effect to a Slide. 274
Applying Preset Animations 276
Modifying Animations 278

TABLE OF CONTENTS

Animating a Bulleted List. 279
Fine-Tuning an Animation. 282
Using Triggers 286
Animating Charts. 288
Animating the Slide Masters 290
Overriding Animation on the Slide Master 292

Chapter 17: Using Sound and Video   **293**
Inserting Movie Clips. 294
Playing Back Your Clips. 296
Adding Sounds 298
Playing CD Sound Tracks 300
Using the Clip Organizer to Play Sounds and
    Movies. 302

Chapter 18: Taking Your Show on the Road   **305**
Showing Your Presentation on
    Another Computer 306
Using PPS Files 311
Viewing a Slide Show when PowerPoint Is
    Nowhere to Be Found 313
Packaging Your Presentation on CD 314
Sending Out for Review 316
Creating Password-Protection 319

**Chapter 19: From Screen to Toner: Printing Your
               Presentation**   **321**
Selecting a Printer 322
Previewing Slides in Grayscale. 323
Printing Slides 324
Formatting Handout Pages 326
Printing Handouts 327
Stopping a Print Job. 328
Printing the Outline. 329
Adding Speaker Notes. 330
Editing the Notes Master 332
Printing Speaker Notes 333
Creating a PDF File. 334

Chapter 20: Presenting on the Internet   **335**
Linking to a Web Site 337
Saving a Presentation to an FTP Site 341
Creating a Web Page 343
Saving a PowerPoint File for the Web 344
Previewing a Slide Show in a Web Browser 348

Index   **351**

INTRODUCTION

Visual QuickStart Guides offer a unique way to learn software. Most of the pages in this book are self-contained, presenting single topics with concise step-by-step instructions on how to perform certain tasks.

The text is accompanied by illustrations and explanatory captions that help you find your way. This type of organization makes learning a complex program such as Microsoft PowerPoint less overwhelming and allows you to master just the features you need.

At the end of most topics, you'll find lists of helpful tips. These tips provide you with shortcuts, alternative techniques, additional information, and related topics. Some of these tips are undocumented or buried so deep in the documentation that it's unlikely you would ever find them.

We author types would love to believe that you would read this book cover to cover, so riveted by our engaging prose that you couldn't put it down. In the real world, devoid of delusions, you will probably just turn to the specific chapters or topics you want to learn about, and the way this book is organized, you will be able to do so quickly and efficiently.

What's in This Book

This book covers the latest versions of PowerPoint for Windows; however, it is 95% applicable for the previous version and largely relevant for Macintosh users.

New users of PowerPoint might want to begin at Chapter 1 and learn the latest version of PowerPoint with all of its current features. This first chapter introduces you to presentation graphics and PowerPoint's capabilities.

If you consider yourself a quick study, you might prefer to dive into Chapter 2, our Quick Tour, which is like flying a helicopter over the program. Chapter 2 is a great way to learn the main features of PowerPoint, especially if you have a presentation that needs to be out the door yesterday.

Chapters 3 through 8 explain how to create different types of slides (bulleted lists, charts, tables, and organization charts) and format your presentations.

Chapters 9, 10, and 11 cover the colorful world of graphics and the challenges and opportunities that await those who seek to bring tasteful visual variety to their work.

Chapter 12 is required reading for all, as it covers the important topics of global formatting, including working with Slide Masters and presentation-wide defaults.

Chapters 13 and 14 illustrate two additional ways to view and organize presentations: Outline view and Slide Sorter view.

Chapters 15 and 16 focus on what many consider the meat and potatoes of good presentations: creating good navigation and effective animation and preparing for the actual running of your slide show.

Chapter 17 introduces you to the sometimes scary, often risky, and always fun opportunities to add sound and video to your work.

Chapter 18 is a one-stop shop for learning about the issues of presenting while on the road, whereas Chapter 19 covers the often-overlooked questions of how best to make printouts of your slides.

Finally, Chapter 20 covers the many avenues available for using the Internet as a medium for your presentations.

✔ Tip

- The new version of Microsoft Office for Windows is called Office 2003, and the individual applications in the suite are version 11.

Thumbnail miniatures

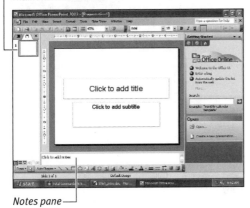

Notes pane

Figure i.1 The Normal view of PowerPoint 11.

Toggle tabs

Figure i.2 By alternating between two tabs, you can toggle between the old Outline view and a new Slide Thumbnail view.

Figure i.3 In addition to viewing the text outline, you can view and drag thumbnails of your slides within Normal view.

First Impressions

When you open PowerPoint and add a new slide, you are in Normal view. This view displays elements on both the right and left columns of the screen (**Figure i.1**).

The tab on the left side of the screen toggles between Slide Thumbnail view and Outline view. You can use these thumbnails to locate slides by their visual content (**Figure i.2**). Also, you can click and drag the thumbnails the same way you move your content in Outline or Slide Sorter view (**Figure i.3**).

New Features

Many Office users skip versions and others barely get around to learning new features when it's time to upgrade again. Therefore, our introduction includes a roundup of features that were added to PowerPoint 2002.

PowerPoint 2003 is not exactly a maintenance update; neither is it a major upgrade. The program is faster, smarter, and a bit more stable, but it does not boast a dizzying number of new features. We welcome that—it gives us a chance to catch up on the new features of the previous version that we never got around to using! If you're like us, you'll welcome the subsequent review of features that were added to PowerPoint 2002.

NEW FEATURES

New to PowerPoint 2003

The biggest news in the current release is the addition of an updated Viewer utility. This applet allows a non-PowerPoint user to view your presentation without having the software. The Viewer itself is not a new concept, but it has not seen an update in more than five years—thus new transitions and animations added since then have not been viewable. The new Viewer can show anything you can whip up in PowerPoint 2003.

The Viewer is part of the Package for CD command, which is also new—at least in name. The old Pack and Go has been eliminated, but much of its functionality has been integrated into Package for CD. In fact, that command is misnamed, as you can do much more than burn files onto a CD. **Figure i.4** shows the dialog box; we predict you'll click the Copy to Folder button just as often as you click the Copy to CD button, after you discover it.

Other new features include the following:

◆ The Research Task pane. This handy service lets you look up pretty much anything, from animations in PowerPoint to amusements at a county fair (**Figure i.5**). This new Task pane also offers a thesaurus.

◆ Windows Media Player Support. PowerPoint 2003 offers better integration with the latest release of Media Player.

◆ Send to a fax service. The entire Office 2003 suite of applications supports the sending of a document directly to an Internet-based fax service.

◆ New pen options. It is easier and more flexible to create annotations in the middle of a slide show. You can even opt to save the annotation as a graphic object on the slide.

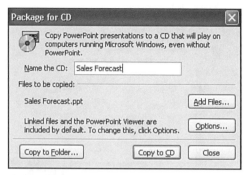

Figure i.4 The Package for CD command offers more than you'd think, with the capability to gather and copy all elements of a presentation to a local folder or network drive.

Figure i.5 The new Research Task pane can help you with your next presentation or your next vacation.

◆ And one of our favorites, you can now press Shift+F5 to begin a slide show at the current slide. With earlier versions, the only way to do that is to click on one of those tiny, migraine-inducing icons at the lower-left of the application window.

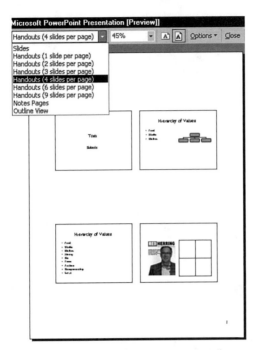

Figure i.6 In the Print Preview area, you can easily use the drop-down menu to see various types of output, including slides with multiple layout choices, notes, and handouts.

Figure i.7 The Office 2003 clipboard holds 24 objects, which are displayed as thumbnails in the task pane to make them easier to paste into a slide.

New to PowerPoint 2002

Some of the new features in the Windows version are common to all the applications in the Office XP suite, and others are particular to PowerPoint.

◆ Automatic Layout. For example, let's say you've created a bulleted list in a slide with a simple title and bullet layout. Then you decide that one of the new diagram options would effectively illustrate the points in your list. When you insert the Diagram object, PowerPoint will automatically alter the layout of your slide to accommodate the diagram.

◆ Multiple Masters. You can create more than one set of masters to apply globally to a presentation. For instance, you can have a set of masters for presenting the slides and a second set for printing them.

◆ Print Preview. Before you print your handouts, notes, or slides, you can use Print Preview to view them in different formats (multiple slides per page, outline, notes, and so on) (**Figure i.6**).

◆ Multiple Monitors or Projectors. For large-scale presentations, PowerPoint 2002 added support for the use of a second monitor, on which presenters might consult their speaker notes.

◆ Anti-aliasing of Text Fonts. This long-awaited feature of PowerPoint 2002 smoothes out fonts and other onscreen elements, such as lines, shapes, rectangles, and ellipses.

◆ Windows Clipboard. The Office XP clipboard holds 24 items, and its contents are visible in its own task pane for quick import (**Figure i.7**).

When you paste an item from the clipboard into a PowerPoint slide, a Smart Tag offers further formatting choices (**Figure i.8**).

Other Smart Tags appear if you change a layout, offering you an additional drop-down menu with more context-appropriate options (**Figure i.9**).

Design Enhancements

PowerPoint 2002's graphics features make pictures easier to use on the Web or in notes, or to move, place, and manipulate them more efficiently.

◆ Compression. The Office XP Compress Pictures technology makes your presentations smaller and easier to transport without compromising quality.

◆ Rotation. You can flip and rotate images more easily within your slides, in addition to resizing them.

◆ Visible Grid. Added to PowerPoint's alignment and spacing options is a visible and user-definable grid to help you lay out a diagram or slide more precisely (**Figure i.10**).

Internet Improvements

PowerPoint 2002 promised improved stability for Webcasts and more options, including support for Netscape Navigator 4. The most notable new feature was the Web Querying. Suppose you want to *really impress* an audience with the very latest data—maybe the sales figures from your warehouse up to five minutes ago? Office 2002 includes a Web Query in Excel that refreshes the data with a click of the mouse. As long as the data resides on a Web page, you can use the Excel Web Query as linked data to a PowerPoint slide.

Figure i.8 The drop-down menu that accompanies the Paste icon when an object is inserted from the clipboard is known as a Smart Tag.

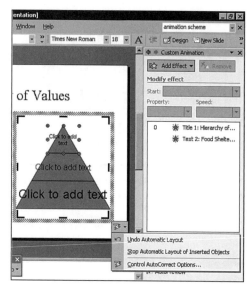

Figure i.9 The new Smart Tags give you a quick way to undo formatting choices or implement other changes.

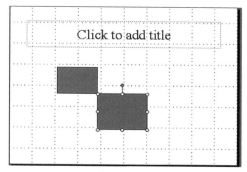

Figure i.10 The new grid option lets you more precisely align objects on your slides.

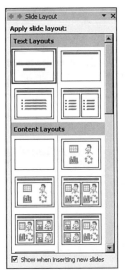

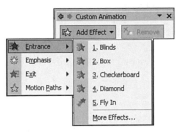

Task Panes

In Normal view, PowerPoint 2002 offers task panes—drop-down menus containing formatting choices.

The Slide Layout task pane appears when you start the program or add a slide (**Figure i.11**).

Figure i.11 Within any content placeholder, you can choose to add a table, chart, picture, gallery clip art, media clip, or diagram.

The new PowerPoint 2002 layouts were reorganized within the Slide Layout task pane into four main areas: Content, Text, Text and Content, and Other (insert media, tables and the older organizational chart).

The Slide Design task pane (**Figure i.12**) integrates the three main design options: Design Templates, Color Schemes, and Animation Schemes.

The Custom Animation task pane lets you fine-tune animation and alter the timing of various objects and elements (**Figure i.13**). New options include Emphasis, Exit, and Motion Paths. Depending on the display capabilities of your system, you can also implement bitmap rotation and levels of transparency in these effects.

Figure i.12 The new Slide Design task pane lets you quickly add a background design, color scheme, or combination of effects to objects in one or more slides.

Figure i.13 The new Custom Animation choices include slide Entry, Emphasis, Exit, and Motion Paths to more precisely manage movement of objects.

NEW TO POWERPOINT 2002

Content Options

Content includes most of the graphical elements that can go into a slide. The icons in the Content area of the Slide Layout task pane let you choose among tables, charts, diagrams, pictures and clip art (**Figure i.14**). Clicking the Picture icon lets you insert any picture from anywhere on your computer.

The Content area also lets you access the Clip Organizer. It lets you easily import your own content from any folder on your computer (**Figure i.15**).

The other main content choices are instantly available: table, chart, media clip, and the new organizational chart/diagram.

The Diagram Gallery provides some interesting charts that you can easily customize and animate to communicate complex ideas (**Figure i.16**).

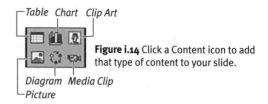

Figure i.14 Click a Content icon to add that type of content to your slide.

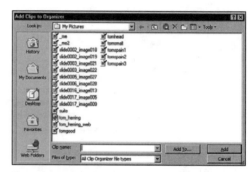

Figure i.15 It's a lot easier to add material to the new Clip Organizer from any folder or from the default folder, My Pictures.

Figure i.16 The new Diagram Gallery offers charts that help illustrate complex ideas.

INTRODUCING POWERPOINT

What exactly can presentation graphics software do? It lets you tell your story visually; and in today's "just-tell-me-what-I-need-to-know" business climate, that can spell the difference between success and failure

Furthermore, it lets you tell your story in a way that a conventional graphics program cannot. If a picture is worth a thousand words, then a PowerPoint presentation might be worth five thousand, as you get to interact with your audience in a robust environment:

◆ You decide what gets shown to your audience and how.

◆ You decide what to emphasize and how to emphasize it.

◆ You choose the order in which elements are introduced.

◆ And you determine the pace of the entire experience.

It is no wonder that an estimated 15 million users turn to PowerPoint at some point in their weekly business activities. Just about every industry can find a reason to create presentations.

Presentation graphics software like PowerPoint can take elements from many sources to create a presentation. As a PowerPoint user, you can use the tools built into the program to create content for your slides, or you can import elements from other programs.

Getting Creative with PowerPoint

PowerPoint gives you everything you need to create slides with a variety of different formats, such as bulleted lists, numeric tables, and organization and business charts (pies, bars, and lines, among others).

You also can easily add graphics to your slides. For example, you can create designs for your slides using the Rectangle, Oval, and Line tools.

If you aren't artistically inclined, don't worry—you can always insert a ready-made drawing from the clip-art library, or you can use a professionally designed template (**Figure 1.1**).

PowerPoint can convey your message visually in several ways: as an onscreen slide show (complete with special transition effects); on paper (one image per page, or several per page for audience handouts); output to 35mm slides; as a Web page or series of pages; or as a self-contained, stand-alone CD.

You can easily revise your graphics content right up until the time it is presented, and you can customize your slides for any specific audience. A bit of restraint is advised in that department, as it is easy to get carried away and continue to tweak a presentation until it is nothing more than an over-designed, over-animated beast. With the proper self-control, however, you can create a balanced, professional presentation and maintain complete control over it until the moment you are ready to deliver it.

Figure 1.1 The graphical objects on this slide were produced by applying a professionally designed template.

Figure 1.2 Outline view shows the structure of your presentation, letting you easily reorganize the presentation if necessary.

PowerPoint offers convenient ways to organize the presentation. Using the Outline view (**Figure 1.2**) or Slide Sorter view (**Figure 1.3**), you can see the structure of the presentation and reorganize the slides easily.

A presentation program presents graphics—it makes your point or tells your story visually. That's why PowerPoint is an excellent choice for all of these tasks.

✔ Tips

- Slide Sorter view lets you see many slides at once, but you can also view more than one slide using the Slide icon. Click the Slide icon in the left pane, and you can see a thumbnail view of your slides while you work on the current slide.

- From this same view, you can enlarge the Notes area to create your own speaker notes and have room on the right side for the task pane to show you one of several specific tasks (such as applying animation or designs). With a sufficiently high-resolution display, you can perform almost every task without changing views.

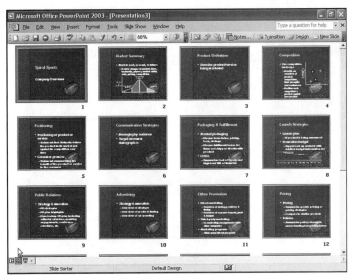

Figure 1.3 Slide Sorter view displays small images of the slides and lets you move them around at will.

GETTING CREATIVE WITH POWERPOINT

The PowerPoint 2003 Interface

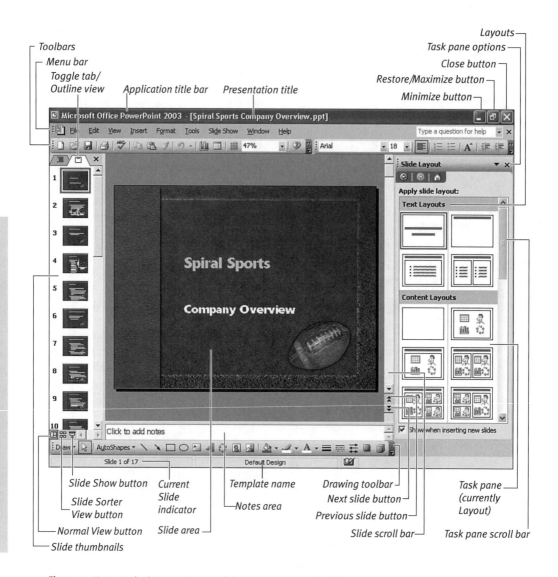

Figure 1.4 Here are the important areas of the PowerPoint window (Normal view). For further information on any of these areas, refer to the key on the opposite page.

Application title bar Displays the name of the current application (Microsoft PowerPoint).

Presentation title Shows the name of the current presentation.

Minimize button Shrinks the application to a button on the taskbar.

Restore/Maximize button Enlarges the window so that it fills the screen. When the window is maximized, the Restore button is displayed; this button restores the window to its previous size.

Close button Closes the window.

Menu bar Contains the range of menus. Clicking a menu name displays a drop-down menu.

Toolbars Contain buttons for frequently used tasks, such as opening, saving, and printing.

Slide thumbnails In Normal view, Slide Thumbnail view alternates with the Outline view when these tabs are clicked.

Toggle tab/Outline view You can access Outline view to organize the text in your presentation by clicking this tab.

Drawing toolbar Contains buttons for drawing and formatting objects.

Normal View button Simultaneously displays the slide area where you can work, an outline that you can revise, and notes for the speaker or audience.

Slide Sorter View button Displays zoomable thumbnails of each slide; lets you see many slides at once and apply formatting to any of them.

Slide Show button Presents the slides one at a time in an onscreen slide show.

Current Slide indicator Indicates the number of the slide currently on the screen.

Template name Displays the name of the current template (design). Double-clicking this area lets you apply another template.

Notes area An area in Normal view where you can enter speaker notes for the current slide.

Slide area The work area where you create, format, and modify slide elements.

Slide scroll bar Displays other slides in the presentation.

Previous Slide button Displays the previous slide in the presentation.

Next Slide button Displays the next slide in the presentation.

Note: The Scroll bar and Previous and Next Slide buttons are visible only when there is more than one slide.

Task panes Let you quickly apply layouts or designs to the current slide.

Task pane options Let you move quickly to other common editing features.

Layouts Automatic formats and placeholders for slide elements.

Task pane scroll bar Navigation tool for the current task pane.

THE POWERPOINT 2003 INTERFACE

Using PowerPoint Menus

You can choose options on the PowerPoint menu bar just as you do in any other Windows application. In their factory settings, however, Office applications menus work a bit differently: They automatically modify themselves as you use them. When you first display a drop-down menu, you see an abbreviated list of the most frequently used options (**Figure 1.5**). This short menu saves you from having to wade through a list of options that you rarely use.

If you don't see the option you want, just pause for a few seconds and the complete list will appear (**Figure 1.6**). If you then choose one of these secondary commands, it will automatically appear on the initial list in the future. (And over time, options you have stopped using will drop off the initial menu.)

✔ Tips

- Many Office users do not like the abbreviated menu system, which can be disabled by going to Tools > Customize > Options > Always Show Full Menus (**Figure 1.7**). If you change that setting in any Office 2003 application, it will change for all applications.

- If you prefer giving commands with the keyboard instead of the mouse, you'll want to use the many shortcut keys that are available. For example, instead of choosing Edit > Select All, you can press Ctrl+A. All menus show their available hotkeys.

Indicates that some of the commands are hidden

Figure 1.5 Use the initial abbreviated menu for frequently used options.

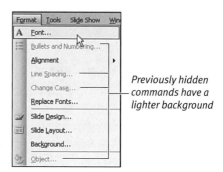

Previously hidden commands have a lighter background

Figure 1.6 You can choose more options from the expanded menu.

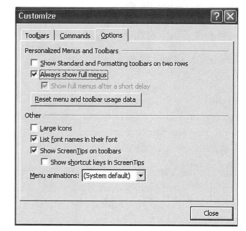

Figure 1.7 If you don't like the abbreviated menu system, eliminate it.

More Buttons icon

Figure 1.8 Click the More Buttons icon to select a tool not currently on the toolbar.

Figure 1.9 These additional buttons are displayed.

Standard toolbar

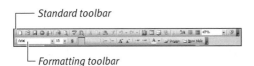

Formatting toolbar

Figure 1.10 After you drag it down, the Formatting toolbar appears on its own line.

Figure 1.11 Another way to separate toolbars onto their own lines.

Using Toolbars

PowerPoint has toolbars for drawing, outlining, creating tables, formatting text, formatting pictures, adding animation effects, and more. You can turn these toolbars on and off, depending on your needs.

To display or hide a particular toolbar:

1. Choose View > Toolbars.

2. Select the toolbar you want to display or hide.

PowerPoint 2002 offers dynamic toolbars that automatically update to reflect the buttons you use most often. (You might notice that the screen images throughout this book gradually change, as we ourselves work the product.)

To use the dynamic toolbars:

1. Click the More Buttons icon (**Figure 1.8**) to see additional icons (**Figure 1.9**).

2. Select the icon you want to use. It will automatically be added to the toolbar.

✔ Tips

- You can toggle toolbars on and off by right-clicking on any part of any toolbar. A list of all toolbars will display, and you can check or uncheck any toolbar from there.

- The Standard and Formatting toolbars are combined on one line, but you can separate them by clicking the left edge of the toolbar (the cursor will change to a four-way arrow) and dragging down until the Formatting toolbar jumps down onto a line of its own (**Figure 1.10**).

- Another way to change the toolbars is to choose Tools > Customize > Options. You can choose to have your Formatting and Standard toolbars separated onto two lines (**Figure 1.11**).

Using Shortcut Menus

A shortcut menu lists the most common commands pertaining to a selected object (**Figure 1.12**). These menus are commonly referred to as context menus (because they show commands that are relevant to the task at hand) and right-click menus (because that is how you access them). Options on a shortcut menu vary depending on what is selected. If nothing is selected, a menu with options for formatting your presentation will appear.

To display the shortcut menu:

1. Hover your mouse pointer over an object.

2. Press the right mouse button (**Figure 1.12**).

Right-click anywhere along the edge of this text box... *...to get a shortcut menu like this*

Figure 1.12 This Shortcut menu displays all of the commands you might want to use on a block of text.

USING SHORTCUT MENUS

Click here to cycle through recently used task panes   *Click here to change the task pane*

Click here to close the task pane

Figure 1.13 One of the many task panes available in PowerPoint.

Using Task Panes

Many of the most common formatting options in PowerPoint are accessible through task panes, which pop up on the right side of the screen. **Figure 1.13** shows the Custom Animation task pane that appears when you issue the command to add animation to an element. In this case, the title and subtitle have had animations applied to them.

You can also view the various task panes by clicking the drop-down menu on the top of the task pane.

Some of the task pane options are also available from the shortcut menu; others are found only within the appropriate area in a task pane.

You will become more familiar with the features in the various task panes as you perform specific tasks in PowerPoint.

USING TASK PANES

Getting Help

As with all Windows applications, when in doubt, you can press F1 for Help. But Office 2003 applications provide you with a different front door—the so-called Assistance page (**Figure 1.14**). If you type a keyword or two into the Assistance text box, PowerPoint will search all of microsoft.com for you. Otherwise, click Table of Contents to navigate the traditional way.

You can also go to Help > Show the Office Assistant to display the usually cute and often annoying animated helper. The Assistant is handy for typing a freeform query (like "how do I animate bullets"), but most users prefer to use the Type a Question for Help box on the menu line. It does the same thing with a bit less fanfare.

Figure 1.14 The new Assistance pane in Help.

Figure 1.15 The Undo button is handy for those really big messes that you make.

Using Undo

PowerPoint offers plenty of opportunity for you to fix boo-boos—up to 99 times. So, even if you make a lot of mistakes, you may be able to backtrack step by step. There are three ways to Undo:

1. Choose Edit > Undo.

2. Press Ctrl+Z.

3. Use the handy Undo icon in the toolbar (**Figure 1.15**); this gives you a drop-down history of your recent actions.

✔ Tips

■ If you perform an Undo and then decide to undo your Undo, you can issue the Redo command: Edit > Redo or Ctrl+Y.

■ The Undo history button must be used in order. For example, if you change a font, add a transition, and then change the page size, you cannot undo the transition without first undoing the page size change. You do the action by walking in; you undo it by backing out.

■ On major projects, you may also want to save incrementally, which means saving different stages of your project with different names. As you make design decisions, you can always return to a previous version.

USING UNDO

A Quick Tour
of PowerPoint

Suppose you need to create a set of charts by the end of the day, but you have never used PowerPoint. Don't panic—just by reading this chapter, you'll learn the most important things you need to know about creating a presentation in PowerPoint. One of the things you might discover is that learning the mechanics of PowerPoint really isn't that hard—it's no wonder that many millions of people use the product. However, you might also discover that learning how to create an attractive and effective presentation is an altogether different challenge—it's no wonder that so many people create so many bad-looking slides.

After taking the quick tour in this chapter, you'll be able to create bulleted lists and charts, format your slides, print them, run an onscreen slide show, and use the Outline and Slide Sorter views to reorganize a presentation.

You'll also learn how to use simple animation, and when to use it effectively.

This chapter gives you the bare-bones information—for details, turn to the referenced chapters. To create presentations that are not overdone and that will not embarrass you takes lots and lots of practice!

Launching PowerPoint

You can launch PowerPoint in a number of ways, depending on how your system is set up. But just about every user can start the program by doing this:

To launch PowerPoint:

◆ Click the Start button, point to or click All Programs, click Microsoft Office, and then click Microsoft Office PowerPoint 2003 (**Figure 2.1**).

PowerPoint opens, with the Getting Started task pane in the right column (**Figure 2.2**).

The task panes are important elements introduced in PowerPoint 2002. Click the arrow at the top-right corner to see some of the other task panes that are available (**Figure 2.3**).

You will be using some of the other task panes regularly, so take a look at how they work (**Figure 2.4**). To access task panes when they are closed, simply select View > Task Pane.

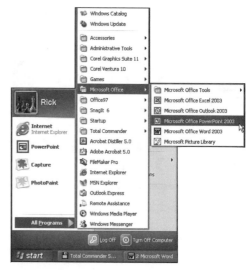

Figure 2.1 Choose Microsoft Office PowerPoint 2003 from the All Programs menu.

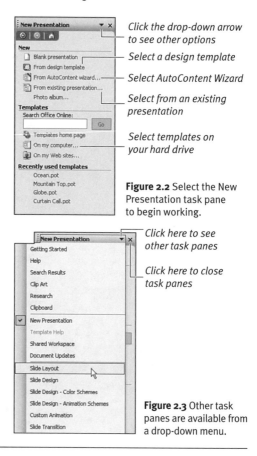

Click the drop-down arrow to see other options

Select a design template

Select AutoContent Wizard

Select from an existing presentation

Select templates on your hard drive

Figure 2.2 Select the New Presentation task pane to begin working.

Click here to see other task panes

Click here to close task panes

Figure 2.3 Other task panes are available from a drop-down menu.

LAUNCHING POWERPOINT

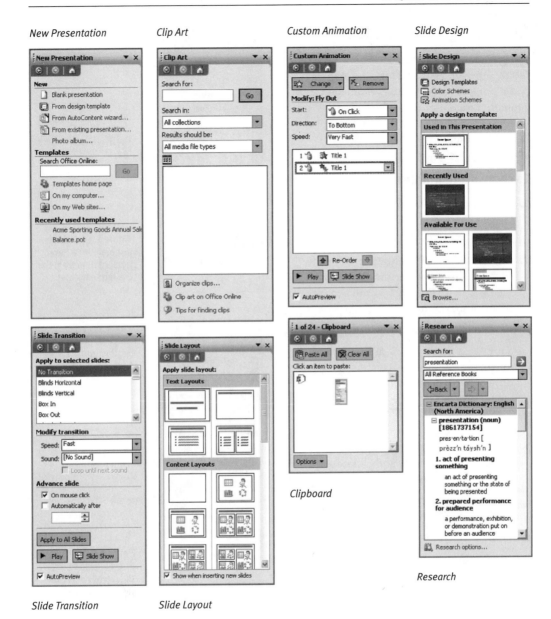

Figure 2.4 The task pane system opens many formatting options.

Choosing a Template

A template controls the look of your presentation—the colors, the format, the graphics placed on each slide. It can even include content. PowerPoint comes loaded with dozens of templates, and there are literally tens of thousands available in the user community, many for free.

To choose a template:

1. When you open PowerPoint, the Getting Started task pane appears in the right column.

2. Choose the New Presentation task pane from the drop-down arrow at the top of the task pane (**Figure 2.2**) and choose From Design Template.

3. Browse the Available for Use section.

   You can also click Browse at the very bottom of the task pane to navigate your hard drive or network drives for more templates.

4. Select the Design Templates tab (**Figure 2.5**).

5. When you find a template you like (like Ocean.pot), right-click and choose Apply to All Slides (**Figure 2.6**).

   To learn more about templates, see Chapter 12, "Making Global Changes."

✔ Tips

- Content options and the AutoContent Wizard give you suggestions regarding the text and design of your slides.

- You can start with a Content or Design template and customize it for your own use by using the techniques in this book.

- You can use any presentation file as a template for creating another, including presentations that you have already created. Just click Browse to find it.

Figure 2.5 Choose a template for a new presentation from the Design Templates window.

Figure 2.6 You can apply a new design to one slide, a few selected slides, or to all slides.

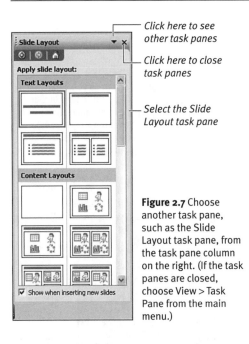

Click here to see other task panes

Click here to close task panes

Select the Slide Layout task pane

Figure 2.7 Choose another task pane, such as the Slide Layout task pane, from the task pane column on the right. (If the task panes are closed, choose View > Task Pane from the main menu.)

Choosing a Layout

PowerPoint offers various layouts to help you define and place the elements you want on a slide, such as a bulleted list, a chart, a table, or an organization chart.

To choose a layout:

1. Choose a layout from the Slide Layout task pane. If task panes are not open in the right column, choose View > Task Pane and then choose the Slide Layout task pane (**Figure 2.7**).

2. Click the desired layout to apply it to the current slide.

✔ Tip

■ With the Slide Layout task pane, you can request a new slide and a specific layout together. Pick the desired layout, click the drop-down list, and choose Insert New Slide. PowerPoint creates a new slide with that layout.

Creating a Bulleted List

A bulleted list is one of the most common slide types used in presentations. It helps organize your information into short, understandable segments. When you create a new bulleted list slide, the text and title areas display placeholders surrounded by dotted lines.

To create a bulleted list:

1. Choose Insert > New Slide, click the New Slide button on the toolbar, or press the hotkey Ctrl+M.

2. From the Slide Layout task pane, choose the Bulleted List layout (**Figure 2.8**).

3. Click the title placeholder and type the title of your bulleted list.

4. Click the text placeholder and type your bulleted text (**Figure 2.9**). Follow these simple rules:

   ▲ Press Enter to type another bullet.

   ▲ Press Tab to "demote" the bullet to the next level down.

   ▲ Press Shift+Tab to "promote" the bullet up one level.

Note in **Figure 2.9**: When typing bullets, PowerPoint assigns a dark background to the typing area to make it easier for you.

✔ Tips

■ To change the bullet shape, choose Format > Bullets and Numbering. See Chapter 3, "Creating Text Slides," for more information.

■ If you change the Navigation pane on the left to Outline view, you can enter bulleted text there or directly onto the slide.

If you don't see the options you want, use the scrollbar

Figure 2.8 Choose a layout as you create a new slide. To see the layout options, move the mouse over the icon. If you don't see the layouts, click the options arrow.

Bullet and title slide in the task pane

Title placeholder

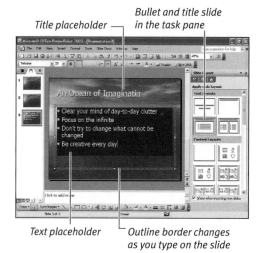

Text placeholder   *Outline border changes as you type on the slide*

Figure 2.9 Select a bullet and title layout for a new or existing slide, and a bulleted list slide will appear before any text has been added.

CREATING A BULLETED LIST

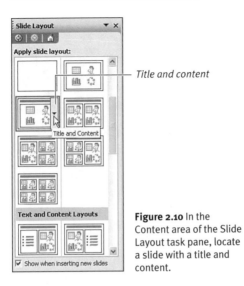

Title and content

Figure 2.10 In the Content area of the Slide Layout task pane, locate a slide with a title and content.

Figure 2.11 Add a title to your slide.

Click here for a chart

Figure 2.12 Click the little image of the bar chart in the Content box.

Creating a Chart

Instead of showing your audience columns and rows of numbers, use a chart to illustrate your data graphically. PowerPoint offers a wide variety of chart types—line, column, area, and pie are a few examples.

When you create charts in PowerPoint, you actually use the Microsoft Graph program, included with Office.

To create a chart:

1. Click the New Slide button on the toolbar, or choose Insert > New Slide (Ctrl+M).

2. From the Slide Layout task pane, select the Title and Content layout (**Figure 2.10**).

3. Click the title placeholder and type the title of your chart (**Figure 2.11**).

4. Click the small bar chart in the Content box (**Figure 2.12**).

continues on next page

CREATING A CHART

5. You can now enter your data into the Microsoft Graph datasheet. As you do, watch the chart change interactively (**Figure 2.13**).

Note that you have to delete the sample data in the datasheet and replace it with new data in order to see the chart change.

6. To close the datasheet and view the chart, click the "x" in the datasheet window, or just click outside the chart on the slide.

Your chart with new data is now in the slide's content placeholder (**Figure 2.14**).

✔ Tips

■ Chart remembers if the datasheet was visible from your last editing session, and if it was, it redisplays the datasheet. If not, click the View Datasheet button.

■ Sometimes double-clicking a selected object doesn't work because you are still in Microsoft Graph. Just press the Esc key and reselect or try again.

■ If you erase over existing data, make sure to delete columns that were used in the sample data but not in your chart. Otherwise, Chart might consider that column part of the chart. To delete a column, place your cursor in a cell in that column, right-click, choose Delete, and choose Entire Column.

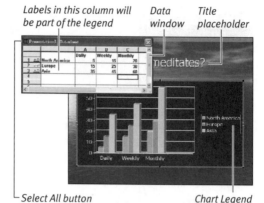

Labels in this column will be part of the legend — *Data window* — *Title placeholder*

Select All button — *Chart Legend*

Figure 2.13 A new slide with a sample bar chart appears, as well as a datasheet with sample data. Enter your chart data in the datasheet.

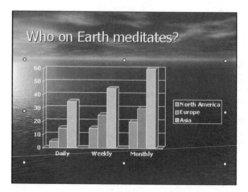

Figure 2.14 When you have revised the datasheet and title, you have a new slide with a chart like this one.

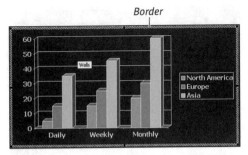

Border

Figure 2.15 The border around this chart indicates that you are in Microsoft Graph.

Select a chart type...   ...then choose a sub-type

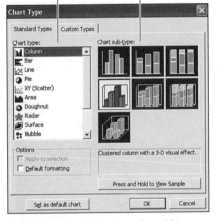

Figure 2.16 Select a chart type from this dialog box.

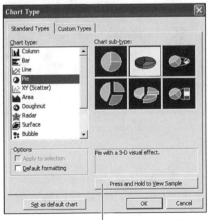

Click here and hold to see how the data will look

Figure 2.17 Select another chart type to change the view of the data.

Choosing a Chart Type

To format a chart, you must still be in Microsoft Graph. To determine whether you are in Graph, look for a border with diagonal lines around the chart (**Figure 2.15**). If you aren't in Microsoft Graph, double-click the chart placeholder.

To change the chart type:

1. While working in Microsoft Graph, choose Chart > Chart Type.

   The Chart Type dialog box appears (**Figure 2.16**).

2. To change the chart, choose a different type and sub-type (**Figure 2.17**).

3. Click and hold the Press and Hold to View Sample button for a preview of the new chart type.

4. Your data will appear in the new chart type instead of the placeholder. If it meets with your satisfaction, click OK.

✔ Tips

- You can select the chart type either before or after you fill in the datasheet.

- All relevant charting commands are on the shortcut menu (the right-click menu) as well as on the Chart menu.

- If you use one type of chart frequently, you can make it the default by clicking Set as default chart (**Figure 2.17**).

Formatting a Chart

To format an element on a chart, just double-click to select the chart and then double-click the item you want to format. The appropriate Format dialog box will then appear. For example, suppose you want to place the legend at the bottom of the chart.

To format the legend:

1. Working in Microsoft Graph, point to the legend with the mouse; you will see a ToolTip indicating that you are about to select the legend (**Figure 2.18**).

2. Double-click the legend to display the Format Legend dialog box (or right-click and choose Format Legend).

3. Select the Placement tab (**Figure 2.19**).

4. Choose the Bottom radio button.

5. Click OK.

   Figure 2.20 shows the chart with the legend placed at the bottom.

   See Chapter 5 for information on formatting charts. See Chapter 6 for information on formatting pie charts.

✔ Tips

■ Some of the chart elements are so close together that it is difficult to select the one you want. To make sure you have selected the element you want, read the ToolTip that appears when you point to an element.

■ Many chart elements have sub-elements, and it may be difficult to select only the part of the chart you want to change. For instance, after clicking on the legend to select it, click again on one of the categories within the legend to select just it. Now, any formatting you do will be applied just to that one category.

■ To move a legend, just drag it to a new location with your mouse.

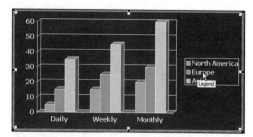

Figure 2.18 When you point to an object, a ToolTip appears with the name of the object.

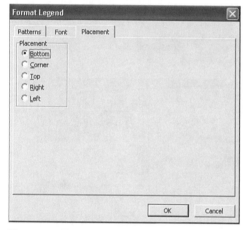

Figure 2.19 Choose a placement option from the Placement tab of the Format Legend dialog box.

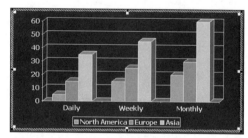

Figure 2.20 The legend now appears at the bottom of the chart.

■ To exit Microsoft Graph, click the slide outside of the chart placeholder.

■ To reload Microsoft Graph, double-click the chart on the PowerPoint slide.

FORMATTING A CHART

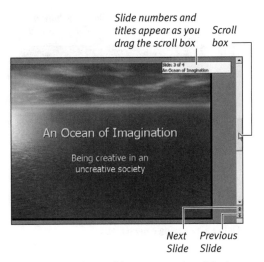

Slide numbers and titles appear as you drag the scroll box

Scroll box

Next Slide   Previous Slide

Figure 2.21 Use the scroll bar to go to other slides in the presentation.

Table 2.1

Navigation Keys	
To Move To	Press
Next Slide	Page Down
Previous Slide	Page Up
First Slide	Ctrl+Home
Last Slide	Ctrl+End

Navigating a Presentation

The status line at the bottom of the PowerPoint window indicates the current slide number. The slide numbers and titles also appear as you drag the vertical scroll box (**Figure 2.21**). In Slide or Normal view, you can use the keyboard commands listed in **Table 2.1** to display other slides in the presentation.

You can also use the Next Slide and Previous Slide buttons on the scroll bar. Use the following guidelines when navigating with the scroll bar:

◆ Drag the scroll box to the top of the scroll bar to go to the first slide.

◆ Drag the scroll box to the bottom of the scroll bar to go to the last slide.

◆ Drag the scroll box up or down to go to a specific slide.

✔ Tips

■ In Normal view, you can scroll through the outline or the slide thumbnails and click the slide title you want to see in Normal view.

■ In Normal view, the scroll bar will be to the left of the task pane unless you close the pane.

Saving, Opening, and Closing Presentations

The commands for saving, opening, and closing presentations are on the File menu.

To save a new presentation:

1. Choose File > Save As (Ctrl+S), or click the Save button on the toolbar. With a new, untitled presentation, Save and Save As function the same.

   The Save As dialog box appears (**Figure 2.22**).

2. Type a descriptive name in the File Name text box.

3. If necessary, choose a different disk or folder by navigating the dialog box as you would any standard Windows file dialog.

4. Click Save.

✔ Tip

■ You can do this entire operation from the keyboard, if you prefer (it's often faster). Press Ctrl+S to invoke the Save As dialog box; if necessary, type the path into the File Name box (like c:\my documents\pres), press Enter, type the filename, and then press Enter.

The current folder *The Up One Level button displays the previous folder*

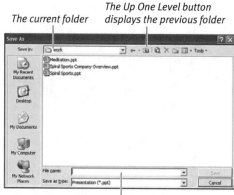

Enter the filename here

Figure 2.22 Saving a presentation.

To open an existing presentation:

1. Choose File > Open, or click the Open button on the toolbar.
   The Open dialog box appears.

2. If necessary, choose a different disk or folder by navigating the dialog box as you would any standard Windows file dialog.

3. Click the name in the list and click Open.

To close the current presentation:

◆ Choose File > Close (Ctrl+F4), or click the Close Window button (the X) in the presentation window. (Of the two Xs at the top-right of the application windows, the lower one closes the current presentation and the top one closes all of PowerPoint.)

✔ Tips

■ The names of recently opened presentations appear at the bottom of the File menu. To open one of these files, just click the name.

■ When saving presentations, don't use names like "My Presentation." Instead, name your files so you will remember what they contain. Presentation filenames can be many characters long and contain several words.

SAVING, OPENING, AND CLOSING

Printing a Presentation

Before showing your final presentation to an audience, you may want to print the slides on paper so you can see and correct any mistakes or use them as handouts for your audience.

To print a presentation:

1. Choose File > Print (Ctrl+P).

   The Print dialog box appears, shown in **Figure 2.23**.

2. Select the range to print.

3. In the Print What box, make sure Slides is selected.

4. Click OK.

   See Chapter 16, "Presentation Output," for more information on printing a presentation.

✔ Tips

- You can also print by choosing the Print button on the toolbar.

  However, this button does not display the Print dialog box. It prints the range last specified, and it doesn't give you a chance to change your print range.

- If you don't have a color printer, you might want to choose Grayscale or Pure Black and White from the Color/grayscale drop-down menu.

- You can preview your print output in various formats in Windows by selecting File > Print Preview.

- Printing successfully from PowerPoint with all of its options often involves trial-and-error. If you own Adobe Acrobat, test your printouts by printing to Acrobat (PDF) files. It is faster and doesn't waste paper.

Be sure to select a print range   Current printer   Click here to select a different printer

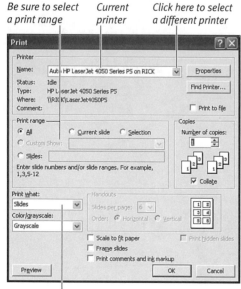

To print full-page slides, make sure the Print What option says Slides

Figure 2.23 Select options from the Print dialog box.

Using Normal View

PowerPoint's Normal view has a view of the current slide, an area for notes, the task pane on the right, and the Slide Thumbnail/Outline pane on the left (**Figure 2.24**).

To use Normal view:

1. Choose View > Normal or click the Normal View button at the bottom of the window.

2. Work on the current slide in the slide pane (the main part of the view).

3. Click the Notes pane and type any speaker notes pertinent to the current slide.

4. To display a different slide, click its title in the Outline pane, or navigate to it with the scroll bar or the Page Down and Page Up keys. (You could also select the slide's thumbnail.)

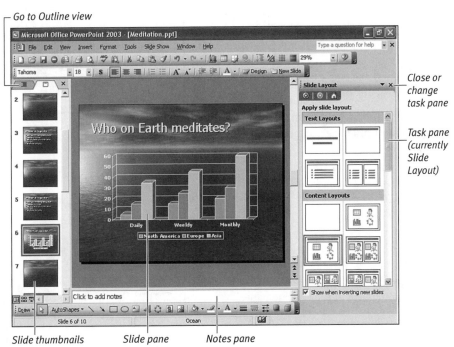

Go to Outline view

Close or change task pane

Task pane (currently Slide Layout)

Slide thumbnails   *Slide pane*   *Notes pane*

Figure 2.24 Use Normal view to display three window areas: the slide, the Notes pane, and the Outline/Slide Thumbnail pane.

Using the Outline Pane

The Outline pane in Normal view (**Figure 2.25**) displays an outline of your presentation that includes the slide titles and any main text, such as bulleted items.

With the Outlining toolbar, you can hide or collapse part of the outline so that you see only the slide titles. Outline view is ideal for seeing the textual structure of your presentation and for quickly adding bullets to existing slides or an entirely new slide of bullets. For reordering slides, it is easier to use the Slide Thumbnails or Slide Sorter view.

To use the Outline pane:

1. Select Normal view and click the Outline tab on the Outline/Slide Thumbnail pane.

2. If the Outlining toolbar is not displayed, choose View > Toolbars > Outlining (**Figure 2.26**).

3. To display only the slide titles, click the Collapse All button on the Outlining toolbar.

4. To redisplay the entire outline, click the Expand All button.

5. To display or hide text formatting, click the Show Formatting button (**Figure 2.27**).

   See Chapter 13, "Working in Outline View," for more information about Outline view.

✔ Tip

- To move a slide, select it by clicking the icon in front of the slide title. Then, click the Move Up or Move Down button until the slide is in its new position, or simply drag it into place in the Outline pane.

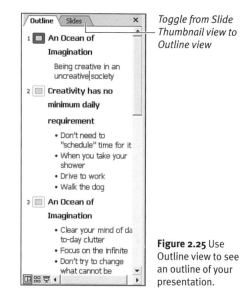

Toggle from Slide Thumbnail view to Outline view

Figure 2.25 Use Outline view to see an outline of your presentation.

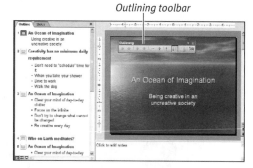

Outlining toolbar

Figure 2.26 The Outlining toolbar provides options for creating outlines directly in PowerPoint.

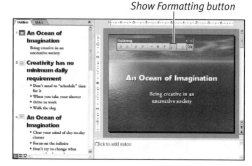

Show Formatting button

Figure 2.27 The Show Formatting choice displays text formats in Outline view.

USING THE OUTLINE PANE

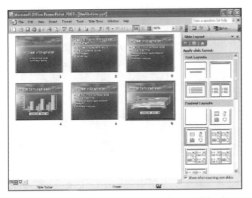

Figure 2.28 You can see miniatures of your slides in Slide Sorter view.

Click in the Zoom box and type any percentage up to 100%...

...or click the arrow and choose a percentage

Figure 2.29 You can zoom in and out while in Slide Sorter view.

Using Slide Sorter View

Slide Sorter view (**Figure 2.28**) gives you the big picture of your presentation. In this view, you can easily reorder, delete, or duplicate slides. The size of the slides in Slide Sorter view can be controlled in the Zoom drop-down, shown in **Figure 2.29**.

To use Slide Sorter view:

1. Choose View > Slide Sorter or click the Slide Sorter View button.

2. To see more slides but less detail, choose a lower zoom percentage in the Zoom field.

   See Chapter 14, "Working in Slide Sorter View," for more information on Slide Sorter view.

✔ Tips

- To move a slide, drag it to a new location.

- To return to Normal view, double-click any slide.

- To select more than one slide, hold down the Shift button while clicking on slides. To select noncontiguous slides, hold down the Ctrl button and click the slides.

Using Transitions and Animation

Transitions and animations are more advanced functions, but they can be very helpful even now, as you are just getting started.

Unobtrusive slide transitions can keep the eyes of your audience on the screen between slides. A simple animation, like a fade or wipe, can introduce your slide elements as you get to them without being too flashy or annoying.

To use transitions or simple animation:

1. Click the Slide Sorter View button.

   All your slides will be displayed as thumbnails (**Figure 2.30**).

2. To quickly add transitions to all of your slides, choose Select All or click Ctrl+A; then choose a transition from the Slide Transition task pane.

   You will see a preview of the effect on the selected slides.

3. To add an animation scheme (for example, having all elements fade in, one at a time), you can select the slides in Slide Sorter view and choose the animation scheme from the Slide Design – Animation Schemes task pane (**Figure 2.31**).

✔ Tips

- Animation schemes are divided into three categories: subtle, moderate, and exciting. You could apply exciting effects to all of your bullets...please don't, lest your audience might think they took a wrong turn and ended up at the circus.

- Animation schemes are complete packaged sequences. (You will learn about customized animations in Chapter 15, "Producing a Slide Show.")

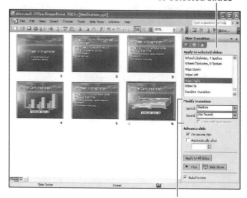

Click one to apply to selected slides

Slide Transition task pane

Figure 2.30 In Slide Sorter view, you can quickly add transitions to selected slides.

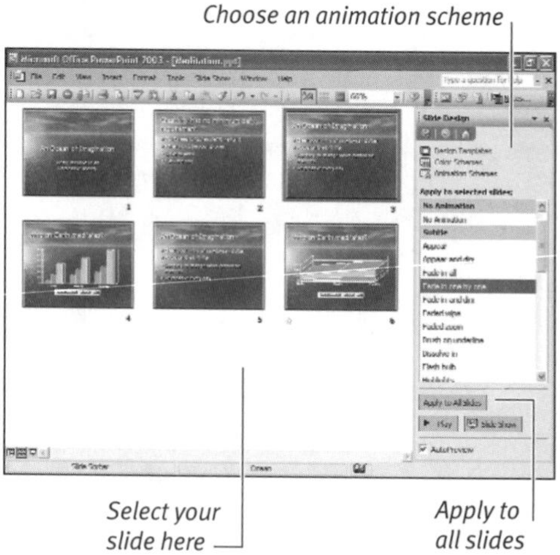

Choose an animation scheme

Select your slide here

Apply to all slides

Figure 2.31 Add an animation scheme to one slide or to all of them.

Viewing a Slide Show

A slide show displays each of the slides in the presentation in sequence in full-screen view. For a large audience, you can project the slide show from a laptop's video output, saving you the time, cost, and trouble of producing 35mm slides (to say nothing about losing out on any animations you have created).

To view a slide show:

1. Choose View > Slide Show, or press F5.

2. To view the next slide, press the space-bar, the Page Down key, the right-arrow key, the down-arrow key, or just click the left mouse button.

3. To cancel the slide show, press Esc.

   See Chapter 15 for additional information on slide shows.

✔ Tips

■ Editing mode and presentation (Show) mode are completely separate. During a slide show, all editing menus and toolbars are invisible and unavailable.

■ To preview a slide show starting with the current slide, click the Slide Show button at the lower-left of the application window.

■ To run a slide show directly from Windows Explorer or My Computer, without launching PowerPoint, just right-click the presentation's filename and choose Show from the shortcut menu.

■ During a slide show, practice advancing to the next slide or element with the right arrow key, and going to the previous slide with the left arrow key.

■ During a slide show, experiment with the right-mouse click to display the Shortcut menu. This gives you the option of marking up your slide or going to any slide by title.

CREATING
TEXT SLIDES

Figure 3.1 A bulleted list slide.

Figure 3.2 A two-column text slide.

In this chapter, you'll learn how to create slides that contain text and how to edit and format the text. The types of slides that consist primarily of text are title slides, bulleted lists (**Figure 3.1**), and two-column text (**Figure 3.2**).

Other slide types combine text with elements such as clip art, charts, or media clips (**Figure 3.3**).

When you create a new slide using the New Slide button on the toolbar or the task pane, PowerPoint's layout options let you efficiently place text and graphic elements in your slide.

Figure 3.3 Text combined with a diagram.

Choosing a Text Layout

When you insert a slide into a presentation, you can choose a layout for the new slide. Of the many layouts for new slides, most have a text placeholder—a container for text. **Figure 3.4** shows some of the layouts that have placeholders for body text.

To create a slide with a text layout:

1. In Slide or Normal view, choose Insert > New Slide (Ctrl+M), or click the New Slide button on the Standard toolbar.

   The Apply Slide Layout pane (**Figure 3.4**) shows the first set of AutoLayouts.

2. Use the scroll bar to see additional layouts, if necessary.

3. Click the desired layout to apply it to the slide, or click the drop-down arrow for a list of other options.

   See also "Choosing a Layout" in Chapter 2, "A Quick Tour of PowerPoint."

✔ Tips

- If you don't find an AutoLayout that fits your needs perfectly, don't despair; you can modify, move, or delete placeholders. See "Manipulating Text Placeholders" later in this chapter.

- In **Figure 3.4**, you will notice that we expanded the task pane to show more layouts without having to scroll. That is a simple matter of dragging and stretching the border of the task pane.

- To select a different layout for an existing slide, choose Format > Slide Layout, or open the Slide Layout task pane and click another layout type.

Move your mouse over a layout ...

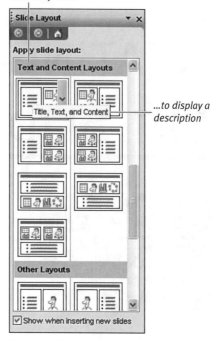

...to display a description

Figure 3.4 Choose a layout in the Slide Layout task pane.

Dotted lines surround empty
AutoLayout text placeholders

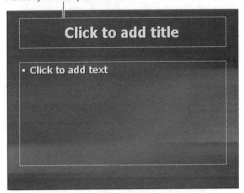

Figure 3.5 Choosing the bulleted list layout creates two text placeholders: one for the title and one for the bulleted text.

Table 3.1

Editing Text Within a Placeholder	
TO MOVE CURSOR TO...	DO THIS
Beginning of line	Press Home
End of line	Press End
Next word	Press Ctrl+right arrow
Previous word	Press Ctrl+left arrow
TO DELETE...	DO THIS
Character to the right	Press Delete
Character to the left	Press Backspace
Any amount of text	Select text and press Delete
TO SELECT...	DO THIS
Word	Double-click word
Paragraph	Triple-click paragraph
All text in placeholder	Click text and press Ctrl+A
Any amount of text	Click and drag across characters

Entering Text into a Placeholder

Text placeholders that are created with an AutoLayout have a dotted-line boundary (**Figure 3.5**). They tell you exactly what to do to enter text in them: Click to Add Title or Click to Add Text.

To enter text into a placeholder:

1. Click inside the placeholder.

2. Start typing.

   Refer to **Table 3.1** for ways to edit your text.

3. Click outside the placeholder when you're finished.

   The text will appear on your slide and in the Outline pane.

✔ Tip

- If you start typing on a new slide without clicking a placeholder, the text is placed in the title placeholder.

Creating a Text Box

Sometimes you'll need to add your own text boxes—for example, to annotate a chart (**Figure 3.6**) or to insert a footnote, like a date, on a title slide (**Figure 3.7**).

To create a text box:

1. Click the Text Box tool on the Drawing toolbar.

2. To insert a single line only, just click where the text should go and start typing. **Figure 3.8** shows a text box that was inserted this way.

3. To create a text box that allows multiple lines and will word wrap, drag a box to the desired width and start typing.

   When you type, text will word-wrap inside the box. The text box shown in **Figure 3.9** was created with this technique.

✔ Tips

- If you don't see the Drawing toolbar, choose View > Toolbars > Drawing.

- The text boxes in **Figures 3.8** and **3.9** have a rotational tool attached to them so that the textbox can be turned at an angle.

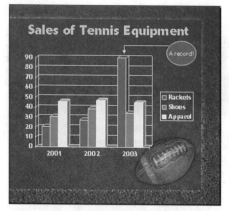

Figure 3.6 The "A record!" annotation is inside a text box, attached to an oval, and added to the slide.

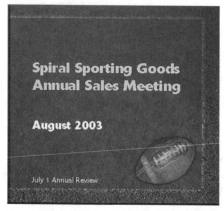

Figure 3.7 The date appears at the bottom of the slide in a text box.

The rotation circle lets you turn the text

Figure 3.8 This type of text box is ideal for single-line labels. The box grows wider as you type.

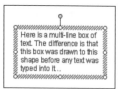

Figure 3.9 This type of text box will word-wrap text within the box.

Selection handles   Selection box

Spiral Sporting Goods
Annual Sales Meeting

Drag a top or bottom   Drag a side handle
handle to adjust the   to adjust the width
height

Drag a corner handle
to adjust the height
and width

Figure 3.10 A selection box with selection handles appears around the text placeholder when you click inside.

✔ Tips

- Selecting a placeholder can be tricky if the text cursor is not already within the text—you won't be able to see it at all! The easiest way to select the placeholder is to click within the text and then press Escape. To delete a text placeholder, therefore, click once on the text, press Escape, and then press Delete.

- Sometimes if you cut or delete a placeholder with text already entered, the original placeholder (Click to Add Title) reappears. You can delete the placeholder, change the layout, or ignore it—the placeholder will not appear on the slide when it's shown in slide show view.

Manipulating Text Placeholders

Text placeholders and boxes can be moved, copied, resized, and deleted.

To move a text placeholder:

1. Click the text.
   You will see a selection box around the placeholder (**Figure 3.10**).

2. Place the pointer on the selection box (but not on a selection handle).
   The pointer becomes a four-way arrow.

3. Drag the placeholder to the desired location on the slide.

To copy a text placeholder:

1. Click the text.

2. Place the pointer on the selection box (but not on a selection handle).
   The pointer becomes a four-way arrow.

3. Press and hold Ctrl as you click and drag to a new location.
   The text is copied.

To resize a text placeholder:

1. Click the text.

2. Place the pointer on a selection handle.
   The pointer becomes a double-headed arrow.

3. Drag the selection handle until the placeholder is the desired size.

Moving Text

One way to move text is to use the cut-and-paste technique (**Figure 3.11**). An alternative method for moving text is drag and drop (**Figure 3.12**).

To cut and paste text:

1. Select the text that you want to move (**Figure 3.13**).

2. Choose Edit > Cut (Ctrl+X).

3. Place the cursor inside of a text layout.

4. Choose Edit > Paste (Ctrl+V).

✔ Tip

■ Step 3 is not required, but usually recommended. If you do not click inside a layout before pasting, PowerPoint places the text on the page as a text box. That might be perfectly fine for your needs, but it's helpful to understand how PowerPoint behaves with pasted text and why.

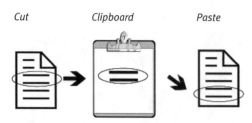

Cut   Clipboard   Paste

Figure 3.11 Cut-and-paste is a way to move text. The Clipboard is a temporary storage area for cut or copied objects.

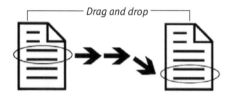

Drag and drop

Figure 3.12 The drag-and-drop technique is another way to move text.

The bullets are not highlighted

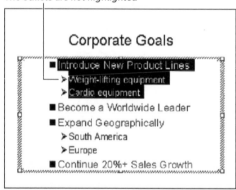

Figure 3.13 The selected text can be moved by using either cut and paste or drag and drop.

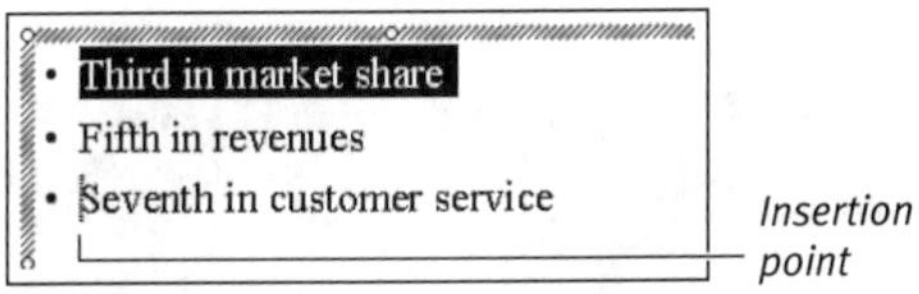

Figure 3.14 When you begin to drag, an insertion point appears where the text object can be dropped.

Figure 3.15 When released, the text becomes the middle bullet.

Copy — Paste

Cut —

Figure 3.16 Icons for cutting, copying, and pasting are found on the Standard toolbar.

To drag and drop text:

1. Select the text to be moved.

2. Place the pointer in the selection.

3. Hold down the mouse button and begin dragging.

   A vertical line indicates the insertion point (**Figure 3.14**).

4. Release the mouse button when the vertical line is positioned where you want to insert the text.

   The text will then drop into place (**Figure 3.15**).

   See Chapter 13, "Working in Outline View," for information on moving bullet items in Outline view.

✔ Tips

■ The Standard toolbar contains buttons for cutting, copying, and pasting (**Figure 3.16**).

■ To select a bullet item and all of its subbullets, click the main bullet or triple-click the first bullet line.

■ The Office Clipboard can now hold up to 24 items. To view the content, open the Clipboard from the task pane drop-down menu options. To paste any item at the cursor location, just click the item in the list.

MOVING TEXT

Using the Spelling Checker

The spelling checker searches all text place-holders in the presentation and stops at words that aren't in the dictionary. You can either spell check the entire presentation or correct misspellings of single words.

To correct a misspelled word:

1. Go to Tools > Options > Spelling and Style and verify that Check Spelling As You Type is checked.

2. Place the mouse pointer on a word that has a red wavy line underneath it.

3. Right-click the word.

4. Select the correct spelling from the list in the shortcut menu that appears (**Figure 3.17**).

To check the presentation:

1. Choose Tools > Spelling or click the Spelling button on the Standard toolbar. The Spelling dialog box appears (**Figure 3.18**), displaying a misspelled word in the Not in Dictionary text box.

2. If the word is spelled correctly, choose Ignore or Ignore All. Or, if you'll use the word frequently, choose Add to add it to the custom dictionary.

3. For misspelled words, choose the correct spelling from the Suggestions list or edit the Change To field and then choose Change or Change All.

✔ Tip

■ If the mistyped word is an actual word (such as *meat* for *meet*), the spelling checker isn't smart enough to consider the word suspect. Therefore, it's important that you still proofread the text.

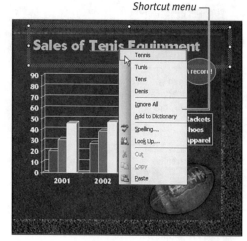

Figure 3.17 Select the correct spelling from the list.

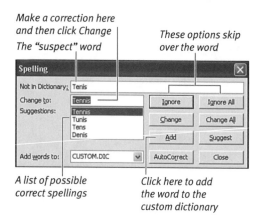

Figure 3.18 Choose Tools > Spelling to display the Spelling dialog box.

Mistake or Abbreviation	Correction
ANnual	Annual
wednesday	Wednesday
seperate	separate
adn	and
(c)	©
insted	instead

Figure 3.19 These are examples of the types of corrections the AutoCorrect feature makes.

Uncheck to turn off this feature

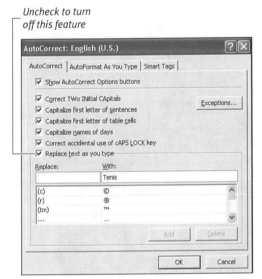

Figure 3.20 You can customize the replacement list in the AutoCorrect dialog box.

■ The AutoCorrect option appears in the shortcut menu displayed when a spelling error is right-clicked—along with a sub-menu of choices for words with which the misspelled word can be replaced.

Correcting Mistakes Automatically

AutoCorrect automatically corrects mistakes as you type. It will correct capitalization errors, common misspellings, and transpositions (**Figure 3.19**). If AutoCorrect is turned on, mistakes are corrected when you press the spacebar after the word.

The AutoCorrect feature is turned on by default when you enter the program. If you want to turn off this feature or customize the replacement list, you will need to go to the AutoCorrect dialog box (**Figure 3.20**).

To correct mistakes automatically:

1. Choose Tools > AutoCorrect.
   The AutoCorrect dialog box appears.

2. Select or deselect options, as desired.

3. To add your own replacement item, click the Replace field and type the word you want replaced. Click the With field, type the replacement word or phrase, and then click Add.
   The word will be added to the replacement list.

4. Click OK when you are finished.

✔ Tips

■ You can automatically replace abbreviations with their longer counterparts. For instance, you can type a code for your company name (such as asg), and AutoCorrect will replace it with the full company name (Spiral Sports).

■ To turn off AutoCorrect, uncheck the Replace Text as You Type check box in the AutoCorrect dialog box.

■ You can use the Spelling dialog box to add entries to the AutoCorrect replacement list.

Working with Smart Tags

New to the Office 2003 suite, a smart tag recognizes text by its pattern and offers you a menu of actions relevant to it. For instance, with Smart Tags enabled, if you type an address on a bullet slide, PowerPoint can offer to show you driving directions to that address or add it to a contact in Outlook.

To enable Smart Tags:

1. Choose Tools > AutoCorrect Options > Smart Tags.

2. Check Label Text with Smart Tags (**Figure 3.21**).

3. Click OK.

To work with Smart Tags:

1. Create a bullet that includes a full date (**Figure 3.22**). A dotted line should appear below the date, similar to the one used by Spell Check.

2. When the Smart Tag icon appears, click it to see the options available (**Figure 3.23**).

Figure 3.21 Turn Smart Tags on to tell PowerPoint to recognize data patterns.

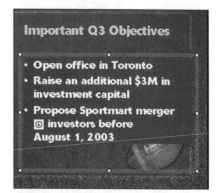

Figure 3.22 This date has been empowered with a smart tag.

Figure 3.23 Here are the actions that can be taken with this date.

*Shows how the selected
text will be formatted*

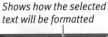

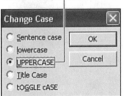

Figure 3.24 Change
the capitalization of
selected text in the
Change Case dialog box.

Changing Case

The Change Case command lets you choose different combinations of uppercase and lowercase orthography for selected text.

To change the case of selected text:

1. Select the text you want to change.

2. Choose Format > Change Case.
   The Change Case dialog box appears (**Figure 3.24**).

3. Select one of the case options and click OK.
   The selected text will change.

✔ Tips

- Toggle Case is handy when you have mistakenly typed text with Caps Lock on—it turns lowercase letters into uppercase and vice versa.

- Title Case capitalizes each word in the selected text, except for small words such as *the, and, or, of, at.*

- Use Shift+F3 to toggle among UPPERCASE, lowercase, and Title Case.

- Use the Style Checker to make sure you have used uppercase and lowercase consistently throughout your presentation.

Correcting Style Inconsistencies

PowerPoint can ensure that you have capitalized and punctuated your slide titles and body text consistently throughout your presentation. It can also check for visual clarity by making sure you haven't used too many fonts (or made them too small), placed too many bullet items in a list, or used too many words in a title or bullet item.

When PowerPoint finds a style inconsistency, a yellow light bulb appears on the slide. Note that to use this feature, the Office Assistant must be turned on.

To correct style inconsistencies:

1. If you have turned off the Assistant, choose Help > Show the Office Assistant. Then choose Tools > Options > Spelling and Style, and click Check Style.

   PowerPoint automatically checks your presentation for inconsistencies. If it finds any, a light bulb is displayed on the slide.

2. Click the light bulb to see the Office Assistant's commentary on your slide.

   In **Figure 3.25**, the Style Checker has noticed that one of the bullets is set in a different typeface and is recommending against that practice.

✔ Tip

■ You might have to install the Office Assistant; it is not a default part of the program installation.

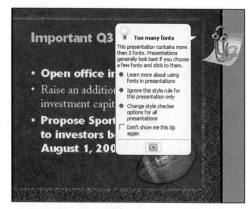

Figure 3.25 When you click the light bulb, a list of recommendations appears.

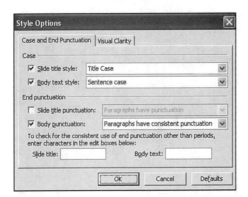

Figure 3.26 Have PowerPoint check your style in the Style Options dialog box (the Office Assistant must be installed).

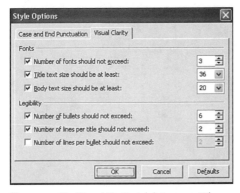

Figure 3.27 The Visual Clarity tab lets you set the options you want PowerPoint to check for you. Here, if you add a seventh bullet, the light bulb will appear.

To set your style preferences:

1. Choose Tools > Options > Spelling and Style, and then click Style Options.

2. On the Case and End Punctuation tab (**Figure 3.26**), specify the case and end punctuation style for titles and body text.

3. Select the Visual Clarity tab and change any of the fonts and legibility options (**Figure 3.27**).

4. Click OK to close the Style Options dialog box.

5. Click OK again to close the Office Assistant window.

CORRECTING STYLE INCONSISTENCIES

Numbering a List Automatically

The list in **Figure 3.28** was numbered automatically with the Format > Bullets and Numbering command.

To number a list automatically:

1. Select the text in the list you want to number.

2. Choose Format > Bullets and Numbering.

   The Bullets and Numbering dialog box appears.

3. Select the Numbered tab (**Figure 3.29**).

4. Click the desired numbering style.

5. Use the controls on the dialog box to change the starting number, color, or size.

6. Click OK.

✔ Tips

■ If there are second-level bullets between the numbered items (**Figure 3.30**), you cannot select all of the text (because the subbullets would be numbered also). Here's a quick way to number this type of list:

   ▲ Use the Format > Bullets and Numbering command to number the first line.

   ▲ Click each line that you want numbered and press Ctrl+Y to repeat the command.

■ You can quickly remove bullets and numbering from a list and deselect bullets or numbering using the Bullets and Numbering buttons on the Formatting toolbar.

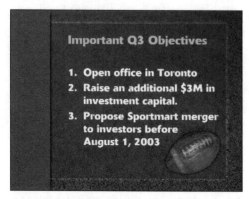

Figure 3.28 This list was numbered automatically.

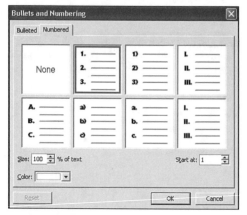

Figure 3.29 Choose a numbering style on the Numbered tab of the Bullets and Numbering dialog box.

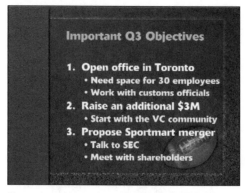

Figure 3.30 This numbered list has subbullets.

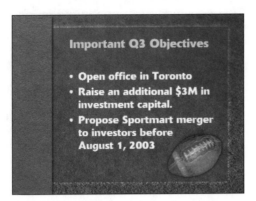

Figure 3.31 This slide uses default bullets.

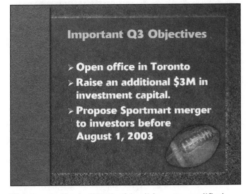

Figure 3.32 The bullets in this slide were modified.

To change the type of bullet, click on Customize

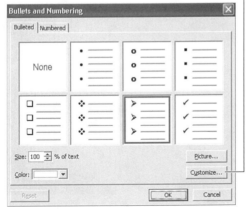

Figure 3.33 If you click Customize, you can choose a different bullet shape.

Choosing Bullet Shapes

Figure 3.31 shows a bulleted list slide that uses the default bullets. **Figure 3.32** shows this same list with different bullets selected.

To choose a different bullet shape:

1. Click anywhere on the line whose bullet you want to change. To change the bullets in several consecutive lines, select them by clicking and dragging.

2. Choose Format > Bullets and Numbering.

   The Bullets and Numbering dialog box appears (**Figure 3.33**).

3. On the Bulleted tab, click a bullet style or click the Customize button.

   The Symbol dialog box appears.

   continues on next page

4. In the Font field, click the arrow to display a list of fonts (**Figure 3.34**).

5. Choose the desired typeface.

Wingdings and Zapf Dingbats are two typefaces that contain many symbols appropriate for bullets.

6. Click the desired symbol.

7. Change the bullet's color or size, if you like.

8. Click OK.

See "Changing the Default Format for Text" in Chapter 12, "Making Global Changes."

✔ Tips

■ To remove a bullet from a line, click the Bullets button on the Formatting toolbar.

■ The Picture option in the Bullets and Numbering dialog box allows you to use any graphic file as a bullet (**Figure 3.35**). This option opens the Picture Bullet dialog box. Remember that bullets need to be small images, without many fine details.

■ To change the bullets for all slides, see Chapter 12.

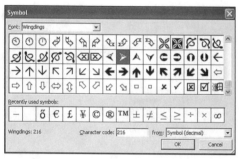

Figure 3.34 Changing the font to Wingdings gives you some interesting choices.

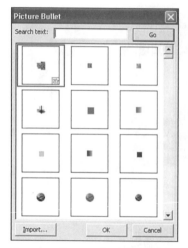

Figure 3.35 You can also use pictures as bullets. The Picture button opens the Clip Organizer.

Vertical ruler   Horizontal ruler

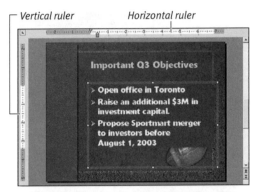

Figure 3.36 To display the rulers, choose View > Ruler.

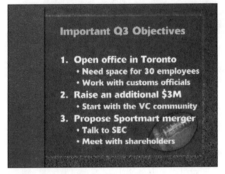

Figure 3.37 A bulleted list slide before any adjustment of indents.

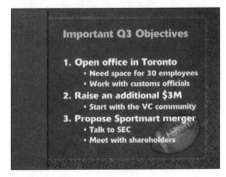

Figure 3.38 The same list after the indents have been increased slightly.

Left indent   First-line indent   Square
marker   marker   marker

Figure 3.39 Move the indent markers in the horizontal ruler to adjust the bullet placement.

Adjusting Bullet Placement

To change the horizontal spacing between the bullet and the text that follows it, you need to display the rulers (**Figure 3.36**) and drag the appropriate markers. **Figure 3.37** shows a bulleted list slide before any spacing change; **Figure 3.38** shows the same list after a bit of space has been added between the bullets and text.

To adjust the placement of bullets:

1. Choose View > Ruler to display the ruler.

2. Click anywhere on the text.

   For each bullet level, the horizontal ruler shows a set of indent markers that can be individually adjusted (**Figure 3.39**): If there are two bullet levels, the ruler displays two sets of indent markers.

3. Drag the left-indent marker in the ruler to change the spacing between the bullet and the text by moving the text.

4. To adjust the position of the bullet, drag the first-line indent marker in the ruler.

5. To adjust the position of both the bullet and the text without changing the spacing between the two, drag the square marker in the ruler. Bullets and text will move together.

✔ Tips

■ You don't need to select all of the text in the placeholder before adjusting the indents—the ruler automatically controls the entire placeholder.

■ To hide the ruler, choose View > Ruler again.

■ To control the placement of the indents, hold Ctrl while you drag the indent markers.

Changing the Font

You can format text by using either the Formatting toolbar or the Font dialog box.

To change the font:

1. Select the text by dragging across the characters. To select an entire text place-holder, first click inside the text and then click the selection box border (or press Escape after clicking the text).

2. On the Formatting toolbar, use the Font and Font Size fields to change the font. Click the Bold or Italic button, if desired (**Figure 3.40**).

Or

1. Choose Format > Font.

    The Font dialog box appears (**Figure 3.41**).

2. Choose a font, font style, and size.

3. Click the Preview button so you can see how the formatted text looks without closing the dialog box.

4. Click OK.

✔ Tip

- If the toolbar doesn't display one of the formatting buttons you want to use, click the More Buttons icon on the Formatting toolbar and select the formatting button you want.

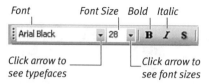

Figure 3.40 You can format text with the Formatting toolbar.

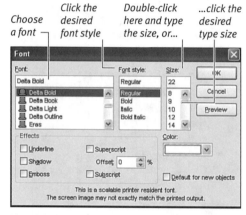

Figure 3.41 Choose Format > Font to display the Font dialog box.

Small color palette *Large color palette*

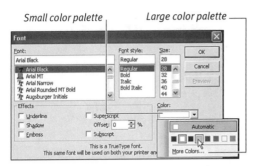

Figure 3.42 The Font dialog box gives you quick access to color.

Click any circle here... *...and the new color is shown here*

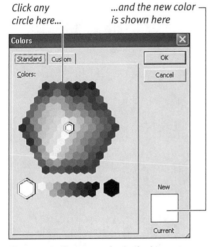

Figure 3.43 Choose a color in the large color palette.

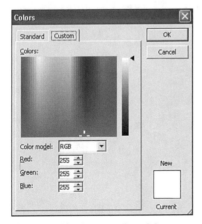

Figure 3.44 The Custom color tab lets you select within a range of hues.

Adding Text Effects and Color

In addition to options for typeface, size, and style of text, the Font dialog box has options for special effects (such as underline, shadow, and emboss) and color.

To add effects and color to your text:

1. Select the text by dragging across the characters. To select an entire text place-holder, first click inside the text, and then click the selection box border.

2. Choose Format > Font.
   The Font dialog box appears (**Figure 3.41**).

3. Choose an effect from the Effects area. (Consider using Shadow if you are not sure you have enough contrast between the font color and the background.)

4. To choose a color, click the color swatch and pick one of the eight colors that appear on the pop-up.
   This first set of choices includes the basic colors of this color scheme (**Figure 3.42**).

5. Click More Colors to see a wider selection.
   The system Color Picker appears. The Standard tab lets you choose from a wide assortment of screen-friendly colors (**Figure 3.43**), whereas the Custom tab lets you work from a graded palette of colors (**Figure 3.44**).

continues on next page

ADDING TEXT EFFECTS AND COLOR

6. Choose a color that will contrast with your background and complete other elements.

7. Click OK in the Color Picker and OK in the Font dialog box.

✔ Tips

■ Use the Font Color button on the Drawing toolbar or the Standard toolbar to quickly access and reuse the color palette.

■ Use the Superscript effect to raise text above the baseline (for example, x^2). Use the Subscript effect to lower text below the baseline (for example, H_2O).

■ When underlining text, if you need to control the spacing between the text and the line, you can draw a line with the Line tool on the Drawing toolbar instead of using the Underline effect.

See "Drawing Lines" in Chapter 10, "Importing Graphics."

ADDING TEXT EFFECTS AND COLOR

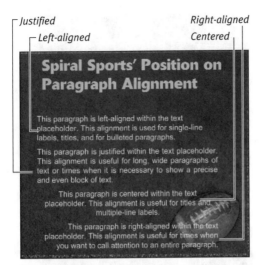

Figure 3.45 These paragraphs illustrate the four types of alignment.

Aligning Paragraphs

Figure 3.45 shows examples of the four types of paragraph alignment.

To align paragraphs:

1. Select the paragraphs to be aligned.

2. Choose Format > Alignment.

3. Choose Left, Center, Right, or Justify.

✔ Tips

■ The Formatting toolbar contains buttons for left-, right-, and center-aligned text, but not justified text. For that you will need to go to Format >Alignment

■ To select all of the text in a placeholder, first click inside the text and then click the selection box border (or press Escape). When you give an alignment command, all text will be aligned.

■ Text is aligned within the text place-holder. If the text isn't positioned quite where you want it, try adjusting the size or position of the placeholder.

ALIGNING PARAGRAPHS

Formatting a Text Placeholder

To control the horizontal and vertical placement of a block of text within a placeholder, you set a text anchor. Compare **Figures 3.46** and **3.47**. In **Figure 3.46**, the list is anchored on the top-left side of the placeholder; in **Figure 3.47**, the list is anchored along the top center. Whereas the Alignment command centers each paragraph separately, the text anchor controls the position of the text as a whole unit. This command also lets you align text vertically.

To format a text placeholder:

1. Click anywhere in the text placeholder.

2. Choose Format > Placeholder (or right-click and choose Format Placeholder). The Format AutoShape dialog box appears.

3. Select the Text Box tab (**Figure 3.48**).

4. Click in the Text Anchor Point field and choose where you want the text anchored in the placeholder.

5. Click OK.

✔ Tips

■ The Top, Middle, and Bottom anchor points are all anchored to the left side of the placeholder.

■ To add extra space between the placeholder boundary and the text, adjust the internal margin settings.

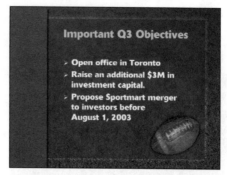

Figure 3.46 The list is anchored along the top-left side of the placeholder.

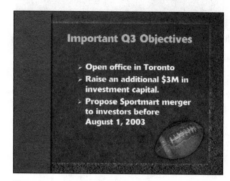

Figure 3.47 The list is anchored in the top center of the placeholder.

Controls left and right padding   *Click here to display a list of anchor points*   *Controls top and bottom padding*

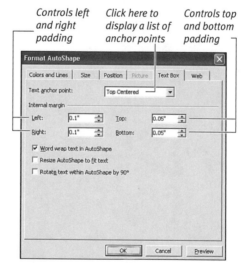

Figure 3.48 Click the Text Box tab to set the horizontal and vertical positioning of all the text in a placeholder.

Line spacing within a paragraph

Spacing before a paragraph

Spacing after a paragraph

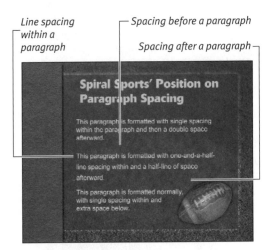

Figure 3.49 Various spacing effects.

Double-click in the box and enter a new value, or...

...click here to adjust the value in 0.05 increments

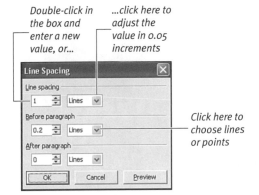

Click here to choose lines or points

Figure 3.50 Choose Format > Line Spacing to display this dialog box.

Controlling Line and Paragraph Spacing

PowerPoint helps you control spacing between lines in a paragraph as well as between each paragraph. **Figure 3.49** illustrates these types of spacing.

To adjust line and paragraph spacing:

1. Select the paragraphs to be formatted.

2. Choose Format > Line Spacing.

   The Line Spacing dialog box appears (**Figure 3.50**).

3. Enter the new values for Line Spacing, Before Paragraph, and/or After Paragraph.

4. Click the Preview button so you can see how the formatted text looks without closing the dialog box

5. Click OK.

✔ Tips

■ You won't usually want to choose both Before Paragraph and After Paragraph spacing. If you choose both, the two spacing values will be added together.

■ Do not use the Enter or Return key to add extra space between paragraphs. The Line Spacing dialog box gives you more precise control over spacing.

■ However, to break a paragraph before its natural wrapping point and continue typing in that paragraph, press Shift+Enter to insert a line break.

■ To select a single paragraph, just click inside it—you don't need to select any text.

■ To select all of the text in the placeholder, click the text and then the border of the selection box. Then, when you give a spacing command, all text will be formatted.

■ You will rarely want to go below .75 in the line spacing setting. Smaller than this, and the ascenders and descenders of your text will often be clipped off.

Table 3.2

Types of Formatting You Can Copy
Font
Style
Size
Effects
Color
Alignment
Line spacing
Paragraph spacing
Bullets

Copying Formatting Attributes

If you want the text in one placeholder to be formatted exactly like the text in another placeholder, you can do so by "painting" the format. **Table 3.2** lists the types of formatting you can paint.

To copy formatting attributes:

1. Click the text placeholder whose format you want to copy and then click the border of the selection box.

2. Click the Format Painter button on the Formatting toolbar.

3. Place the pointer (which now includes a paintbrush) on the text to which you want to apply the format, and click.

✔ Tips

- You can use the Format Painter to "paint" the format of other types of objects (such as boxes, circles, and arrows).

- You can also use the Format Painter to copy from and apply formatting to specific text as opposed to the entire placeholder.

- If the Formatting toolbar isn't displayed, choose View > Toolbars > Formatting.

- If you don't see the Format Painter button on the Formatting toolbar, click the More Buttons button to see other formatting buttons.

- Double-clicking the Format Painter makes it "sticky" so that you can apply formatting to more than one object. Clicking it again toggles it off.

COPYING FORMATTING ATTRIBUTES

INSERTING CHARTS

In PowerPoint, you can create a wide variety of two- and three-dimensional charts, such as area, bar, column, line, pie, doughnut, stock, and cone. This chapter concentrates on the types that have axes. Typically, you would create these charts to show relative values and relationships between multiple categories (comparing sales between this year and last, how the East did with respect to the West, which processor speed is the fastest, which country produces more Olympic skaters).

Chapter 6, "Creating Pie Charts," covers pie and doughnut charts, where the emphasis is on determining percentages of a whole.

Launching Graph

When you create charts in PowerPoint, you actually use the Microsoft Graph program. In Graph, you'll notice that the toolbar offers buttons specific to graphing, and the menu bar contains two new options: Data and Chart.

You can open Microsoft Graph from within PowerPoint. Many long-time users did not even realize that they were launching a separate application to create their charts. Here's how it works.

To launch Microsoft Graph:

1. Create a new slide that contains a chart placeholder, or use any of the slide layouts that include "Content"—from those flexible layouts, you can create just about anything, including charts.

or

Open an existing slide that contains a chart.

2. Double-click the chart placeholder or existing chart.

You'll see a thick border around the chart (**Figure 4.1**). If this is a new chart, Graph creates some data for you.

✔ Tip

■ To return to PowerPoint, click anywhere on the slide outside the chart border.

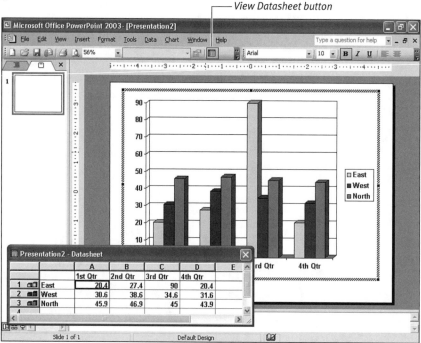
View Datasheet button

Figure 4.1 The border around the chart indicates you're working in Microsoft Graph.

LAUNCHING GRAPH

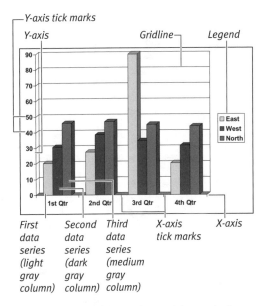

Y-axis tick marks

Y-axis   Gridline   Legend

First data series (light gray column)   Second data series (dark gray column)   Third data series (medium gray column)   X-axis tick marks   X-axis

Figure 4.2 It's helpful to understand the terminology used for charts.

Chart Terminology

Figure 4.2 points out the key areas of a column chart; many chart types have these same areas.

The *y-axis* is known as the *value axis* because it always displays values on its scale. The *x-axis* is known as the *category axis* because it displays categories of data (such as quarters, months, years, and names).

Tick marks appear next to each value on the y-axis and between categories on the x-axis. *Gridlines* may extend from the tick marks to help you interpret the values at each *data point*. A set of data points makes up a *data series*.

When a chart has more than one data series (**Figure 4.2** has three: East, West, and North), you can use a *legend* to identify each series.

✔ Tip

- On a three-dimensional chart, the value axis is called the *z-axis*, and the *series axis* running along the depth of the chart is called the *y-axis*.

Creating a Chart Slide

PowerPoint 2002 includes charts in its numerous content layouts in the Slide Layout task pane. When you select any layout that includes content, you can click the bar chart icon to create a chart placeholder. **Figure 4.3** shows the many layouts that include charts.

To create a chart slide:

1. Click the New Slide button on the toolbar, or choose Insert > New Slide, or press Ctrl+M.

   The Slide Layout task pane opens in the right column. If it is not open, select View > Task Pane and then from the Other task panes drop-down menu, choose Slide Layout.

2. From the Slide Layout task pane, select one of the content layouts (**Figure 4.3**).

   A slide with content options appears (**Figure 4.4**).

Content layouts

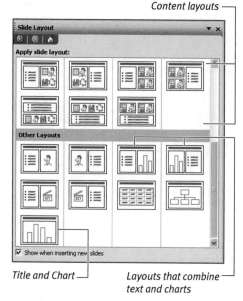

Title and Chart   *Layouts that combine text and charts*

Figure 4.3 Choose a chart layout in the Slide Layout task pane.

When you choose a content layout with a title and/or text, you can add those elements first

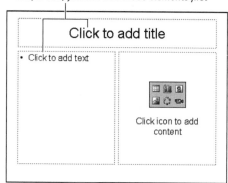

Figure 4.4 Content layouts also can include titles and text.

Double-click the chart object to launch Microsoft Graph and enter your data.

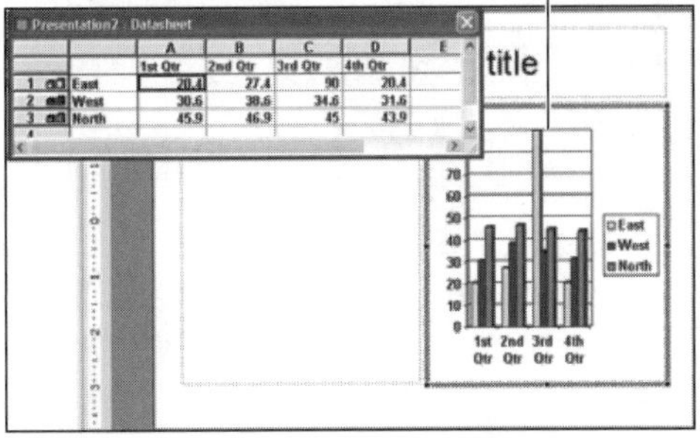

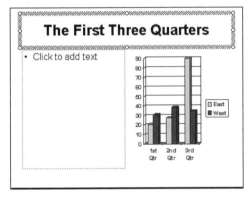

Figure 4.5 This slide uses the content with the title and text layout.

The First Three Quarters

Figure 4.6 The title for the slide.

3. Click on the small bar chart icon.

A chart with a generic dummy datasheet appears on your slide (**Figure 4.5**).

4. Right-click on Column D (the one labeled 4th Qtr) and choose Delete.

5. Right-click on Row 3 (the one labeled North) and choose Delete.

As you make these deletions, the chart behind the datasheet automatically updates.

6. If you choose a layout with a title, click the title placeholder and compose a title for your slide (**Figure 4.6**).

Graph closes automatically (because you clicked on the slide outside of the chart).

✔ Tips

■ In the text placeholder of a Text and Chart or Chart and Text layout, you can provide details about the chart, such as an interpretation of the data or a conclusion that can be drawn from the data.

■ PowerPoint doesn't care the order you go when creating new content slides. You can either create a new slide and then determine the content type with the Slide Layout task pane (as in the steps above), or you can start in the Slide Layout task pane, pick a layout, right-click on it, and choose Insert New Slide.

CREATING A CHART SLIDE

Entering Data

You enter your chart data in the datasheet window (**Figure 4.7**). The datasheet initially appears with sample data. You can erase it before entering your own data or overwrite the data with your own numbers and labels.

To enter data in the datasheet:

1. If you haven't already done so, double-click the chart placeholder to launch Microsoft Graph.

2. If you don't see the datasheet window, click the View Datasheet button on the toolbar.

3. To erase the sample data, click the Select All button (**Figure 4.7**) and press Delete.

4. Enter your chart data.

5. To view the chart, move the datasheet aside (by dragging the window's title bar) or close the datasheet window (by clicking the View Datasheet button).

   If your system display is at a sufficiently high resolution, you should be able to see the datasheet and the chart underneath it.

✔ Tips

■ Be sure to use the Select All button when deleting the sample data. If you just delete a range of cells and your data consumes fewer rows and columns than the sample data, Microsoft Graph still reserves space for this data on the chart. **Figure 4.8** shows what happens if you use your cursor to remove data from a row: Graph thinks that it is still part of the chart. To fix this problem, right-click the unwanted row and choose Delete.

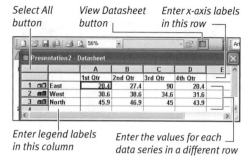

Select All button · View Datasheet button · Enter x-axis labels in this row

Enter legend labels in this column · Enter the values for each data series in a different row

Figure 4.7 Enter chart data in the datasheet.

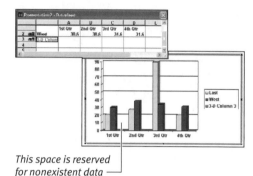

This space is reserved for nonexistent data

Figure 4.8 The Exclude Row/Col command on the Data menu will fix the problems on this chart.

■ If you have a row or column that you do not want to remove but also do not want included in the chart, select it and choose Data > Exclude Row/Col. This command tells Graph not to chart the data in the selected row or column.

■ You can enter legend labels in the top row and x-axis labels in the first column of the datasheet. But you must use the Data > Series in Columns command to let Graph know that the data series are entered in columns instead of rows.

Choose the file type first

Figure 4.9 Select a file to import from the Import File dialog box.

Figure 4.10 Choose whether to import the entire file or a range.

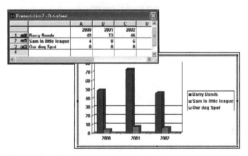

Figure 4.11 The data appears in the chart.

- If one of your data points is too long for the column width (like "Sam in little league" in **Figure 4.11**), increase the width of the column by dragging its right edge to the right. To automatically optimize the width of the column, double-click at its right edge and it will automatically stretch to accommodate the widest entry in that column.

Importing Data

If the chart data already exists in a spreadsheet or text file, you don't need to retype it in the datasheet—you can import the data.

To import data from a file:

1. Open or create a slide containing a chart and then double-click the chart placeholder to open Microsoft Graph.

2. Delete the sample data in the datasheet.

3. Click the first cell of the datasheet.

4. Choose Edit > Import File or click the Import File button on the toolbar.

   The Import File dialog box appears (**Figure 4.9**).

5. Click the Files of Type field and choose the desired file type (such as Microsoft Excel or Lotus 1-2-3).

6. Choose the drive and folder where the file is located and click the filename.

7. Click Open.

   The Import Data Options dialog box appears (**Figure 4.10**).

8. Select the sheet containing the data you want to import.

9. Choose Entire Sheet.

   or

   Choose Range and type the range of cells (such as A5:H10) or enter a range name.

10. Click OK.

    Your imported data will appear in the datasheet (**Figure 4.11**).

✔ Tips

- It is common for imported data to enter the datasheet one row down from the top, turning the categories into the first row of data. If this happens, just delete that first row.

Linking Data

Another way to import data is to link it from an existing spreadsheet file. When you link data, changes you make to the source file are automatically reflected in the PowerPoint datasheet and chart.

To link from a file to a datasheet:

1. With PowerPoint open, launch the application that created the source file and then open the file (**Figure 4.12**).

2. Select the data to be linked and choose Edit > Copy.

3. Switch back to PowerPoint.

4. Create a new chart slide, double-click the chart icon in the content placeholder, and then delete the sample data in the datasheet.

5. Click the first cell of the datasheet.

6. Choose Edit > Paste Link and click OK to continue.

   You might get a box asking if you want to replace existing data, even if the sample data has already all been deleted.

7. Move or close the datasheet to see your new chart.

✔ Tips

- Changes to the source file are instantly reflected in the chart. Also, if the chart is open in Graph, the datasheet updates automatically.

- If you forget the name or location of the source file, choose Edit > Links to display the Link dialog box (**Figure 4.13**).

- A fast way to open your source file is to click Open Source in the Link dialog box.

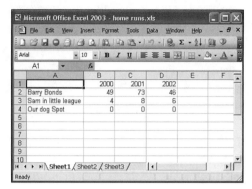

Figure 4.12 The selected range in a Microsoft Excel spreadsheet will be copied and then paste-linked in a PowerPoint datasheet.

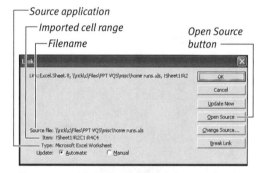

Figure 4.13 While in the datasheet, choose Edit > Links to display the Link dialog box.

- Use the Change Source option in the Link dialog box if you have moved or renamed the source file.

- If you move your PowerPoint file, make sure you move your source file along with it; keeping them together in a folder is a good idea.

- To avoid problems if Graph inserts an extra row with imported data, consider entering the categories (the first row) yourself and then paste-linking just the values into the second row.

LINKING DATA

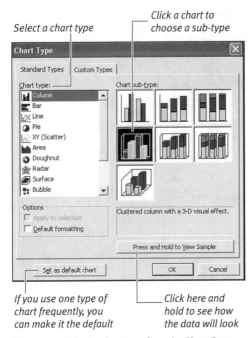

Select a chart type

Click a chart to choose a sub-type

If you use one type of chart frequently, you can make it the default

Click here and hold to see how the data will look

Figure 4.14 Select a chart type from the Chart Type dialog box.

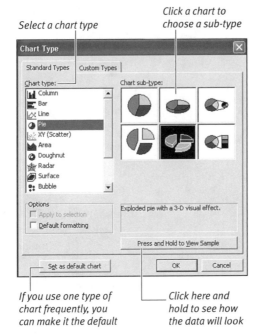

Select a chart type

Click a chart to choose a sub-type

If you use one type of chart frequently, you can make it the default

Click here and hold to see how the data will look

Figure 4.15 Select another chart type to change the view of the data.

Choosing a Chart Type

The default chart type is 3-D clustered column. You can choose a different chart type before or after you enter data in the datasheet. In addition to choosing a chart type, you can choose a sub-type. Sub-types are variations on the selected chart type. For example, a column chart has sub-types of clustered columns, stacked columns, 100 percent stacked columns, and so forth.

To choose a chart type:

1. Open or create a slide containing a chart, and then click the Chart icon in the content placeholder to open Microsoft Graph.

2. Choose Chart > Chart Type.

   The Chart Type dialog box appears (**Figure 4.14**).

3. Select the desired chart type.

   A description of the chart type appears beneath the Chart Sub-Type area. Change to another type of chart if you like (**Figure 4.15**).

4. Choose a sub-type (**Figure 4.15**) and click OK.

5. Hold down the preview button (Press and Hold to View Sample) to get a quick look at how your chart will look.

CHOOSING A CHART TYPE

67

✔ Tips

■ Another way to change the chart type is with the Chart Type button on the toolbar (**Figure 4.16**). Clicking the arrow next to the button will display a palette of 18 chart types.

■ You can also change the shape of individual series in a 3D bar or column chart. Select the series, choose Format > Selected Data Series, and select the Shape tab. You can then select a shape, such as a cylinder, pyramid, or cone. We don't recommend it, but see **Figure 4.17** for an example.

Click here to display a palette of chart types

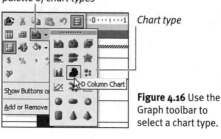

Chart type

Figure 4.16 Use the Graph toolbar to select a chart type.

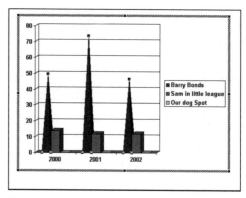

Figure 4.17 You can change just one data series. (Now please change it back!)

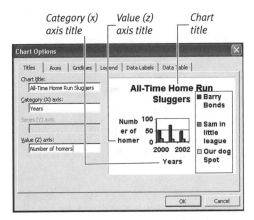

Figure 4.18 Enter the title, categories, and values.

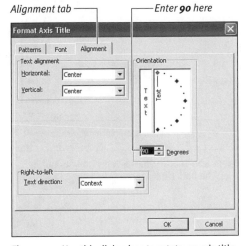

Figure 4.19 Use this dialog box to rotate an axis title.

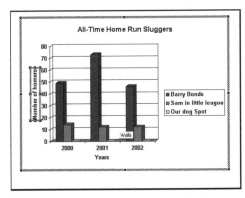

Figure 4.20 The value axis title is rotated 90 degrees.

Inserting Titles

You can insert titles at the top of a chart or on any of the axes (**Figure 4.18**).

To insert titles on a chart:

1. Double-click the chart to open it in Graph and choose Chart > Chart Options.
   The Chart Options dialog box appears.

2. Select the Titles tab.

3. Type the title text in the appropriate box.

4. Enter Years for the Category Axis and Number of Homers for the Value axis (**Figure 4.18**).
   You'll learn not to trust the little preview window in Chart Options, as it is unable to show the axis titles small enough.

5. Click OK.

To rotate an axis title:

1. Select the value axis title

2. Choose Format > Selected Axis Title and then click the Alignment tab.
   The Format Axis Title dialog box appears.

3. Use the Orientation wheel or the value box below it to set the title to 90 degrees (**Figure 4.19**).

4. Click OK.
   Figure 4.20 shows the rotated axis title.

Inserting Data Labels

You can place data labels at data points to show their exact values (**Figure 4.21**).

To insert data labels:

1. Double-click the chart and choose Chart > Chart Options.

   The Chart Options dialog box appears.

2. Select the Data Labels tab (**Figure 4.22**).

3. Under Label Contains, choose Value.

4. Click OK.

✔ Tips

- Data labels are not appropriate for all charts. If the chart has many data points or many data series, the chart may look too busy with data labels, or the labels may run into one another.

- To change the number of decimal places displayed in a data label, choose Format > Selected Data Labels and select the Number tab in the Format Data Labels dialog box.

- To change the size and color of data labels, choose Format > Font.

- If a label appears above the plot area, you can either move the label or change the upper value on the y-axis scale.

  See "Repositioning Data Labels," the next section in this chapter, and "Scaling the Axis" in Chapter 5.

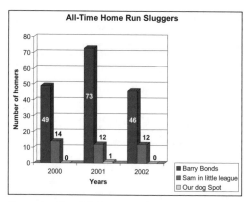

Figure 4.21 Data labels appear above each data point.

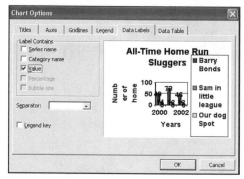

Figure 4.22 Choose Chart > Chart Options and select the Data Labels tab.

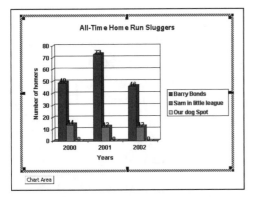

Figure 4.23 With the data labels in the default positions, the values are difficult to read.

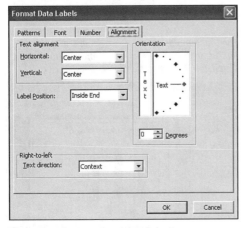

Figure 4.24 For two-dimensional charts, you can reposition the data labels automatically.

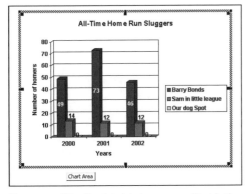

Figure 4.25 After the data labels are moved inside the columns and the font color is changed, the values become easier to see.

Repositioning Data Labels

Graph inserts data labels near the data point, but sometimes the labels from one series will overlap the labels from another, or the label may not be easily read in its current position (**Figure 4.23**). Fortunately, you can position the data labels exactly where you want them.

To reposition data labels automatically (2D charts only):

1. Select the data labels in a series.

   Make sure there are selection handles around each label in the series, but note that you only have to click on one label to achieve this.

2. Choose Format > Selected Data Labels. The Format Data Labels dialog box appears.

3. Select the Alignment tab.

4. In the Label Position field, choose the desired position (such as Inside End) (**Figure 4.24**).

5. Click OK.

Repeat these steps for each series you want to reposition.

To move data labels manually (for any chart type):

1. Click the data label you want to move; click until you see selection handles around the one label only.

   Clicking once on any data label selects the entire series of data labels. Clicking a second time on a data label reduces the selection to just that data label.

2. Drag the border of the selected label to the desired position.

Repeat these steps for each label to be repositioned. In **Figure 4.25**, the font for Barry Bonds' data series has also been set to white, using the Font Color control on the toolbar.

71

Revising a Chart

To revise a previously created chart, you need to reopen it in Microsoft Graph.

To revise a chart:

1. In PowerPoint, double-click the embedded chart (**Figure 4.26**).

   If you want to change only the formatting, go to step 6.

2. If you need to update the data and the datasheet is not currently displayed, click the View Datasheet button.

3. To replace the contents of a cell, click the cell and type the new value. The chart instantly reflects the change to the datasheet.

4. To edit the contents of a cell, double-click the cell.

   A text cursor appears.

5. Position the cursor where you want to make the change and then insert or delete characters. Press Enter or Return when you are finished.

6. Make any desired formatting changes to the chart (insert titles, insert data labels, change the chart type, and so forth).

7. To reposition the Legend, select it and drag it somewhere else. To remove the legend altogether, choose Format > Chart Options > Legend and uncheck Show Legend (or just select the Legend and press Delete).

8. To return to PowerPoint, click the slide outside of the chart.

✔ Tips

- Check **Figure 4.27** for some clues if you're unsure whether the chart is still active in Microsoft Graph, or you're in PowerPoint.

Double-click the embedded chart

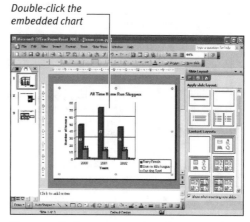

Figure 4.26 Before you can revise a chart, you must open it in Microsoft Graph.

The Graph toolbar is one indication that you are in Graph, not PowerPoint...

...and this border around the chart is another clue

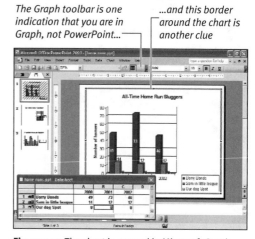

Figure 4.27 The chart is opened in Microsoft Graph.

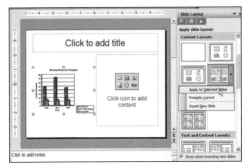

Figure 4.28 Two charts can be shown on one slide.

Creating Two Charts on a Slide

Adding a second chart to a slide can be tricky in that both charts need to be taller than they are wide (or else they will be tiny). You can use a multiple-content layout to accomplish this, or you can copy and paste one chart to create another on the same slide.

To add a second chart to a slide:

1. Open the Slide Layout task pane and click on any of the layouts that show side-by-side content (**Figure 4.28**).

   PowerPoint automatically shrinks the existing chart and adds the second content placeholder.

2. Create the second chart by clicking the Insert Chart icon in the new content placeholder, and use PowerPoint's charting tools to build and format the second chart. Click outside the chart to return to the slide when your second chart is complete.

✔ Tips

- To align the two charts with one another, select both of them, click the Draw button on the Drawing toolbar, and choose the Align or Distribute command from the pop-up menu. If the Drawing toolbar is not available, select View > Toolbars > Drawing Toolbar.

  See "Aligning Objects" in Chapter 11.

- It's easier to compare data in the two charts when the axes use the same scale.

  See "Scaling the Axis" in Chapter 5.

- You can title each chart on the Titles tab of the Chart Options dialog box.

  See "Inserting Titles" earlier in this chapter.

FORMATTING CHARTS

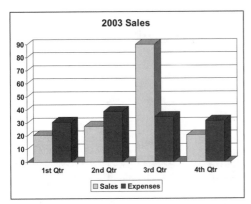

Figure 5.1 This 3D column chart uses Graph's default settings.

Microsoft Graph offers an abundance of ways to format your charts. You can reposition the legend, add and remove gridlines, change the color of the data series, change the upper and lower limits on the value axis, and more.

Figure 5.1 shows a chart with Graph's default settings, and **Figure 5.2** shows the same chart after formatting.

Don't forget that these formatting options are for charts created in PowerPoint; for charts copied from or linked to Excel, these formatting changes must be made in the original program (Excel).

See "Chart Terminology" in Chapter 4.

Elevation of 3D
columns changed

New colors assigned
to data series

Scale units adjusted

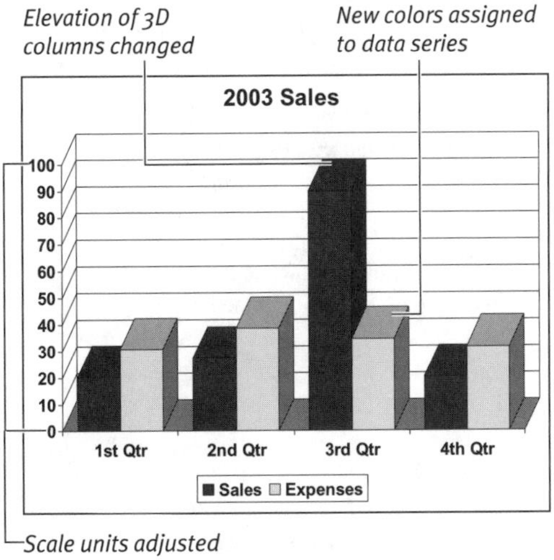

Figure 5.2 The same 3D column chart after formatting.

Formatting Charts

No matter what type of chart element you are formatting, the procedure is basically the same.

To format a chart:

1. If you're not already in Microsoft Graph, double-click the embedded chart on your slide.

2. Select the area of the chart that you want to format—you may need to click more than once.

   For example, to format the legend, click the legend until you see selection handles around it (**Figure 5.3**).

   When you select an item that's part of a larger group—such as a single point in a data series—the first click selects the group, and the second click selects the single item.

3. Choose Format > Selected *xxx*, where *xxx* is the name of the selected area.

   For example, if a data series is selected, the command will be Selected Data Series (**Figure 5.4**). The appropriate dialog box will open.

4. Make your desired choices in the dialog box and click OK to implement them.

✔ Tips

- A quick way to display the appropriate Format dialog box is to double-click the chart element you want to format.

- To make sure you have selected the object you intended, just point to the object and pause for a second—you'll see a ToolTip with the name of the object you are pointing to (**Figure 5.3**).

- Another way to select an area of a chart is to select its name in the Chart Objects field on Graph's toolbar (**Figure 5.5**).

Figure 5.3 A selected object has selection handles.

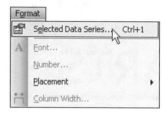

Figure 5.4 When a data series is selected, the Format menu offers the command Selected Data Series.

Click here to display the list

Figure 5.5 You can select an area on the chart from the Chart Objects field on the toolbar.

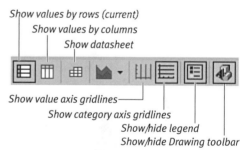

Show values by rows (current)
  Show values by columns
    Show datasheet

Show value axis gridlines
  Show category axis gridlines
    Show/hide legend
      Show/hide Drawing toolbar

Figure 5.6 You can quickly change the chart type; add and hide gridlines, the legend, and the drawing toolbars; and reorient your data.

- When Microsoft Graph is active, additional toolbar items appear to let you format easily (**Figure 5.6**).

Figure 5.7 This legend uses the default border.

Figure 5.8 After formatting, the legend border has a shadow.

A preview of your current formatting selections

Patterns tab

Color palette

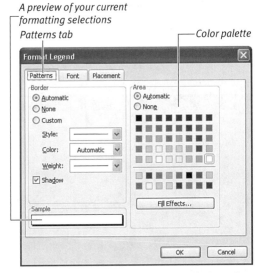

Figure 5.9 Use this dialog box to format the legend.

Figure 5.10 Click the Style field to display this list.

Figure 5.11 Click the Weight field to display this list.

Formatting the Legend

By default, the legend has a thin border around it (**Figure 5.7**). If you like, you can thicken the border, add a shadow, shade the background, or remove it altogether. In **Figure 5.8**, the legend is formatted with a heavier line weight and a shadow.

To format the legend:

1. Select the legend and then choose Format > Selected Legend.

   or

   Double-click the legend.

   The Format Legend dialog box appears.

2. Select the Patterns tab (**Figure 5.9**).

3. To choose a different border style (such as dashed lines), click the arrow by the Style field to display the drop-down menu (**Figure 5.10**). Choose one of the styles.

4. To choose a different line thickness, click the arrow by the Weight field to display a drop-down menu (**Figure 5.11**). Choose one of the weights.

5. To add a shadow, select the Shadow check box.

6. To shade the background of the legend, click one of the colors on the palette.

7. Click OK.

   To format the legend text, see "Formatting Chart Text" later in this chapter.

✔ Tips

- To enlarge the legend, drag the selection handles.

- To remove the legend border, go to the Patterns tab of the Format Legend dialog box and choose None, under Border.

FORMATTING THE LEGEND

Repositioning the Legend

You can place the legend in a variety of standard positions on the chart (**Figure 5.12**).

To reposition the legend:

1. Select the legend and choose Format > Selected Legend, or press Ctrl+1.

   or

   Double-click the legend.

   The Format Legend dialog box appears.

2. Select the Placement tab (**Figure 5.13**).

3. Choose one of the placement positions.

4. Click OK.

✔ Tips

- Another way to reposition the legend is to drag it to the desired location.

- To remove a legend, select it and press Delete.

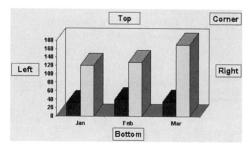

Figure 5.12 Graph offers five standard positions for the legend.

Placement tab

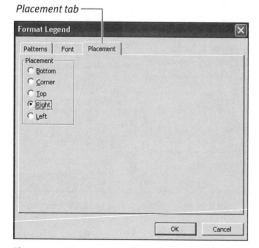

Figure 5.13 Choose a legend position on the Placement tab.

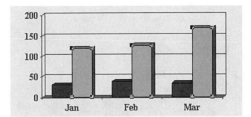

Figure 5.14 The second data series is selected in this column chart.

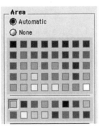

Figure 5.15 Choose a color in the Area palette.

Changing the Color of a Data Series

You can assign new colors to each of the data series in a chart to help differentiate the series.

To change the color of a data series:

1. Click any one of the points in the data series (selection handles will appear on all the points, as shown in **Figure 5.14**) and choose Format > Selected Data Series.

   or

   Double-click any point in the series.

   The Format Data Series dialog box appears.

2. Select the Patterns tab.

3. Choose a color in the palette in the Area section (**Figure 5.15**).

4. Click OK.

✔ Tip

- The Format Data Series dialog box contains different tabs and options depending upon the chart type.

Filling a Data Series with Textures or Patterns

You can assign textures to chart elements to help define data. **Figure 5.16** shows a wood texture applied to the data series.

To fill a data series with textures or patterns:

1. Click any one of the points in the data series (selection handles should appear on each point in the series) and choose Format > Selected Data Series.

   or

   Double-click the series.

   The Format Data Series dialog box appears.

2. Select the Patterns tab.

3. Click Fill Effects.

   The Fill Effects dialog box appears.

4. Select the Gradient tab and choose a shading style (**Figure 5.17**).

   or

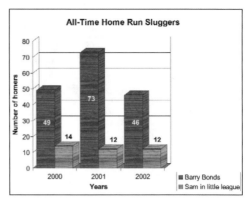

Figure 5.16 Both of these data series have wood textures. Baseball bats and all...

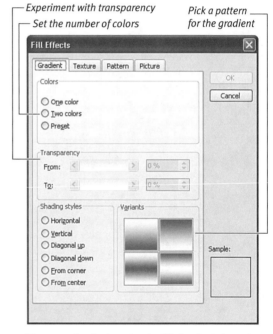

Figure 5.17 Gradients make nice fills for chart elements.

Texture tab

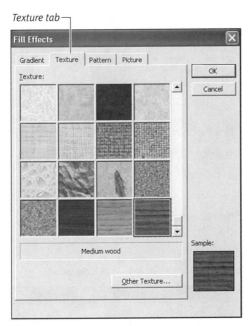

Figure 5.18 You can choose from a variety of textures.

Select the Texture tab and click a texture (**Figure 5.18**).

or

Select the Pattern tab and click a pattern (**Figure 5.19**).

5. Click OK to close the Fill Effects dialog box, and click OK again to close the Format Data Series dialog box.

Choose the colors of the pattern here   Pattern tab

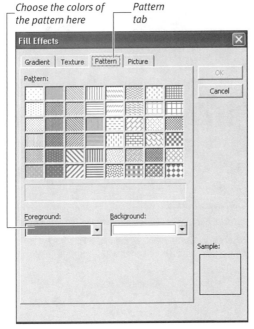

Figure 5.19 Use the Pattern tab to choose from among dozens of patterns.

FILLING A DATA SERIES

Filling a Data Series with a Graphics File

Suppose your sales team wins a tropical vacation for meeting certain goals. You can include a picture of a palm tree in the top data values to motivate your team. **Figure 5.20** shows a column chart that has one of its data series filled with a photograph.

To fill a data series with a graphics file:

1. Select the data series you want to fill (selection handles should appear on each point in the series) and choose Format > Selected Data Series.

   or

   Double-click the series.

   The Format Data Series dialog box appears.

2. Select the Patterns tab.

3. Click Fill Effects.

   The Fill Effects dialog box appears.

4. Select the Picture tab.

5. Click Select Picture.

   The Select Picture dialog box opens.

6. Navigate to the drive and folder containing the graphics file.

   The Microsoft Office folder contains a ClipArt folder with dozens of graphics files, but you can use your own images as well.

7. Choose the filename and click Insert to return to the Picture tab of the Fill Effects dialog box (**Figure 5.21**).

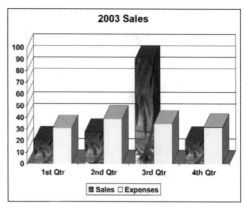

Figure 5.20 The first data series is filled with a photo of a palm tree.

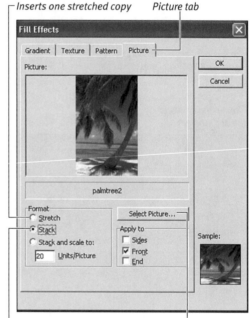

Figure 5.21 Use the Picture tab in the Fill Effects dialog box to fill a data series with a graphics file.

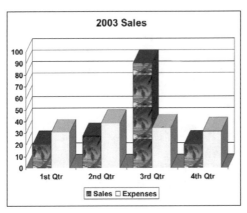

Figure 5.22 The first data series contains stacked graphics.

8. To insert a single copy of the graphic (as in **Figure 5.20**), choose Stretch in the Format area.

9. To have multiple copies of the graphic sit on top of each other (as in **Figure 5.22**), choose Stack in the Format area.

10. For 3D charts, select the Front check box in the Apply To area to place the graphic on the front face of the area, and deselect the Sides and End check boxes.

11. Click OK twice to return to the chart.

FILLING A DATA SERIES WITH A GRAPHICS FILE

Formatting Data Markers

Data markers are symbols, such as circles or squares, that appear at data points on line-, XY-, and radar-type charts. The markers also appear in the legend to help you identify each data series (**Figure 5.23**). The data markers can be reformatted, but before you can do this, you need to change the chart type.

To create a line chart:

1. Choose Chart > Chart Type.

2. Choose Line as the Chart Type and Line with Markers Displayed at Each Data Value as the Chart Sub-Type (**Figure 5.24**).

3. Choose OK.

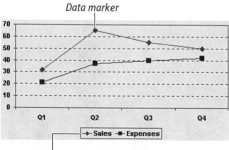

Data marker

Markers also appear in the legend

Figure 5.23 Data markers help you identify data series in this line chart.

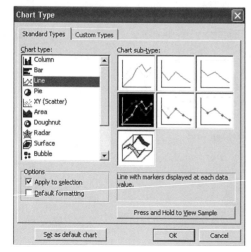

Figure 5.24 Change the chart to a Line chart.

Patterns tab *Marker section* *Click here to display the marker styles*

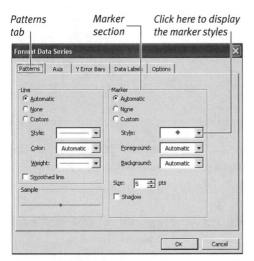

Figure 5.25 Choose a marker style on the Patterns tab.

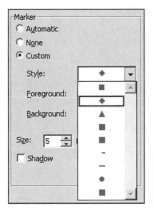

Figure 5.26 Click the Style field to display a list of marker styles.

To format data markers:

1. Click one of the data series (there should be selection handles at each data point) and choose Format > Selected Data Series.

   or

   Double-click the series.

   The Format Data Series dialog box appears.

2. Select the Patterns tab (**Figure 5.25**).

3. In the Marker section, display the Style list and choose a marker style (**Figure 5.26**).

4. If desired, increase the marker size by clicking the arrows or typing in a new number for the size.

5. Click OK.

✔ Tip

■ In the Marker section, choose None if you don't want any markers on the line. Make sure, though, that each line is a different color so you have some way of differentiating the series.

FORMATTING DATA MARKERS

Inserting/Removing Gridlines

Gridlines are the lines that extend from the tick marks on a chart's axes (**Figure 5.27**). They are useful for interpreting the actual values of the data points when you're not using data labels. Horizontal gridlines extend from the value axis, and vertical gridlines extend from the category axis.

To insert or remove gridlines:

1. Choose Chart > Chart Options.

2. Choose the Gridlines tab.

3. Choose which guidelines to display (**Figure 5.28**).

✔ Tip

■ The Chart Options dialog box also allows you to insert minor gridlines—lines that extend from the minor tick marks (ticks between the scale increments). Minor gridlines are rarely used because they often make the chart too busy.

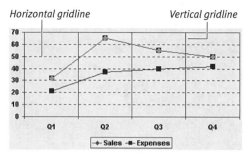

Figure 5.27 A line chart with horizontal and vertical gridlines.

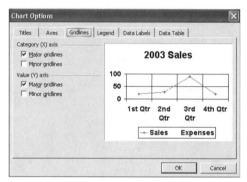

Figure 5.28 You can select gridlines from the Gridlines tab in the Chart Options dialog box.

Patterns tab

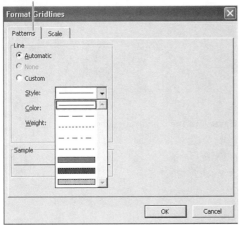

Figure 5.29 Minor gridlines can make a chart look too busy.

Formatting Gridlines

You can change both the thickness and the style of the gridlines. **Figure 5.23** shows the dotted style.

To format a gridline:

1. Select one of the gridlines and choose Format > Selected Gridlines.

   or

   Double-click a gridline.

   The Format Gridlines dialog box appears.

2. Select the Patterns tab.

3. To choose a different line style (such as dashed lines), display the Style list, and choose one of the styles (**Figure 5.29**).

4. To choose a different color, click the Color field and choose a color.

5. To choose a different line thickness, display the Weight list and choose one of the weights.

6. Click OK.

Formatting Tick Marks

Tick marks are tiny lines next to the labels on an axis, similar to divisions on a ruler. You can place tick marks inside, outside, or crossing the axis (**Figures 5.30** and **5.31**). You can also choose to have minor tick marks between the major tick marks.

To format the tick marks:

1. Select the axis whose tick marks you want to format and choose Format > Selected Axis.

   or

   Double-click the axis.

   The Format Axis dialog box appears.

2. Select the Patterns tab (**Figure 5.32**).

3. In the Major Tick Mark Type section, select the type of mark: None, Inside, Outside, or Cross.

4. Select the Minor Tick Mark Type: None, Inside, Outside, or Cross.

5. Click OK.

✔ Tip

■ The frequency of the tick marks depends on the major and minor units.

   See the next section, "Scaling the Axis," for information on specifying the major and minor units.

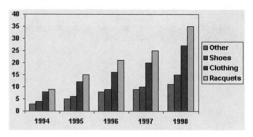

Figure 5.30 The x- and y-axes have outside tick marks.

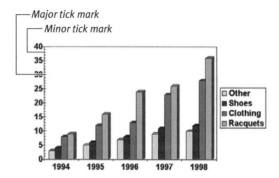

Figure 5.31 On this chart, the major tick marks cross the y-axis and minor tick marks are on the inside; no marks appear on the x-axis.

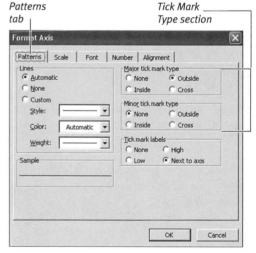

Figure 5.32 Choose types of tick marks from the Patterns tab.

Major unit (10)
   Maximum value (100)

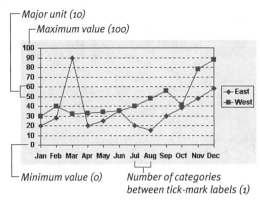

Minimum value (0)   *Number of categories*
between tick-mark labels (1)

Figure 5.33 This chart uses the default y-axis and x-axis scales.

Major unit (20)
   Maximum value (100)

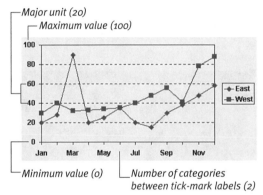

Minimum value (0)   *Number of categories*
between tick-mark labels (2)

Figure 5.34 On this chart, the number of categories on the x-axis and the major unit on the y-axis were changed.

Scaling the Axis

On the value axis (such as the y-axis in **Figure 5.33**), Microsoft Graph lets you adjust the maximum value (the value at the top of the axis), minimum value (the value at the bottom), and major unit (increments between values). On the category axis (such as the x-axis in **Figure 5.33**), you can adjust the number of categories between labels and tick marks. **Figure 5.34** shows the line chart after adjusting the scales.

To scale the value or category axis:

1. Select the axis to be scaled and choose Format > Format > Selected Axis.

   or

   Double-click the axis.

   The Format Axis dialog box appears.

2. Select the Scale tab for the formatting choices of the axis you have selected.

   continues on next page

3. For the value axis (**Figure 5.35**), enter new values for the Minimum, Maximum, Major Unit, and/or Minor Unit.

The checkmark disappears in the Auto column when you change a value from its default.

4. For the category axis (**Figure 5.36**), enter new values for Number of Categories Between Tick-Mark Labels and/or Number of Categories Between Tick Marks.

5. Click OK.

Turn on an Auto check box to return to the default scale value   Scale tab

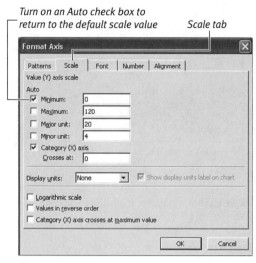

Figure 5.35 Change the scale of the value (Y) axis under the Scale tab.

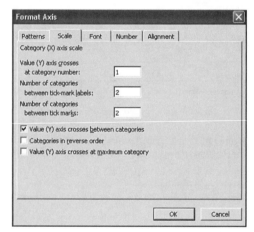

Figure 5.36 Under the Scale tab of the category (X) axis, you can adjust values for number of categories between tick marks and/or tick mark labels.

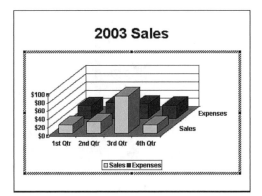

Figure 5.37 The numbers on the value axis have been given Currency format.

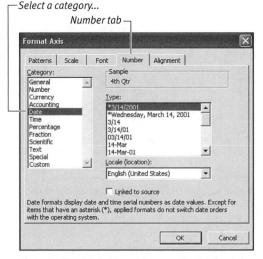

Figure 5.38 Format axis numbers on the Number tab.

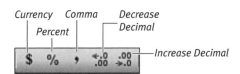

Figure 5.39 You can use the Formatting toolbar to format numbers on the chart.

Formatting Axis Numbers

You can format axis values to indicate date, time, currency, and other specifics. **Figure 5.37** shows a value axis in which the numbers have been formatted to display dollar signs.

To format the axis numbers:

1. Select the axis whose numbers you want to format and then choose Format > Selected Axis.

   or

   Double-click the axis.

   The Format Axis dialog box appears.

2. Select the Number tab (**Figure 5.38**).

3. From the Category list, choose the appropriate formatting category (such as Number, Percentage, or Currency).

4. If desired, change the value in the Decimal Places field.

5. Click OK.

✔ Tips

- You can also apply currency, percent, and comma format using buttons on the Formatting toolbar (**Figure 5.39**).

- Look at the sample in the dialog box to preview the number formatting.

- Instead of formatting all of the numbers as currency, you can insert an axis title that explains that the values are in dollars. *See "Inserting Titles" in Chapter 4.*

Formatting Chart Text

You can format the text in each chart area (legend, titles, and so forth) with a particular typeface, size, and style (**Figures 5.40** and **5.41**).

To format chart text:

1. Select the area with the text you want to format.

   or

   Within a selected text box, drag across the individual characters you want to format.

2. Choose Format > Font.

   The appropriate Format dialog box appears. Choose the Font tab (**Figure 5.42**).

3. In the Font list, choose the desired typeface.

4. Select the desired font style (Regular, Italic, Bold, Bold Italic), size, and color.

5. Click OK.

✔ Tips

- To format all the chart text to the same font, select the entire chart area. An easy way to select the chart area is to choose it from the Chart Objects field on the toolbar.

- To find a typeface in the drop-down menu, start typing its name and PowerPoint will head directly to it.

- If a typeface is bold by nature (that is, if it has bold in its name), do not choose the Bold attribute also. That will make it *very* bold.

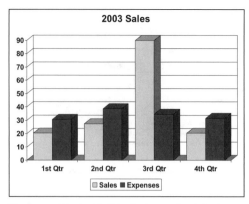

Figure 5.40 The text in this chart uses the default typeface (Arial) and size (18 points).

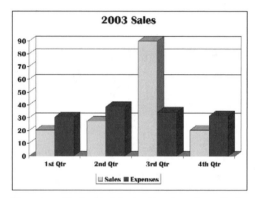

Figure 5.41 The text in this chart has been formatted to 22-point Bookman.

Choose a typeface   Choose a style   Choose a point size

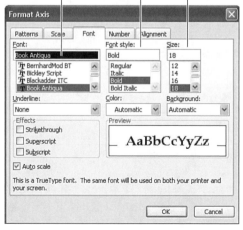

Figure 5.42 You can format chart text on the Font tab.

Gap depth (0)

Gap width (70)   Chart depth (100)

Figure 5.43 This 3D column chart uses the default 3D settings.

Gap depth (40)

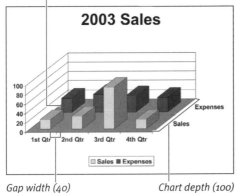

Gap width (40)   Chart depth (100)

Figure 5.44 The same 3D column chart has been altered.

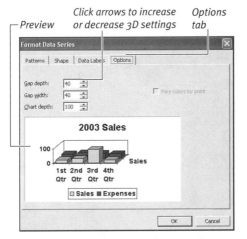

Preview   Click arrows to increase   Options
     or decrease 3D settings   tab

Figure 5.45 Adjust 3D settings for a 3D column chart on the Options tab.

Adjusting 3D Effects

You can adjust the dimensionality of your 3D charts—their gap depth, gap width, and chart depth. **Figure 5.43** shows a 3D column chart with the default 3D settings and **Figure 5.44** shows the same chart after formatting.

You can see in the figures that the gap depth is the vertical distance between each data point, the gap width is the horizontal distance between each data point, and the chart depth is the depth of the chart's base.

To adjust 3D effects on a chart:

1. Select any one of the data series. For this procedure, it doesn't matter which one— the effect will be for every data series in the chart.

2. Choose Format > Selected Data Series. The Format Data Series dialog box appears.

3. Select the Options tab (**Figure 5.45**).

4. Click the arrows to adjust each 3D setting. Watch the preview in the dialog box to see how the new values affect the three-dimensionality of the chart.

5. Click OK.

✔ Tips

- You can also adjust the 3D view of a chart (that is, the viewer's perspective). Choose Chart > 3-D View to open the 3-D View dialog box (**Figure 5.46**). You can adjust a chart's elevation, rotation, and perspective.

- One thing to watch out for is the Apply button in the 3-D View dialog box. It is not a preview button; it actually performs the change, as if you had pressed OK. In addition, because it's fun to experiment and go wild with this effect, you should note what the settings are before playing—or save first—so you can close without saving if you can't find your way back.

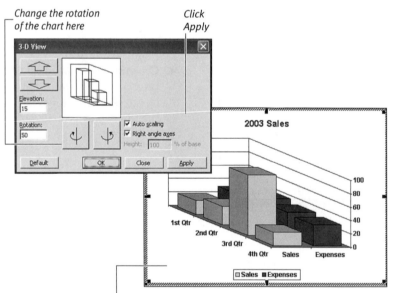

Change the rotation of the chart here

Click Apply

Chart rotates within the slide

Figure 5.46 In the 3-D View dialog box you can change the view of the chart from the viewer's perspective.

ADJUSTING 3D EFFECTS

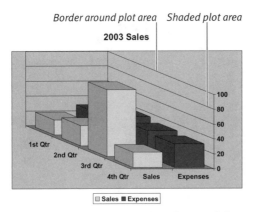

Border around plot area   *Shaded plot area*

Figure 5.47 This area chart includes a formatted plot area.

Figure 5.48 Select the Plot Area using the Chart Objects field on the toolbar.

Formatting the Plot Area

The plot area is the rectangle formed by the horizontal and vertical axes. **Figure 5.47** shows a chart with a formatted plot area.

To format the plot area:

1. Click the Chart Objects field on the toolbar and choose Plot Area (**Figure 5.48**).

2. Choose Format > Selected Plot Area.

   or

   Double-click the border of the plot area. The Format Plot Area dialog box appears (**Figure 5.49**).

3. To place a border around the plot area, select Automatic or Custom in the Border section.

4. To shade the plot area, choose a color from the palette.

5. Click OK.

✔ Tips

- In the Format Plot Area dialog box, you can also adjust the line style, weight, and color of the border.

- Click the Fill Effects button (**Figure 5.49**) to select a texture or gradient for the plot area.

- Be careful with background colors in charts. You must ensure that there is sufficient contrast between your data series, which are likely to be different colors.

  See "Filling a Data Series with Textures or Patterns" earlier in this chapter.

Places a border around the plot area   *Click here to choose a gradient or texture*   *Shades the plot area*

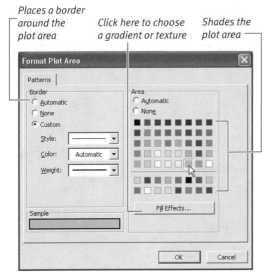

Figure 5.49 Add a border and shade to the plot area in the Format Plot Area dialog box.

FORMATTING THE PLOT AREA

Choosing a Custom Chart Type

With Microsoft Graph's custom chart types, you can create a professional-looking chart that is preformatted with a coordinated set of options. **Figures 5.50** and **5.51** show a chart before and after applying a custom chart type and adjusting the legend position.

To choose a custom chart type:

1. Choose Chart > Chart Type.
   The Chart Type dialog box appears.

2. Select the Custom Types tab (**Figure 5.52**).

3. Make sure the Built-in radio button is selected in order to use one of PowerPoint's built-in chart types.

4. Click a chart type in the list; look at the sample, and read its description.

5. When you have found a built-in custom chart type you like, click OK.

✔ Tips

- After you have a chart close to how you want it, make sure you save your work.

- If you want to refine a chart but not commit to the changes, make a copy of the slide and work with it. The easiest way to do that is to copy and paste the slide thumbnail from Outline view.

  See the next section, "Defining a Custom Chart Type," for information on creating your own custom formats.

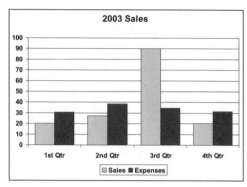

Figure 5.50 A column chart before applying a custom chart type.

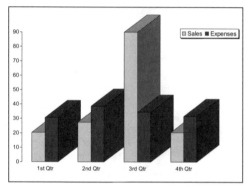

Figure 5.51 The same chart after applying a custom chart type.

First select Built-in... *...then choose a chart type*

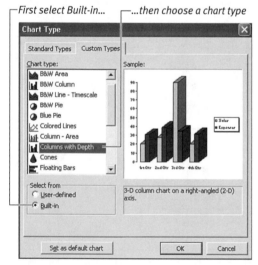

Figure 5.52 Choose a custom chart type on the Custom Types tab.

First select User-Defined...

    ...then click here to add a custom chart type

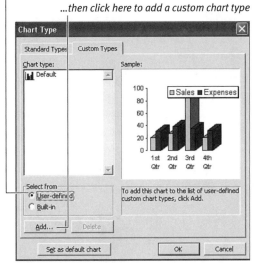

Figure 5.53 Once you select the User-Defined option, you can add and delete your own custom chart types.

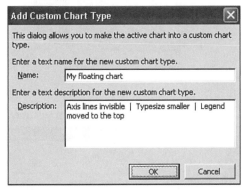

Figure 5.54 Enter the name and description for the custom chart type.

Defining a Custom Chart Type

Suppose you want to format a series of charts with the same settings. You can create your own chart type and then apply its format to any chart; this is called a user-defined chart type.

To define a custom chart type:

1. Format a chart with the exact settings you want to save.

   This chart should be the active chart.

2. Choose Chart > Chart Type.

   The Chart Type dialog box appears.

3. Select the Custom Types tab.

4. Select the User-defined radio button (**Figure 5.53**).

5. Click Add.

   The Add Custom Chart Type dialog box appears (**Figure 5.54**).

6. In the Name field, type a name for the format (up to 31 characters).

7. In the Description field, describe the format in more detail.

8. Click OK to return to the Chart Type dialog box, and click OK again to return to the chart.

DEFINING A CUSTOM CHART TYPE

Applying a User-Defined Chart Type

After you create a user-defined style, you can apply it to existing charts.

To apply a user-defined chart type:

1. Display the chart you want to format.

2. Choose Chart > Chart Type.
   The Chart Type dialog box appears.

3. Select the Custom Types tab.

4. Select the User-defined radio button (**Figure 5.53**).

5. In the Chart Type list, click the name you want to use.

6. Click OK.

CREATING
PIE CHARTS

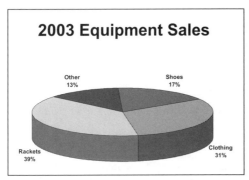

Figure 6.1 Use a pie chart to clearly show relative values.

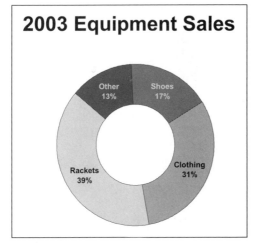

Figure 6.2 Doughnut charts show the breakdown of a total at a certain point in time.

A pie chart shows the relative proportions of several items. By looking at the relative size of the pie slices and their accompanying percentage figures, you can clearly see the relationship between the items (**Figure 6.1**).

Unlike column and line charts, which typically show different values over time, pie charts show values at a particular point in time (such as 2001 sales). Pie charts are one of the simplest types of charts to create because they can have only one data series.

Microsoft Graph offers a number of ways to enhance your pie charts. For instance, you can explode a slice, assign new colors or patterns to the slices, and rotate the pie.

A chart type similar to the pie is the doughnut (**Figure 6.2**). Like pie charts, doughnut charts show the breakdown of a total at a certain point in time.

Inserting a Pie Chart Slide

Like all charts, pie charts use one of the Content layouts.

To insert a pie chart slide:

1. Click the New Slide button on the Standard toolbar or select Ctrl+M.

2. From the Slide Layout task pane, choose a content or chart layout from the task pane (**Figure 6.3**).

   For this example, we chose the Title, Text, and Content layout, providing a title placeholder, a bullet list placeholder, and a content placeholder with which we can create a chart.

3. Click the Insert Chart icon in the Content box (**Figure 6.4**).

   The slide appears with the title (and possibly text) placeholders, and a default column chart is already in place with a data table.

4. You can edit the chart first (working in Microsoft Graph) (**Figure 6.5**).

   or

   Click inside the title placeholder to enter the title of your slide, or click the text placeholder to create your bullets.

5. To edit the chart first, double-click the chart placeholder to activate Microsoft Graph.

   With Microsoft Graph active, the Chart and Data items appear on the menu bar (**Figure 6.6**).

Title placeholder   *Pick a Content Layout (these include text and content)*

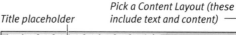

Bullet (text) placeholder

Figure 6.3 Choose a Content Layout on the Slide Layout task pane.

Insert Chart icon

Figure 6.4 Click the Insert Chart icon.

Datasheet   *Dummy chart*   *Title placeholder*   *Click here to enter your title*

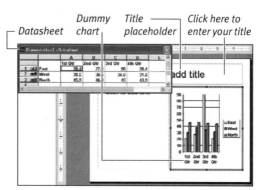

Figure 6.5 A slide appears with a dummy chart (generic data), a datasheet, a title, and possibly a text placeholder.

New Data and Chart items on the main menu

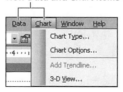

Figure 6.6 With Microsoft Graph active, Data and Chart items appear on the main menu.

First choose the
Pie chart type...

...then choose
a sub-type

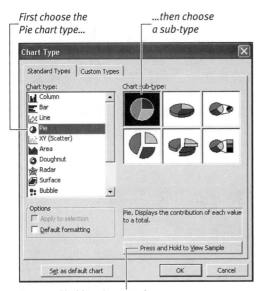

Press and hold to view sample

Figure 6.7 Choose a chart type from the Chart Type dialog box's Standard Types tab.

Change from rows to
columns, or vice versa

Oops, all the data
is the same color

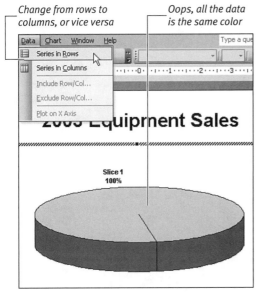

Figure 6.8 Sometimes when you change chart types, the results are not what you expected. Here the pie slices all use the same color. This may happen if you try to chart too much data for a pie chart.

6. Choose Chart > Chart Type.

The Chart Type dialog box appears (**Figure 6.7**).

7. Click the Pie chart type.

8. Click the desired chart sub-type.

9. Click Press and Hold to View Sample for a preview.

10. Click OK.

You are now ready to fill in the datasheet.

See the next section, "Entering Pie Data."

✔ Tip

- If you attempt to convert another type of chart, such as a column or bar chart, to a pie chart and get strange results (**Figure 6.8**), make sure your data can be represented as a pie. Try changing the data orientation, from Series in Rows to Series in Columns, or vice versa. And remember, you can have only one data series for a pie chart.

INSERTING A PIE CHART SLIDE

Entering Pie Data

You enter your chart data in the datasheet window. The datasheet contains sample data that you erase before entering your own data.

To enter pie chart data:

1. If you haven't already done so, double-click the chart placeholder to launch Microsoft Graph.

2. If the datasheet window isn't already displayed, click the View Datasheet button in the toolbar.

3. To erase the sample data, click the Select All button and press Delete.

4. Enter the chart data (**Figure 6.9**).

5. To view the chart, move or close the datasheet.

✔ Tips

- Alternatively, you can enter slice labels in the first column and values in the second column of the datasheet (**Figure 6.10**). But you must use the Data > Series in Columns command to let Graph know that the data series are entered into columns instead of rows.

- Be sure to use the Select All button when deleting the sample data. If you just delete a range of cells and your data consumes fewer columns than the sample data, Microsoft Graph will still insert a slice label for this data on the chart. If you want to keep the data in the graph for later use but you do not want it included in the current chart, use the Exclude Row/Col command on the Data menu. This command tells Graph not to chart the data in the selected row or column.

Enter slice labels in this row   *Enter slice values in this row*

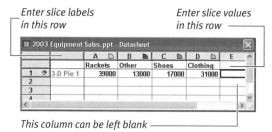

This column can be left blank

Figure 6.9 Enter pie data in the datasheet.

Figure 6.10 Another way to enter pie data is to type the labels and values into columns.

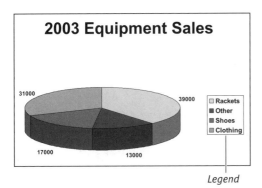

Legend

Figure 6.11 This chart shows values next to each slice.

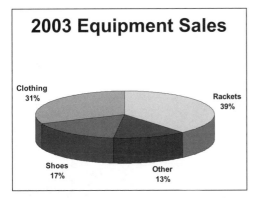

Figure 6.12 This chart shows category names and percentages next to each slice.

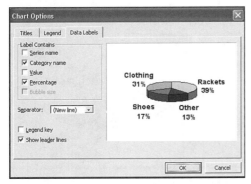

Figure 6.13 Choose the type of data labels you want to appear on your pie chart.

Showing Data Labels

When you first create a pie chart, it includes a legend but no data labels. **Figures 6.11** and **6.12** show some of the types of data (slice) labels you can add to a pie chart.

To place data labels on a pie chart:

1. In Microsoft Graph, choose Chart > Chart Options.

    The Chart Options dialog box appears.

2. Select the Data Labels tab.

3. Choose one or more of the options in the dialog box (**Figure 6.13**).

4. As each check box is selected, the data label appears in the chart. To remove the label, uncheck the check box.

5. Click OK.

✔ Tips

■ When you display only value or percent labels, you will need a legend to identify the slices (**Figure 6.11**).

■ If you choose to display text labels, the text will match the text in the legend. If you show percentages, Microsoft Graph calculates the values for you.

■ If your pie chart has identifying labels next to its slices, you don't need a legend. You can remove the legend from Chart > Chart Options, or just select it and press Delete.

■ To reposition a data label, select it and drag it to the desired location.

Using Leader Lines

When a data label is moved away from the edge of the pie, you can use a leader line to point to its slice (**Figure 6.14**).

To use leader lines on a pie chart:

1. Choose Chart > Chart Options.

   The Chart Options dialog box appears.

2. Select the Data Labels tab.

3. Make sure the Show Leader Lines check box is selected (**Figure 6.15**).

4. Click OK.

   If you have already moved your data labels away from the pie, your leader lines will automatically appear. If you haven't moved your data labels yet, continue on with step 5.

5. Click the data label you want to move: Click once to select the data labels, and then click again on one to select the individual data label.

6. Drag the border of the selected label to the desired position (**Figure 6.16**).

   A leader line will automatically appear.

7. Repeat steps 5 and 6 for each data label.

✔ Tips

- A leader line will not appear if the label is close to or inside the slice.

- Double-click a leader line to format its style, color, and weight.

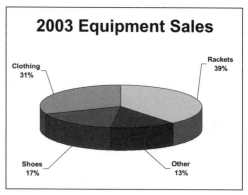

Figure 6.14 This pie chart shows leader lines between the labels and the slices.

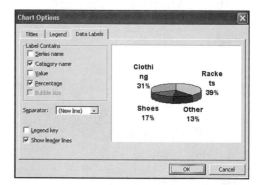

Figure 6.15 Go to the Data Labels tab in the Chart Options dialog box to select the leader line option.

Drag the border to move the label

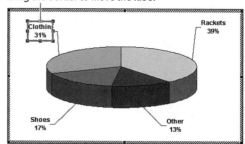

Figure 6.16 The Clothing data label is currently selected.

USING LEADER LINES

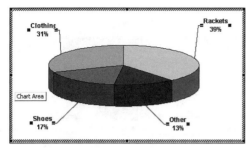

Figure 6.17 The selection handles show that the data labels are currently selected.

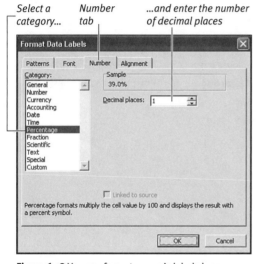

Select a category... *Number tab* *...and enter the number of decimal places*

Figure 6.18 You can format numeric labels here.

Formatting Data Labels

You can format the numbers (percents or values) and the text in the data labels.

To format data label numbers:

1. Select all the data labels by clicking once on any one of them.

   Make sure there are selection handles around all the labels, as shown in **Figure 6.17**.

2. Choose Format > Selected Data Labels. The Format Data Labels dialog box appears.

3. Select the Number tab (**Figure 6.18**).

4. From the Category list, choose the appropriate formatting category (such as Number, Currency, or Percentage).

   If desired, change the value in the Decimal Places field.

5. Click OK.

To format data label text:

1. Select the data labels.

   Make sure there are selection handles around all the labels as shown in **Figure 6.17**.

2. Choose Format > Selected Data Labels. The Format Data Labels dialog box appears.

3. Select the Font tab (**Figure 6.19**).

4. In the Font list, choose the desired typeface.

5. Select the desired font style (Regular, Italic, Bold, or Bold Italic).

6. From the Size list, choose the desired point size.

7. If you like, you can choose a different color from the Color pop-up menu.

8. Click OK.

✔ Tips

- Look at the Preview box (**Figure 6.19**) to preview the formatted text or number.

- One way to select all the data labels is to choose Series 1 Data Labels in the Chart Objects field on the toolbar.

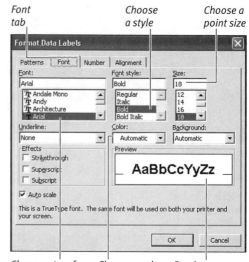

Font tab *Choose a style* *Choose a point size*

Choose a typeface *Choose a color* *Preview*

Figure 6.19 You can format text in data labels.

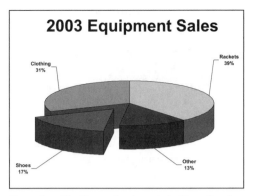

2003 Equipment Sales

Figure 6.20 The Shoes slice is exploded from the pie to emphasize it.

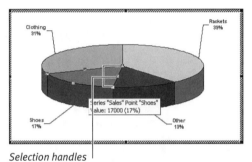

Selection handles

Figure 6.21 Selection handles indicate that the Shoes slice is selected.

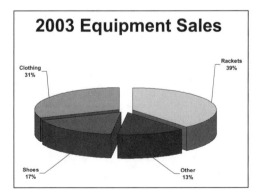

2003 Equipment Sales

Figure 6.22 All slices are exploded in this pie chart.

Exploding a Slice

To emphasize one of the pie slices, you can explode it as shown in **Figure 6.20**.

To explode a pie slice:

1. In Microsoft Graph, click the pie to select it.

2. Click the slice you want to explode. You'll see selection handles around it (**Figure 6.21**).

3. Click the mouse pointer inside the slice and drag away from the pie center until the slice is the desired distance from the rest of the pie.

   The data label moves with the pie slice.

✔ Tips

■ The more space you have between the pie chart and the exploded piece, the greater the emphasis or importance you are placing on the piece.

■ To unexplode a slice, select it and drag it back toward the pie center.

■ To explode all the slices (**Figure 6.22**), select the entire pie and drag any slice—all slices will explode.

■ If you want the exploded slice to be in a particular position (for instance, at the five o'clock position on the pie), rotate the pie until the slice is in the desired place.

See "Rotating a Pie" later in this chapter.

Coloring the Slices

You can assign new colors to any of the slices in a pie chart.

To color the pie slices:

1. In Microsoft Graph, click the pie to select it.

2. Click the slice you want to color. You should see selection handles around it (**Figure 6.23**).

3. Choose Format > Selected Data Point.
   or
   Double-click the slice.
   The Format Data Point dialog box appears.

4. Select the Patterns tab (**Figure 6.24**).

5. Choose a color on the palette in the Area section.

6. Click OK.

7. Repeat steps 2 through 6 for each slice.

✔ Tip

- As an alternative, you can also use the Fill Color button on the toolbar to apply a color to a selected pie slice.

- You can also fill a pie slice with an image, a texture, a gradient, or a pattern, just as you can with column charts as described in Chapter 5.

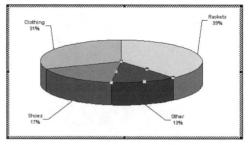

Figure 6.23 The Other slice is selected.

Patterns tab   *Color palette*

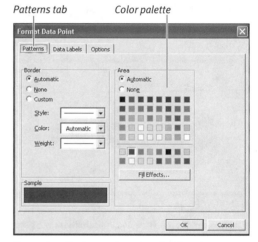

Figure 6.24 To change the color of a slice, choose a color on the palette.

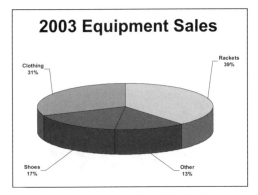

Figure 6.25 The default rotation of the pie slices.

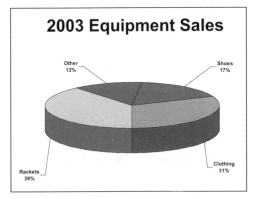

Figure 6.26 After the pie is rotated, the angle is 180 degrees.

Preview box — Options tab — Click arrows to rotate clockwise or counterclockwise

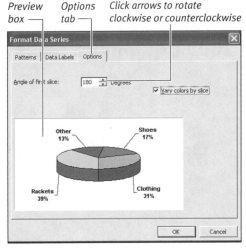

Figure 6.27 To rotate a pie, change the angle of the first slice.

Rotating a Pie

To control the positioning of the slices, you can rotate the pie (**Figures 6.25** and **6.26**).

To rotate a pie:

1. Select the pie.

2. Choose Format > Selected Data Series. The Format Data Series dialog box appears.

3. Select the Options tab (**Figure 6.27**).

4. In the Angle of First Slice field, click the up arrow to rotate the pie clockwise in 10-degree increments, click the down arrow to rotate the pie counterclockwise, or simply type in the angle you want.

5. Click OK.

✔ Tips

■ The angle is measured from the twelve o'clock position on the pie.

■ Watch the preview box (**Figure 6.27**) as you click the arrows in the Angle of First Slice field—the pie rotates with each click.

■ Although data labels will rotate with the slices, you still may need to reposition some of them after rotating.

Formatting 3D Effects

For 3D pies, you can control the height of the pie (**Figure 6.28**) and the angle from which you're viewing it (its elevation, as shown in **Figures 6.29** and **6.30**).

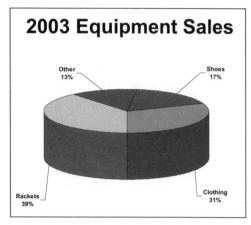

Figure 6.28 This pie chart has a height of 200 percent.

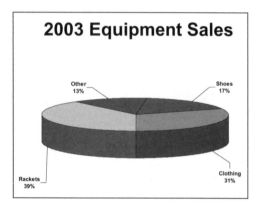

Figure 6.29 This pie chart has an elevation of 10 (the minimum).

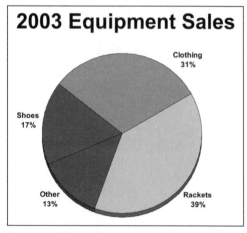

Figure 6.30 This pie chart has an elevation of 80 (the maximum).

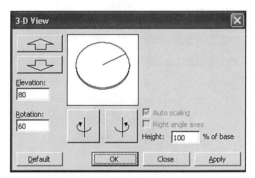

Figure 6.31 Change the elevation and height of a 3-D pie chart in the 3-D View dialog box.

To format a pie's 3D effects:

1. Choose Chart > 3-D View.

   The 3-D View dialog box appears (**Figure 6.31**).

2. Click the large up or down arrow to increase or decrease the elevation angle.

3. Enter a percentage in the Height field.

   The Height value is a percentage of the default height (100%). For instance, 50% is half the default height, and 200% is twice the default height.

4. Click Apply to see the result of your changes without closing the dialog box.

5. Repeat steps 2 through 4 until you are satisfied with the results.

6. Click OK.

✔ Tips

- With a low elevation value, the pie looks as if you are looking at it from the side. With a high value, it looks as if you are viewing the pie from above.

- To return to the default settings, click Default in the 3-D View dialog box.

- Because you may need to rotate your pie after adjusting the elevation and height, the 3-D View dialog box has a Rotation field.

- Labels that are far away from their slice might be sent out of view altogether after you change the elevation. As a precaution, move labels close to their slices *before* increasing the elevation.

FORMATTING 3D EFFECTS

111

Resizing and Repositioning a Pie

After you format and modify a pie chart, you may notice that it seems too small or that it is no longer centered in the chart. You can solve these types of problems by manipulating the plot area.

To resize and reposition a pie:

1. Choose Plot Area in the Chart Objects field on the toolbar (**Figure 6.32**).

   The area of the chart is selected, and selection handles appear at the corners.

2. To resize the pie, drag any corner selection handle (**Figure 6.33**).

3. To reposition the pie, drag from any border line of the selected plot area.

✔ Tip

■ When you resize or move a pie, the data labels move and scale with their respective slices. However, you still may need to manually reposition or resize them. (If you deselect "autoscale" in the Font dialog when formatting the data labels or all chart text, the data labels won't scale—they'll remain the selected font size.)

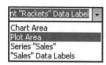

Figure 6.32 Select the plot area in the Chart Objects field on the toolbar.

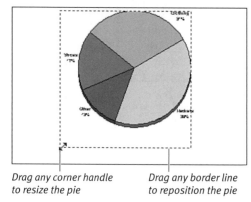

Drag any corner handle to resize the pie

Drag any border line to reposition the pie

Figure 6.33 The selected plot area is being resized.

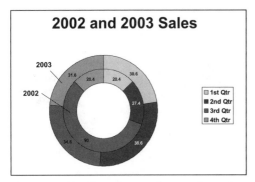

Figure 6.34 A doughnut chart can show two data series.

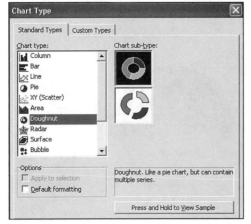

Figure 6.35 Choose the doughnut chart type from the Standard Types tab.

Figure 6.36 You can add labels on the inside of the doughnut pieces.

Creating a Doughnut

A doughnut chart is more than just a two-dimensional pie chart with a hole in the center: Unlike a pie, it can display more than one data series (**Figure 6.34**).

To create a doughnut chart:

1. Insert a new slide with a content layout.

2. Click the Insert Chart icon in the content placeholder.

3. Choose Chart > Chart Type.
   The Chart Type dialog box appears (**Figure 6.35**).

4. Click the Doughnut chart type.

5. Click OK.

✔ Tips

■ You can place labels inside of the doughnut (**Figure 6.36**). To do this, double-click the doughnut to get to the Format Data Series dialog box, choose Options, and decrease the percentage for Doughnut hole size.

■ Because the legend identifies the doughnut pieces, not the data series, you need to identify the data series yourself. In **Figure 6.34**, this was accomplished by returning to PowerPoint and typing the labels **2003** and **2002** with the Text Box tool and drawing the pointers with the Line tool. (These tools are located on the Drawing toolbar.)
   See "Creating a Text Box" in Chapter 3 and "Drawing Lines" in Chapter 10.

113

Creating Linked Pies

The chart shown in **Figure 6.37** contains a second pie that is linked to the first pie—the pie on the right provides a detailed breakdown of a single slice in the main pie. PowerPoint calls this type of chart *pie of pie*. A similar chart type, *bar of pie* (**Figure 6.38**), shows the second pie in a columnar style.

To create linked pies:

1. Create a new slide with a content layout.

2. Click the title placeholder and type the title of your slide.

3. Double-click the chart placeholder to create your chart.

4. Choose Chart > Chart Type.
   The Chart Type dialog box appears.

5. Click the Pie chart type.

6. Click the Pie of Pie or Bar of Pie sub-type (**Figure 6.39**).

7. Click OK.

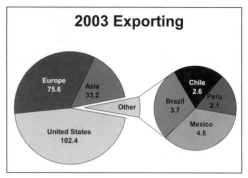

Figure 6.37 The smaller pie is a breakdown of the other slice in the larger pie.

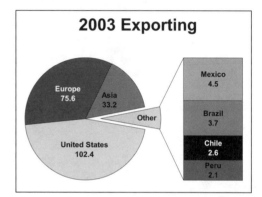

Figure 6.38 The bar shows a breakdown of the other slice.

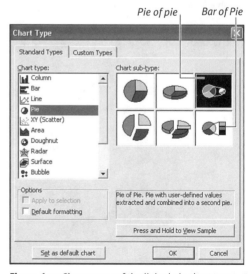

Figure 6.39 Choose one of the linked pie chart types.

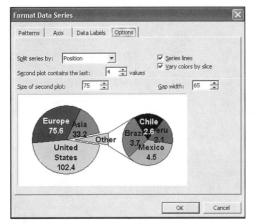

Figure 6.40 Enter the data for both pies as shown. Be sure to enter the values in descending order.

Figure 6.41 The last four values in the datasheet are assigned to the second plot.

Entering Data for Linked Pies

Entering data for a pie of pie or bar of pie chart is not exactly intuitive. The values for both pies are entered into a single column on the datasheet (**Figure 6.40**).

PowerPoint offers a variety of ways to designate how to split the series into two pies. In this example, we've specified that the last four values in the series are for the second plot (**Figure 6.41**).

To enter data for linked pies:

1. Double-click a chart placeholder to open Microsoft Graph.

2. Enter the slice labels in the first column of the datasheet (**Figure 6.40**); do not enter a label for "Other."

3. Enter the slice values in the second column.

4. Choose Data > Series in Columns to show the pies correctly.

5. Select either pie on the chart.

6. Choose Format > Selected Data Series.

   The Format Data Series dialog box appears (**Figure 6.41**).

7. Select the Options tab.

8. To designate how to split the series into two pies, choose one of the options in the Split Series by field (Position, Value, Percent Value, or Custom).

9. Enter a value in the Second Plot Contains the Last x Values field.

10. Click OK.

✔ Tip

- If you want to compare two pie charts on the same slide, but one is not a subset of the other, do not use pie of pie. Instead, use one of the multiple content layouts as described in "Creating Two Charts on a Slide" in Chapter 4.

USING ORGANIZATION CHARTS AND DIAGRAMS

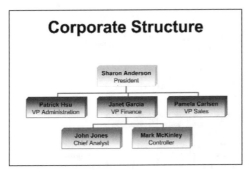

Figure 7.1 PowerPoint includes a complete organization chart, or flowchart, but it cannot be sequentially animated.

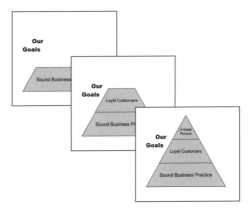

Figure 7.2 These three views of the building pyramid are all within one slide, and each element is built with a mouse click or keystroke.

Because PowerPoint is such an effective tool for visual communications, it has always included the ability to communicate complex ideas using an organization chart (**Figure 7.1**).

PowerPoint 2002 included a new diagram object, with its own organization chart, along with extremely useful cycle, radial, pyramid, Venn, and target diagrams.

These diagrams are great for visual communication, because they present your concepts in sequence (**Figure 7.2**) and can be quickly revised. Using PowerPoint to animate a diagram as a progression keeps the audience in pace with the presentation, making certain that each step is understood.

Using an Organization Chart

All of PowerPoint's organization charts and diagrams are accessible through the now-familiar content layout (**Figure 7.3**). An organization chart (org chart) or flowchart is a great way to show a hierarchical structure of people or ideas.

The first object in the PowerPoint Diagram Gallery (**Figure 7.4**) is such an organization chart or flowchart.

Figure 7.3 Org charts and diagrams are one of the six choices from the content layout.

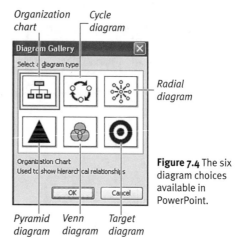

Figure 7.4 The six diagram choices available in PowerPoint.

Organization chart   *Cycle diagram*

Radial diagram

Pyramid diagram   *Venn diagram*   *Target diagram*

Patrick, Janet, and Pamela are co-workers and are subordinates of Sharon
Sharon is manager of Patrick, Janet, and Pamela
Corporate Structure
Sharon Anderson
President
Patrick Hsu
VP Administration
Janet Garcia
VP Finance
Pamela Carlsen
VP Sales
John Jones
Chief Analyst
Mark McKinley
Controller
John and Mark report to Janet

Figure 7.5 This completed organization chart illustrates a corporation's structure.

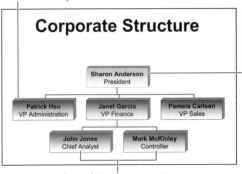

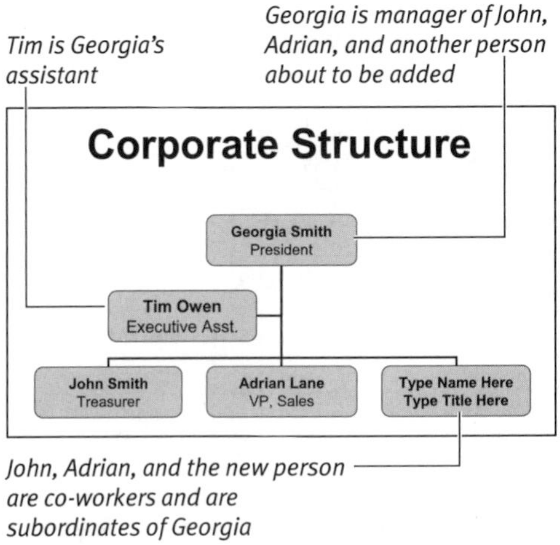

Tim is Georgia's assistant
Georgia is manager of John, Adrian, and another person about to be added
Corporate Structure
Georgia Smith
President
Tim Owen
Executive Asst.
John Smith
Treasurer
Adrian Lane
VP, Sales
Type Name Here
Type Title Here
John, Adrian, and the new person are co-workers and are subordinates of Georgia

Figure 7.6 This chart in progress shows similar relationships.

The most common use for an organization chart is to illustrate a business's structure (**Figure 7.5**). It identifies the names and titles of the key people in a company or division. You can also use org charts to create a simple flowchart, an outline of tasks in a project, a family tree, or even a diagram of your hard disk's directory structure.

Organization charts include various levels, identified as managers, subordinates, co-workers, and assistants (**Figure 7.6**). A manager is someone who has other people—subordinates—reporting to him or her. Co-workers are subordinates that share the same manager. An assistant provides administrative assistance to a manager.

Using the Diagram Objects

Diagram objects are available from the Slide Layout task pane one of two ways: as one of the six choices on the content layout, or as a dedicated choice in the Other Layouts section. You can also use Insert > Diagram.

To insert a diagram object into a slide:

1. Click the New Slide button on the toolbar (Ctrl+M).

2. In the Slide Layout pane, choose one of the combination layouts that includes the standard content layout, or as **Figure 7.7** shows, the Title and Diagram or Organization Chart layout.

3. Double-click anywhere within the placeholder.

   The Diagram Gallery appears (**Figure 7.4**), offering you your choice of the six diagram objects.

4. Click each diagram object to see a description of its features and uses.

5. When you've selected the diagram object you want to use, click OK.

   The diagram object is placed in your slide's content placeholder, and an editing toolbar appears (**Figure 7.8**).

You are now ready to add information to the organization chart diagram object.

See "Editing the Organizational Chart Diagram Object" in the next section.

✔ Tip

- Even after you've selected the diagram object, you can change the slide layout by making another content selection from the Slide Layout task pane.

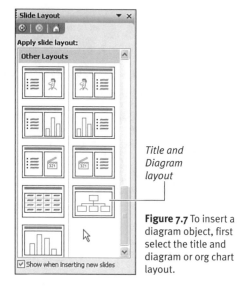

Title and Diagram layout

Figure 7.7 To insert a diagram object, first select the title and diagram or org chart layout.

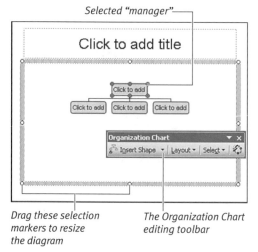

Selected "manager"

Drag these selection markers to resize the diagram

The Organization Chart editing toolbar

Figure 7.8 The organization chart inside the content placeholder.

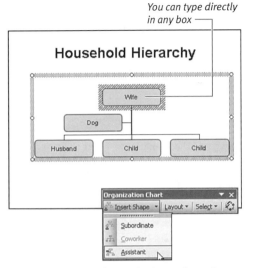

You can type directly in any box

Figure 7.9 The Insert Shape selection on the toolbar lets you add a Coworker, Assistant, or Subordinate box.

Editing the Organization Chart Diagram Object

A described previously, an organization chart (or simple flowchart) shows the structure of a company or concept in a hierarchical view.

The organization chart diagram object starts with two levels: a top level, which consists of a single head (manager), and three subordinates.

Remember that these "people" could be concepts or entities, like a hard drive and folders, or ideas, like a sales cycle or class curriculum.

To edit an organization diagram:

1. Open a slide containing an organization chart and click the chart to select it.

   When the organization chart first appears or is selected within a slide, a toolbar named Organization Chart also appears (**Figure 7.8**).

   The new organization chart has a selection box around it, and selection markers for quick revision. These selection markers let you quickly drag and resize the diagram.

2. Click in any block to enter a name or other text description.

3. To add a new box, click a box beside which, or beneath which, you want to insert a new box.

4. Click Insert Shape on the Organization Chart toolbar.

5. From the drop-down menu, choose the type of new box you want: Subordinate, Coworker, or Assistant (**Figure 7.9**).

   A new box will be added to the chart below (Subordinate), equal to (Coworker), or adjacent to (Assistant) the entry you selected. In this case, we have added a loyal assistant to the head of the household.

   continues on next page

121

6. Click the Layout item on the toolbar.

A drop-down menu appears to let you quickly realign or resize your chart (**Figure 7.10**).

To realign portions of your chart, select a manager box (one that controls a set of subordinates) and then select an alignment option: left hanging, right hanging, or hanging in both directions.

Resize the diagram by using the diagram selection markers, or scale it using ordinary selection handles (**Figure 7.11**).

7. Click an item on the Select drop-down menu to quickly work with a branch or a level. (**Figure 7.12** shows a level of the org chart selected.)

With the Fill Bucket on the Drawing toolbar, the selected branch can be recolored (**Figure 7.13**).

8. To quickly reformat the entire diagram, choose Autoformat from the toolbar (**Figure 7.14**).

The Organization Chart Style Gallery opens, offering a list of choices, with previews (**Figure 7.15**).

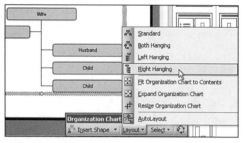

Figure 7.10 The Layout submenu lets you change the orientation of a branch or level or expand the entire diagram. Here, the last two Child items have been made right-hanging.

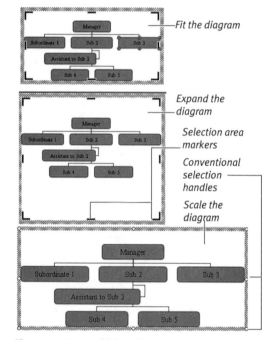

Figure 7.11 You can fit the selection markers to the diagram, expand the selection markers, or rescale the entire diagram with conventional selection handles.

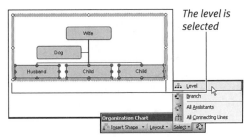

The level is selected

Figure 7.12 The Select item on the toolbar can let you quickly work with an entire group of boxes.

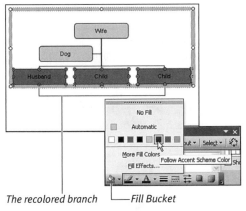

The recolored branch —— Fill Bucket

Figure 7.13 The selected branch is recolored using the Fill Bucket on the Drawing toolbar.

Autoformat opens a Style Gallery

Figure 7.14 The diagram object editing toolbar.

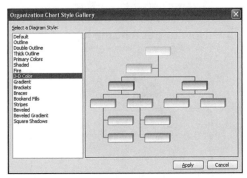

Figure 7.15 The Style Gallery lets you quickly apply a new look to the entire diagram.

✔ Tips

■ To quickly revise an organization chart or any diagram, right-click it; many of the options you might need are offered in a shortcut menu.

■ To add a title to your org chart, first click outside the Org Chart/Diagram box so you're back on the slide itself. Then use the textbox icon on the drawing toolbar to create a textbox and type the title text into it. Select the textbox, cut it, and then click inside the org chart/diagram and paste. Move the textbox where you want it.

■ To reuse an org chart created with an earlier version of PowerPoint, copy the org chart to a new slide in PowerPoint 2003 and double-click it. The new Organization Chart toolbar should appear, and the chart will be converted to a diagram object that you can edit.

■ To select several parts of a diagram for formatting, hold down the Shift key as you select each part in turn.

■ To learn how to animate diagrams sequentially with the Custom Animation and Animation Schemes tasks pane, see Chapter 15.

■ Applying Autoformat overrides any customization (for example, fill and line colors) that you may have already applied to your org chart. And colors cannot be changed on an org chart that uses Autoformat. So use Autoformat on a copy of the org chart to ensure against losing all your work.

EDITING THE ORGANIZATION CHART DIAGRAM

Choosing a Diagram Type

Besides the organization or flowchart, PowerPoint 2002 offers five other diagram objects: cycle, radial, pyramid, Venn, and target diagram objects. Each of these objects uses the same Diagram toolbar.

Use the cycle diagram to show a recurring cycle of events (**Figure 7.16**).

Use the radial diagram to show relationships of one or more elements to a core element (**Figure 7.17**).

Use the pyramid diagram to show a structure where one element supports another (**Figure 7.18**).

Use the Venn diagram to show how elements overlap (**Figure 7.19**).

Use the target diagram to show how steps can lead to a goal (**Figure 7.20**).

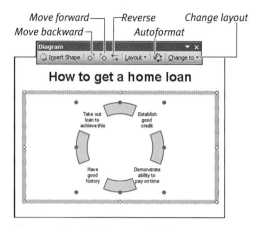

Figure 7.16 A cycle diagram toolbar lets you reverse the order or move elements.

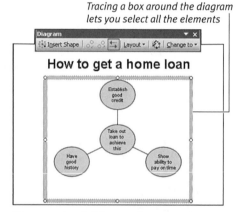

Figure 7.17 A radial diagram shows one element being a core component of the others.

Figure 7.18 A pyramid diagram shows one element supporting or built upon the other.

EDITING THE ORGANIZATION CHART DIAGRAM

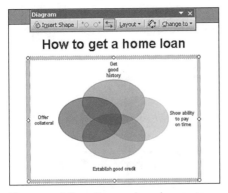

Figure 7.19 A Venn diagram shows how parts of each component overlap the others. (Venn diagrams now also have transparency.)

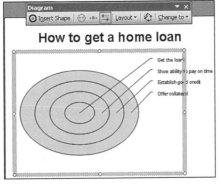

Figure 7.20 A target diagram shows how steps lead to a goal.

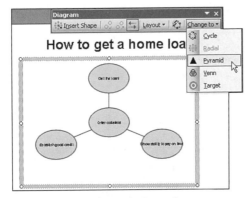

Figure 7.21 You can instantly change from one to the other with the Change To drop-down.

✔ Tips

- To insert any diagram object into your slide, just repeat the steps in "To Insert a Diagram Object into a Slide" presented earlier in this chapter and select the appropriate object.

- To instantly change your diagram type, select Change To from the Diagram toolbar (**Figure 7.21**).

- When using a cycle diagram, click any of the text areas between the cycle segments to insert text (**Figure 7.16**). Use the Change Autoshape option on the Drawing toolbar to change the shapes to arrows.

- Venn diagrams must have Autolayout and Autoformat turned off in order to change fills and lines on the circles. If you then insert another shape into the Venn diagram, it will turn Autolayout back on, but it won't override your customizations the way Autoformat does.

- The Autoformat button on the toolbar gives you access to the Diagram Style Gallery.

EDITING THE ORGANIZATION CHART DIAGRAM

125

Creating a Custom Flowchart or Diagram

If you need to create a complex flowchart or diagram, beyond the capabilities of PowerPoint's tools, don't despair.

You can easily create your own diagrams with the Drawing toolbar and then position them as desired on the slide. Each element will be individually selectable, making it easy to animate.

To learn in more detail how to create these kinds of graphical objects, see Chapter 11.

To create your own diagrams:

1. Create a new slide.

2. Select a blank layout or a slide with just a title.

3. If the Drawing toolbar is not visible, select View > Toolbars > Drawing.

4. Select the Rectangle tool and create a rectangle anywhere on the slide. Begin typing, and your text will automatically appear within the rectangle (**Figure 7.22**).

5. Select an arrow or block arrow (**Figure 7.23**) and draw the arrow to the right of the rectangle.
   This will point to the next box.

6. With the arrow still selected on your slide, press and hold Shift while clicking the rectangle to select it, too. (Or you can drag a marquee around the two objects.)

7. To quickly copy those elements, press and hold Ctrl while you drag the two objects to the right.

   By holding Ctrl, you drag a copy of the objects instead of moving the originals. In this way, you can quickly populate your chart (**Figure 7.24**).

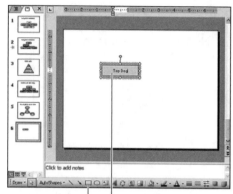

Select rectangle ⎯   *Start typing to enter your text*

Figure 7.22 Select the Rectangle tool and draw one on the slide.

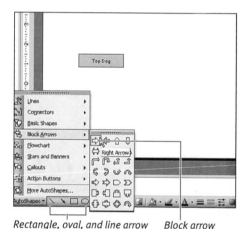

Rectangle, oval, and line arrow   *Block arrow*

Figure 7.23 Select the block arrow and add it to the slide.

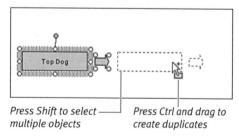

Press Shift to select ⎯   *Press Ctrl and drag to*
multiple objects   *create duplicates*

Figure 7.24 With the Shift key, select multiple objects and drag new ones that look the same.

CREATING A CUSTOM FLOWCHART OR DIAGRAM

✔ Tips

- Rename the boxes and use the Paint Bucket tool to recolor them.

- The Draw drop-down menu on the Drawing toolbar has tools to align your objects and enhance your diagram.

- You can use autoshapes and smart connectors to create org charts and other simple diagrams. These tools give the user much more control over creating and formatting than do some of the new diagramming tools or, for that matter, than the old org chart program. Just choose the Connectors option from the Autoshapes menu.

CREATING A CUSTOM FLOWCHART OR DIAGRAM

Formatting Box Text

You can format any part of the text inside the org chart boxes just as you would ordinary text (**Figure 7.25**).

To format box text:

1. To format a selection of text, click inside the box and then drag across the characters you want to format.

   or

   To format all the text in one or more boxes, select the boxes.

   or

   To format all the text in the entire diagram, select the entire diagram.

2. Choose Format > Font.

   The Font dialog box appears (**Figures 7.26**).

3. In the Font list, choose the desired typeface.

4. Select the desired font style (Regular, Italic, Bold, or Bold Italic).

5. In the Size list, choose the desired point size.

6. Click OK.

✔ Tips

- You can also change the alignment of text within the boxes. From the Text menu, choose Left, Right, or Center. (Center is the default.)

- You can also change the text color. From the Text menu, choose Color and choose a color from the window that appears.

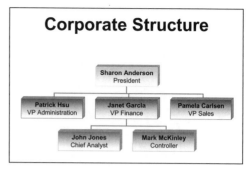

Figure 7.25 All the names are in bold.

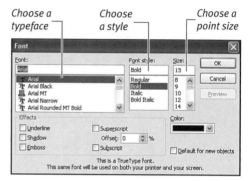

Figure 7.26 Format box text in the Font dialog box.

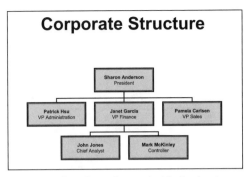

Figure 7.27 These boxes have a double-line border.

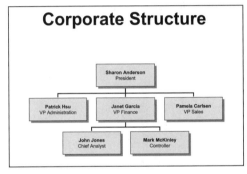

Figure 7.28 These boxes have shadows.

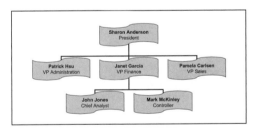

Figure 7.29 Careful with changing autoshapes...

Figure 7.30 Format AutoShape is a handy dialog box to use.

Formatting the Boxes

You can choose a different border style (**Figure 7.27**), add a shadow (**Figure 7.28**), or change the color inside your boxes. *Note:* If you have applied one of the autoformats to your diagram, you cannot apply any additional formats. You must remove any autoformatting before proceeding.

To remove autoformatting:

1. Select any part of the diagram, and click Autoformat on the Organization Chart toolbar.

2. Choose Default for style from the Organization Chart Style Gallery.

3. Click OK.

To format the boxes:

1. Select the boxes you want to format. To select all boxes in a diagram, select the topmost box and then click Select > Branch.

2. Use any of the following formatting commands on the Drawing toolbar:
   - ▲ Choose Fill Color to change the background color of the boxes.
   - ▲ Choose Line Color or Line Style to change the outline of the boxes.
   - ▲ Choose Shadow Style to add a shadow effect, like the one in **Figure 7.28**.
   - ▲ Choose Draw > Change AutoShape to change the shape of the box itself. Because any of the shapes on those menus are available, you could turn the boxes into radically different shapes, like the ones shown in **Figure 7.29**, or into something even wilder. (Please don't...)

✔ Tip

- If you simply double-click on the selected box(es), the Format AutoShape dialog box appears, with which you can make many of the changes listed above (**Figure 7.30**).

Formatting the Connecting Lines

The lines that connect the boxes to each other can also be formatted. You can adjust their thickness and style (**Figure 7.31**).

To format the lines in the org chart:

1. To select all connecting lines, choose Select > All Connecting Lines from the Organization Chart toolbar.

   or

   To select a single line, click the line.

2. Use the Line Color, Line Style, and/or Dash Style menus on the Drawing toolbar.

   or

   Double-click any selected line to invoke Format AutoShape and adjust the lines from there.

✔ Tip

■ To select several lines, hold down Shift as you click each one.

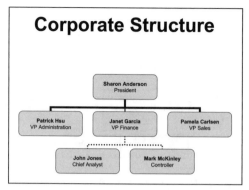

Figure 7.31 The top connecting lines were formatted with a heavy line weight and the ones below it with dotted lines style.

Zooming In and Out

The Zoom option on the View menu (**Figure 7.32**) offers ways to zoom in (get up closer) or zoom out (step back) to change your view of the screen. (It does not affect the printed size of the chart.) You can also change your view using the Zoom button (**Figure 7.33**).

Figures 7.34 and **7.35** show two extreme examples of zooming.

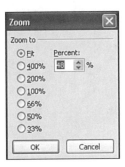

Figure 7.32 Use the Zoom dialog box to change your view of the organization chart.

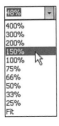

Figure 7.33 The Zoom drop-down on the Standard toolbar is the most convenient way to zoom in and out.

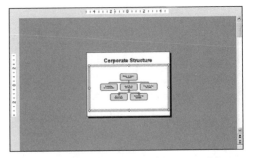

Figure 7.34 For those with better than 20-20 vision.

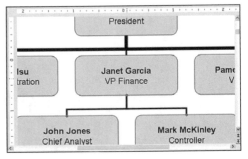

Figure 7.35 And for those with poorer vision...

8

CREATING TABLES

Essential Baseball Statistics		
Player	Home Runs	Covers Bitten Off
Bonds	73	0
Spot	0	73
Weird Al	15	15

Figure 8.1 This table has three columns.

Baseball Commentary	
Why is it bad to bite the cover off the ball?	Baseballs that do not have covers do not travel as far, are more difficult to catch, and if bitten by the wrong species, could contain dog saliva.
What should you do when it happens?	Immediately replace the ball and throw the suspect one into the stands for a fan to enjoy as a souvenir.
Will fans appreciate balls that have drool?	Our conclusion is that fans will take anything that a ballplayer offers them. Even dog slobber.

Figure 8.2 This table has side-by-side paragraphs.

The best way to present columns of data is in a table slide. **Figures 8.1** and **8.2** show examples of tables you can create in PowerPoint.

Unlike in the stone ages of PowerPoint, today you can create tables directly in PowerPoint, without having to use Microsoft Word.

Inserting a Table Slide

PowerPoint 2003 offers one layout specifically for tables (**Figure 8.3**), under Other Layouts in the Slide Layouts task pane; however, you can create a table from any of the content layouts, as Insert Table is the top-left icon of the content icon.

To insert a table slide:

1. Click the New Slide button on the toolbar or choose Ctrl+M.

2. In the Slide Layouts task pane, choose the Title and Table layout (**Figure 8.3**) near the end.

   If the Slide Layout task pane is not visible, choose View > Task Pane > Slide Layout.

   Title and table placeholders appear on the slide (**Figure 8.4**).

3. Click the title placeholder and type the title of your slide.

4. Double-click the table placeholder to create your table.

   You are asked to specify the number of columns and rows (**Figure 8.5**).

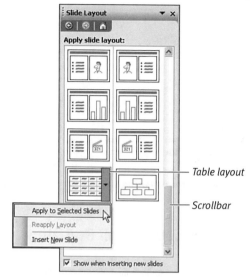

Table layout

Scrollbar

Figure 8.3 To create a table slide, first choose the Table layout under Other Layouts in the Layout task pane. Scroll down if necessary.

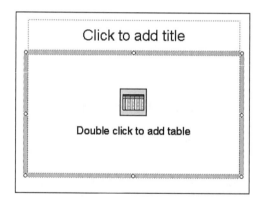

Figure 8.4 Double-click the table placeholder to create your table.

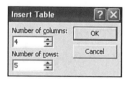

Figure 8.5 Specify the number of columns and rows in your table.

INSERTING A TABLE SLIDE

Tables and Borders toolbar —   *Click the close button to close the toolbar*

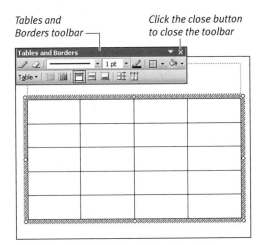

Figure 8.6 A new table with four columns and five rows.

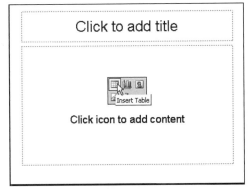

Figure 8.7 Using a content layout provides the third of three ways to add a table to a slide.

5. Specify the number of columns and press Tab to move to the box to input number of rows.

6. Specify the number of rows and click OK.

An empty table appears on the slide, along with a Tables and Borders toolbar (**Figure 8.6**).

✔ Tips

■ You can add a table to any slide without using the task pane—just choose Insert > Table. Also, adding a table is one of the six choices available when you add a generic content layout to a slide (**Figure 8.7**).

■ If the Tables and Borders toolbar does not automatically appear, you can display it from View > Toolbars > Tables and Borders.

■ When you initially create a table, all the columns and rows are the same size. However, the column widths and row heights can be adjusted at any time.

See "Adjusting Column Width" and "Adjusting Row Height" later in this chapter.

Entering Text into a Table

Like an Excel spreadsheet, a table is made up of rows and columns; the rectangular blocks made up by the intersections of rows and columns are called *cells*.

To type text into a table:

1. Click in a cell and start typing.

   As you reach the right edge of the cell, text will wrap automatically to the next line in the cell (**Figure 8.8**).

2. Press Tab to move the cursor to the next cell to the right.

3. After entering text in the last cell in the row, press Tab; this moves the cursor to the first cell in the next row.

✔ Tips

■ If you enter more text than fits in the cell at its original size, the entire row becomes taller to accommodate the extra characters.

■ Pressing Enter in a cell moves the cursor down to the next line in the same cell. It does not move the cursor to a different cell.

■ Pressing Tab from the last cell in a table inserts a new row and places the cursor in the first cell of it.

■ If text wraps in a cell but you want the text to fit on a single line, you can either decrease the type size or adjust the column width.

   See "Formatting Table Text" and "Adjusting Column Width" later in this chapter.

■ Instead of Tab, you can use all four arrow keys to navigate to other cells in the table. Shift+Tab moves you back a cell, and if you need an actual tab in a cell, press Ctrl+Tab.

What is the Smart Health Program?	A health care plan designed to maximize your benefits by utilizing a network of participating physicians and hospitals.
Is my physician a provider in the network?	Check with your physician or get a copy of the Smart Health Program Directory of Physicians. To order a copy, call 800-555-2323.
What about claim forms?	The participating provider is responsible for submitting forms for you.

Figure 8.8 Text automatically wraps within each cell, and the row heights automatically adjust.

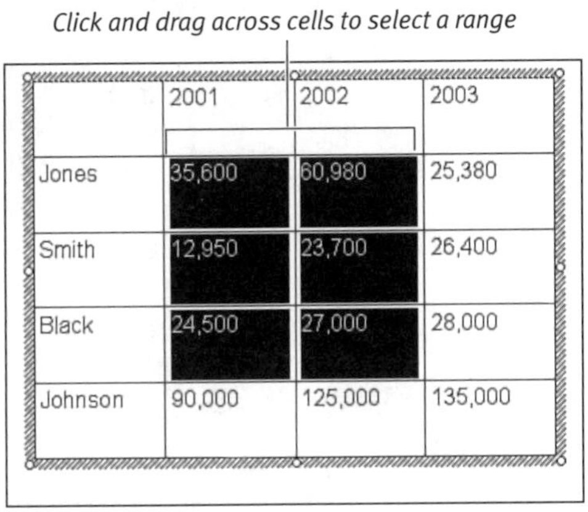

Click and drag across cells to select a range

	2001	2002	2003
Jones	35,600	60,980	25,380
Smith	12,950	23,700	26,400
Black	24,500	27,000	28,000
Johnson	90,000	125,000	135,000

Figure 8.9 A range of cells is currently selected.

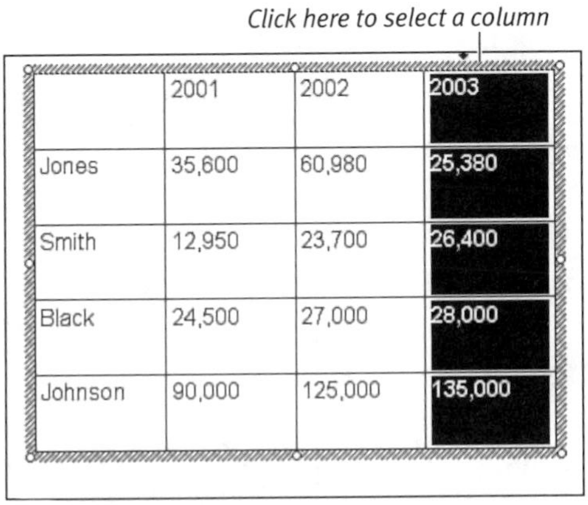

Click here to select a column

	2001	2002	2003
Jones	35,600	60,980	25,380
Smith	12,950	23,700	26,400
Black	24,500	27,000	28,000
Johnson	90,000	125,000	135,000

Figure 8.10 Click above the first cell in a column to select the entire column.

Selecting Cells

Before you can format cells in your table, you need to select them.

To select parts of a table:

Use any of the following techniques to select cells:

- ◆ Click Table on the Tables and Borders toolbar and choose Select Table, Select Column, or Select Row.

- ◆ Select the next cell or the previous cell by pressing Tab or Shift+Tab.

- ◆ With the mouse, you can select a range of cells by dragging across them (**Figure 8.9**).

- ◆ Select an entire column by clicking directly above the column (**Figure 8.10**). The mouse pointer becomes a down arrow when it is positioned properly for selecting the column.

- ◆ Press Shift and use your arrow keys to select multiple cells.

✔ Tips

- ■ Before dragging across cells, make sure that neither the Draw Table nor Eraser tool is selected. If the pointer appears as a pencil or an eraser, press Esc to cancel the tool.

- ■ The keyboard shortcut for selecting the entire table is Ctrl+A.

SELECTING CELLS

Adjusting Column Width

Although a new table starts with columns of equal width, it's easy to make the columns wider or narrower. You can either manually adjust the width of a column or have PowerPoint do it for you automatically.

To adjust the width of a column:

1. Press Esc to make sure that no cells are selected. (If you select certain cells of a column, you would only change the width of those cells—good to know, but perhaps not what you had in mind).

2. Place the pointer on the right border line of the column.

   or

   If your table doesn't have vertical borders, place the pointer between the columns, where the border would be.

3. When the pointer becomes two arrows pointing left and right, do one of the following:

   ▲ Drag to the left to narrow the column (**Figure 8.11**), or drag to the right to widen it.

   ▲ Double-click the column border to automatically find the best fit according to the widest entry. In **Figure 8.12**, double-clicking on the border to the right of the names decreases the width so that Johnson fits snugly.

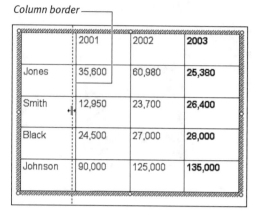

Column border

Figure 8.11 Dragging the column border is one way to adjust the column width.

Double-click here

	2001	2002	2003
Jones	35,600	60,980	**25,380**
Smith	12,950	23,700	**26,400**
Black	24,500	27,000	**28,000**
Johnson	90,000	125,000	**135,000**

Figure 8.12 To quickly set the width of the first column, double-click the column border.

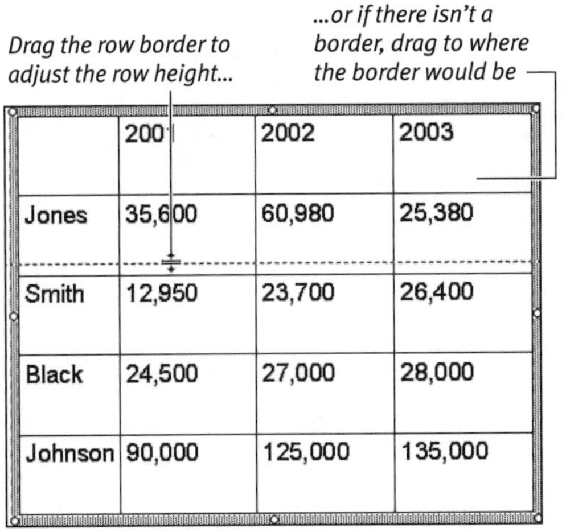

Drag the row border to adjust the row height...

...or if there isn't a border, drag to where the border would be

	200	2002	2003
Jones	35,600	60,980	25,380
Smith	12,950	23,700	26,400
Black	24,500	27,000	28,000
Johnson	90,000	125,000	135,000

Figure 8.13 To adjust the row height, drag the row border.

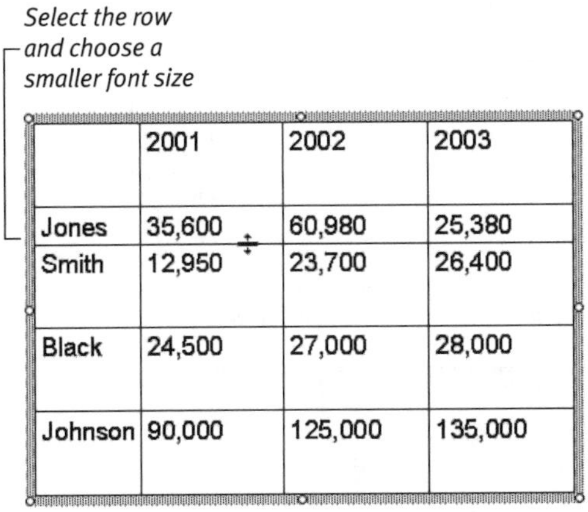

Select the row and choose a smaller font size

	2001	2002	2003
Jones	35,600	60,980	25,380
Smith	12,950	23,700	26,400
Black	24,500	27,000	28,000
Johnson	90,000	125,000	135,000

Figure 8.14 Dragging the row border will not shorten a row below what the text needs to be displayed.

Adjusting Row Height

Although you can increase row height to add extra space between rows, you can't make the row height shorter than the row's tallest entry.

To adjust the height of a row:

1. Place the pointer on the border line beneath the row.

   or

   If your table doesn't have horizontal borders, place the pointer between the rows, where the border would be.

2. When the pointer becomes two arrows pointing up and down, drag up or down to adjust the row height (**Figure 8.13**).

✔ Tip

■ PowerPoint will not allow you to make a row smaller than the text that fits in it. **Figure 8.14** shows the smallest row allowed for the existing text. This holds true for even an empty row, in which PowerPoint reserves sufficient height for one line of type. If you want to make the row shorter than that, select the row and set it to a smaller font size.

Inserting Rows and Columns

If you underestimated the number of rows or columns in your table when initially creating it, you can insert more later. **Figures 8.15** and **8.16** show a table before and after inserting a row.

To insert a row:

1. Click the text cursor in the table where you want to insert the new row.

2. Click Table on the Tables and Borders toolbar.

   The Table menu appears (**Figure 8.17**).

3. Choose Insert Rows Above or Insert Rows Below. You insert columns the same way, by selecting Insert Columns the Left or Insert Columns to the Right.

✔ Tips

- To insert multiple rows (or columns) in the same location, first select the number of rows (columns) you want to insert. For instance, to insert two rows, select two rows and choose Insert Rows Above (or Insert Rows Below) on the Table menu.

- To insert a new row after the last row, position the cursor in the last cell in the table and press Tab.

- You can also insert rows and columns with the Draw Table tool, and rows can be inserted from the shortcut (right-click) menu.

The cursor is located after "Jones"

	2001	2002	2003
Jones	35,600	60,980	25,380
Smith	12,950	23,700	26,400
Black	24,500	27,000	28,000
Johnson	90,000	125,000	135,000

Figure 8.15 You can choose to insert a row either above or below the cursor.

Inserted row

	2001	2002	2003
Jones	35,600	60,980	25,380
Smith	12,950	23,700	26,400
Black	24,500	27,000	28,000
Johnson	90,000	125,000	135,000

Figure 8.16 Use the Table > Insert Rows Above command to insert this row.

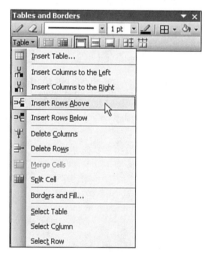

Figure 8.17 Click the Table button on the Tables and Borders toolbar to display this menu.

	2001	2002	2003
Jones	35,600	60,980	25,380
Smith	12,950	23,700	26,400
Black	24,500	27,000	28,000
Johnson	90,000	125,000	135,000

Figure 8.18 A row is selected and can now be deleted.

	2001	2002	2003
Jones	35,600	60,980	25,380
Black	24,500	27,000	28,000
Johnson	90,000	125,000	135,000

Figure 8.19 The row with Smith's data has been deleted from the table.

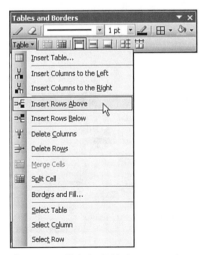

Figure 8.20 Click the Table button on the Tables and Borders toolbar to display this menu. You may need to wait a few seconds for the Delete options to appear.

Deleting Rows and Columns

When you delete rows and columns, you not only remove the contents of the cells, you remove the cells as well (**Figures 8.18** and **8.19**).

To delete rows or columns:

1. Select the rows or columns to be deleted (**Figure 8.18**).

   or

   Just make sure your cursor is somewhere in the column or row.

2. Click Table on the Tables and Borders toolbar.

   The Table menu appears (**Figure 8.20**).

3. Choose Delete Rows or Delete Columns.

✔ Tips

- If the Tables and Borders toolbar isn't displayed, choose View > Toolbars > Tables and Borders.

- If you accidentally delete columns or rows, immediately choose Edit > Undo (Ctrl+Z).

- To erase the contents of selected cells, just press Delete. (The empty cells remain.)

Formatting Table Text

You can apply many kinds of formatting to the text in a table, including typeface, size, and style (**Figures 8.21** and **8.22**).

To format table text:

1. Select the cells whose text you want to format; or within a cell, drag across the individual characters you want to format.

2. Choose Format > Font.

   The Font dialog box appears (**Figure 8.23**).

3. In the Font list, choose the desired typeface.

4. Select the desired font style (Regular, Italic, Bold, or Bold Italic).

5. In the Size list, choose the desired point size.

6. If you like, you can add an underline or other effect to the selection.

7. Click OK.

Essential Baseball Statistics

Player	Home Runs	Covers Bitten Off
Bonds	73	0
Spot	0	73
Weird Al	15	15

Figure 8.21 This text is set in Arial with the table text at 28 points.

Essential Baseball Statistics

Player	Home Runs	Covers Bitten Off
Bonds	73	0
Spot	0	73
Weird Al	15	15

Figure 8.22 After formatting, the text for this table is a mix of Delta Book, Bold, and Heavy.

Click the desired typeface — *Choose a type style from the list* — *Double-click here and type the size or...*

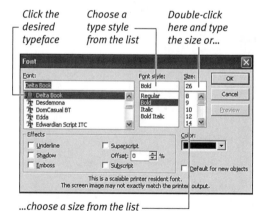

...choose a size from the list —

Figure 8.23 Choose a font for table text in the Font dialog box.

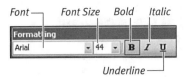

Figure 8.24 You can also format table text using the Formatting toolbar.

✔ Tips

- Instead of displaying the Font dialog box, you can use the Font, Font Size, Bold, Italic, and Underline buttons on the Formatting toolbar (**Figure 8.24**).

- If you select the table placeholder instead of text within the table, you will format the font for the entire table.

Adding Borders

By default, borders appear around the outside and inside of new tables (**Figure 8.25**). These default borders are solid lines with a 1-point line weight. You can remove any of these borders or apply different line styles or weights to existing borders (**Figure 8.26**).

To add new or format existing borders:

1. Select the cells where you want to add or change borders.

2. On the Tables and Borders toolbar (**Figure 8.27**), click the arrow next to the Border Style button and choose a line style from the drop-down menu (**Figure 8.28**).

Essential Baseball Statistics

Player	Home Runs	Covers Bitten Off
Bonds	73	0
Spot	0	73
Weird Al	15	15

Figure 8.25 This table has 1-point borders around all the cells.

Essential Baseball Statistics

Player	Home Runs	Covers Bitten Off
Bonds	73	0
Spot	0	73
Weird Al	15	15

Figure 8.26 This table has only vertical borders, except for a bottom border under the column headings.

Border Style   *Border Width*   *All Borders*

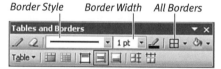

Figure 8.27 Use the Tables and Borders toolbar to apply borders to a table.

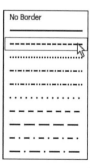

Figure 8.28 Choose a border style from the list.

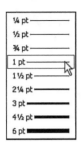

Figure 8.29 Choose a border width from the list.

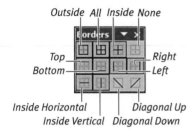

Figure 8.30 Click the Apply Borders button to choose a border type.

Table 8.1

Border Buttons	
BORDER BUTTON	**DESCRIPTION**
Outside Borders	Outline around the selected area
All Borders	Lines around and inside the selected area
Inside Borders	Horizontal and vertical lines inside the selected area
No Border	No lines in the selected area
Top Border	Horizontal line on the top of the selected area
Bottom Border	Horizontal line on the bottom edge of the selected area
Left Border	Vertical line on the left side of the selected area
Right Border	Vertical line on the right side of the selected area
Inside Horizontal Border	Horizontal lines between cells in the selected area
Inside Vertical Border	Vertical lines between cells in the selected area
Diagonal Down Border	Diagonal lines that extend from the upper-left to the lower-right corner of each cell in the selected area
Diagonal Up Border	Diagonal lines that extend from the lower-left to the upper-right corner of each cell in the selected area

3. Click the arrow next to the Border Width button and then choose a line weight from the drop-down menu (**Figure 8.29**).

4. To apply the borders to the selected area, click the arrow next to the Borders button and then choose a border type (**Figure 8.30**).

See **Table 8.1** for a description of the border buttons.

To remove borders:

1. Select the cells whose borders you want to remove.

2. On the Tables and Borders toolbar (refer to **Figure 8.27**), click the arrow next to the Border Style button and choose No Border (refer to **Figure 8.28**).

3. To remove the borders from the selected area, click the arrow next to the All Borders button and choose which border to remove (refer to **Figure 8.30**).

ADDING BORDERS

✔ Tips

- If you have a lot of border work to do, it is often easier to float the Borders menu, so it always stays visible and expanded. Click the arrow to invoke it and then drag it onto the screen from its top (the bubble help should display "Drag to make this menu float").

- To remove all borders from the table, select the table and choose the No Border style on the All Borders button.

- Another way to specify borders is to select the table and choose Format > Table to bring up the Format Table dialog box (**Figure 8.31**). This box will also appear if you right-click the selected table and choose Border and Fill from the shortcut menu. However, the use of the Tables and Borders toolbar is more intuitive than the use of this dialog box.

- Click the Border Color button on the Tables and Borders toolbar to select a different color for the borders.

- Getting a table just the way you want it can be tricky. Remember the Undo option if you make a mistake and, as you get close, save your work and make a duplicate slide to preserve what you've created.

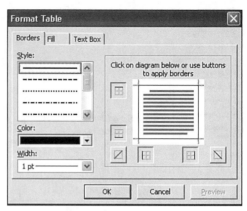

Figure 8.31 Use the Format > Table command to display this dialog box.

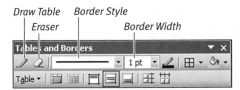

Draw Table *Border Style*
Eraser   *Border Width*

Figure 8.32 The Draw Table tool creates new rows and columns in your table; the Eraser tool removes the borders between cells.

Model Number	Options			Mfg. Cost	Retail Price*
	A	B	C		
490	✓	✓		5,348	6,348
500		✓		5,470	6,470
510		✓	✓	5,600	6,600
520			✓	5,850	6,850
530	✓	✓	✓	5,900	6,900
540	✓		✓	6,200	7,200
* Retail price includes approximately $1,000 in markup					

Figure 8.33 With the Draw Table tool, you can easily create complex tables that have columns within columns and rows within rows.

Drawing Table Borders

With the Draw Table and Eraser tools (**Figure 8.32**), you can change the structure of your table by simply drawing on it. These tools allow you to "draw" new rows and columns, or merge cells by "erasing" their borders. It gives you a lot of flexibility in the layout of your table, as shown in **Figure 8.33**.

To draw a new table border:

1. On the Tables and Borders toolbar (**Figure 8.32**), click the arrow next to the Border Style button and choose a line style.

2. Click the arrow next to the Border Width button and choose a line weight.

3. Click the Draw Table button.
   The pointer is now shaped like a pencil.

4. Drag the pencil-shaped pointer where you want to draw a line (such as between two rows or columns).

5. Repeat step 4 to draw additional lines.

6. Press Esc when you're finished drawing.

To erase a border:

1. Click the Eraser button (**Figure 8.32**).

2. Click a border to erase it, or drag across multiple cells to erase all of their borders.

3. Release the mouse button.
   The selected border is removed, and the adjoining cells are merged into one.

4. Press Esc when you're finished erasing.

✔ Tip

■ You can't draw new rows or columns outside of existing table boundaries. Instead, position the cursor and choose the Insert Rows or Insert Columns command.

DRAWING TABLE BORDERS

Shading Table Cells

To emphasize a range of cells, you can shade the cell background (**Figure 8.34**).

To add shading:

1. Select the cells that you want to shade.

2. On the Tables and Borders toolbar (**Figure 8.35**), click the arrow next to the Fill Color button to display a color palette.

3. Choose a color from the palette (**Figure 8.36**).

Model Number	Options			Mfg. Cost	Retail Price*
	A	B	C		
490	✓	✓		5,348	6,348
500		✓		5,470	6,470
510		✓	✓	5,600	6,600
520			✓	5,850	6,850
530	✓	✓	✓	5,900	6,900
540	✓		✓	6,200	7,200
* Retail price includes approximately $1,000 in markup					

Figure 8.34 The top row in this table has a dark gray shade.

Fill Color

Figure 8.35 Use the Fill Color button to apply shades or colors to selected cells in a table.

Click here to display the large palette

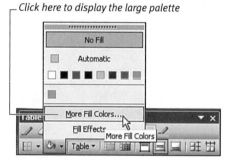

Figure 8.36 The small color palette appears when you click the arrow next to the Fill Color button.

Click one of the color dots to select a color

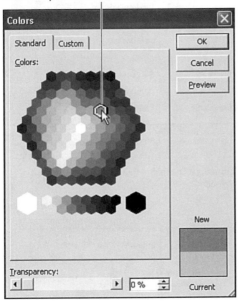

Figure 8.37 Choose from hundreds of colors on the Standard and Custom tabs.

4. If you want a wider choice of colors, click More Fill Colors and choose a color from the Standard or Custom tab of the Colors dialog box (**Figure 8.37**).

5. Click OK.

✔ Tips

- If the Tables and Borders toolbar isn't displayed, choose View > Toolbars > Tables and Borders.

- The Automatic fill color is determined by the slide color scheme.

  See "Changing the Default Colors" in Chapter 12.

Aligning Text within a Cell

By default, table text is aligned at the top-left edge of each cell (**Figure 8.38**). Using PowerPoint's table and paragraph formatting commands, you can adjust the horizontal and vertical alignment of text within a cell, (**Figure 8.39**).

To align text horizontally:

1. Select the cells whose text alignment you want to change.

2. Click an alignment button on the Formatting toolbar (**Figure 8.40**) or use a keyboard shortcut (**Table 8.2**).

	Indemnity Plan	HMO
Services Available	Any doctor	HMO facility
Premium	$100/month	None
Deductible	$500/month	None
Co-insurance	80% / 20%	$7 visit

Figure 8.38 The text in this table has the default alignment.

	Indemnity Plan	HMO
Services Available	Any doctor	HMO facility
Premium	$100/month	None
Deductible	$500/month	None
Co-insurance	80% / 20%	$7 visit

Figure 8.39 By changing horizontal and vertical alignment in the cells, you can improve the appearance of this table.

Align Left   *Align Right*

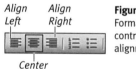

Center

Figure 8.40 Use the Formatting toolbar to control the horizontal alignment of text.

Table 8.2

Keyboard Shortcuts for Aligning Cells	
TYPE OF ALIGNMENT	SHORTCUT
Align left	Ctrl+L
Center	Ctrl+E
Align right	Ctrl+R
Justify	Ctrl+J

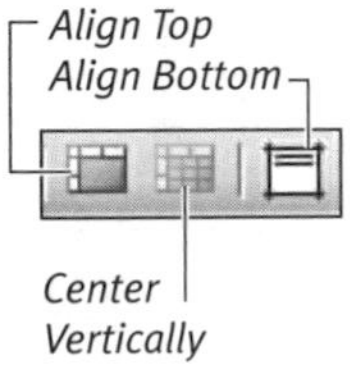

Align Top
Align Bottom

Center
Vertically

Figure 8.41 Use the Tables and Borders toolbar to control the vertical alignment of text.

To align text vertically:

1. Select the cells whose text alignment you want to change.

2. Click a vertical alignment button on the Tables and Borders toolbar (**Figure 8.41**).

✔ Tip

■ If the Tables and Borders toolbar isn't displayed, choose View > Toolbars > Tables and Borders.

ALIGNING TEXT WITHIN A CELL

Inserting a Word Table

An alternative to creating a table using PowerPoint's Table feature is to embed a Word table object onto a slide. Creating a table in this way allows you to take advantage of several advanced table features offered in Word, such as AutoFormatting and calculations.

To insert a Word table:

1. In the task pane, select a Title Only slide layout and use the drop-down menu to insert a new slide (**Figure 8.42**).

2. Choose Insert > Object > Microsoft Word Picture.

   You are now in Microsoft Word; the title bar refers to your PowerPoint file and the Picture toolbar (**Figure 8.43**) appears.

3. Choose Table > Insert > Table (**Figure 8.44**).

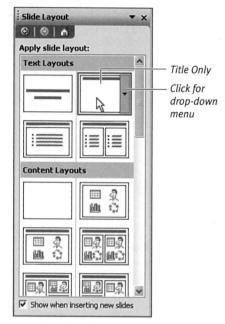

Title Only

Click for drop-down menu

Figure 8.42 The Title Only layout in the task pane is a good choice when you are planning to insert a Word table.

Figure 8.43 The Picture toolbar appears when you're working on a table in Microsoft Word.

You're in Microsoft Word   Insert > Table

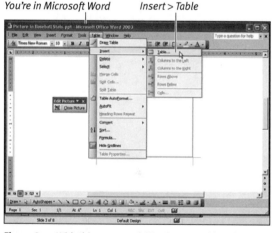

Figure 8.44 With this command, Word opens with a picture object that will become a table.

Notice the AutoFormat option ⎯

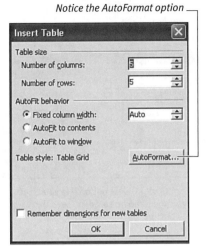

Figure 8.45 Specify the number of rows and columns in your table.

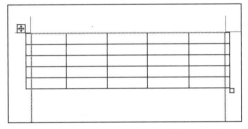

Figure 8.46 When you're creating a table in Word, a border surrounds the object, and rulers appear on the top and left sides.

Spring Semester

Schedule for Classes				
Mon	Tue	Wed	Thu	Fri
8am	2pm	8am	8am	n/a
Essay	Oral	Study	Essay	Exam

Figure 8.47 After you return from Word to PowerPoint, your table is inserted in the slide. Here we've added the slide title "Spring Semester."

4. In the Insert Table dialog box, specify the number of columns and rows (**Figure 8.45**).

An empty table appears on the slide (**Figure 8.46**).

5. Type data into the Word table just as you would in PowerPoint.

6. When you are finished with the table, choose File > Close and Return to [*name of PowerPoint file*]. The outside table border and rulers disappear. You are now back in PowerPoint (**Figure 8.47**).

continues on next page

INSERTING A WORD TABLE

✔ Tips

- To return to the Word table from PowerPoint, double-click the table. (The outside table border and rulers reappear.)

- It's a great idea to save a copy of your table in Word as a Word document for backup. Use File > Save Copy As.Save Copy as from the Word File menu that's available while working on the table.

- If you have already created a table in Word, you can use Insert > Object > Microsoft Word Document and then choose Create from File (**Figure 8.48**).

- You can also select the table within Word and copy and paste it (or a link to it) in PowerPoint. A linked table will update like an Excel chart when it's revised in Word, as long as you don't move either file and break the link.

  See the next sections, "AutoFormatting a Word Table" and "Entering Formulas."

Click to import an existing file

Create a new file with the program that creates the object

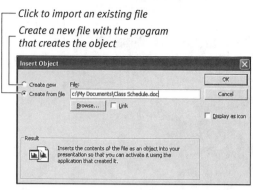

Figure 8.48 The Insert > Object option lets you select a specific file you've already created, by selecting the Create from File button.

Sales Results

	2001	2002	Change
Jones	35,600	40,000	+4,400
Smith	12,950	14,000	+1,050
Johnson	18,000	16,000	-2,000
Totals	68,538	71,999	+3,450

Figure 8.49 This table has not yet been formatted.

Sales Results

	2001	2002	Change
Jones	35,600	40,000	+4,400
Smith	12,950	14,000	+1,050
Johnson	18,000	16,000	-2,000
Totals	68,538	71,999	+3,450

Figure 8.50 This table has been formatted with the Classic 2 AutoFormat.

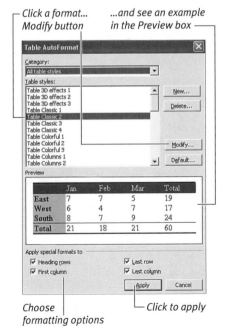

Click a format...
Modify button
...and see an example
in the Preview box

Choose
formatting options
Click to apply

Figure 8.51 Select a predesigned format in the Table AutoFormat dialog box.

AutoFormatting a Word Table

With Word's Table AutoFormat feature, you can add borders, shading, and other formatting attributes by choosing one of several dozen predesigned formats. **Figures 8.49** and **8.50** show a table before and after choosing an AutoFormat. Not only is this feature a big time-saver, but it also assures you of professional-looking results.

Note that you can apply an AutoFormat to an embedded Word table only—not to a table created in PowerPoint.

To AutoFormat a Word table:

1. If you aren't currently editing the table in Word, double-click the embedded table. Microsoft Word opens.

2. Choose Table > Table AutoFormat. The Table AutoFormat dialog box appears.

3. Click different formats in the Table Styles list and look at the Preview box to see what each one looks like (**Figure 8.51**).

4. Uncheck any formatting options you don't want to apply: Heading Rows, First Column, Last Row, and Last Column.

continues on next page

5. Click the Modify button to access more formatting choices for the style you have selected (**Figure 8.52**). Click OK to exit the Modify Style box.

6. Click Apply to make the table look like the style you have selected.

✔ Tips

■ If you don't like an AutoFormat after you have applied it, choose Edit > Undo (Ctrl+Z).

■ If you've modified the style in AutoFormat, you can save it as a template for future use.

Figure 8.52 The Modify Style dialog box lets you further refine your formatting choices.

	2001	2002	Change
Jones	35,600	40,000	+4,400
Smith	12,950	14,000	+1,050
Johnson	18,000	16,000	-2,000
Totals			

Figure 8.53 Click where you want the sum to appear.

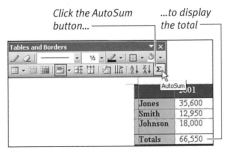

Click the AutoSum button... ...to display the total

Figure 8.54 After you click the AutoSum button, the result of the calculation appears in the cell.

Entering Formulas

Just as in a spreadsheet program, Word tables can perform some simple calculations, such as totaling and averaging. Summing a column or row of numbers is particularly easy with the AutoSum button.

Note that you can perform calculations in an embedded Word table only—not on a table created in PowerPoint.

To sum a column or row:

1. If you aren't currently editing the table in Word, double-click the embedded table.
    Microsoft Word opens.

2. Click the cell at the end of the row or bottom of the column that you want to sum (**Figure 8.53**).

3. If the Tables and Borders toolbar isn't displayed, choose View > Toolbars > Tables and Borders.

4. Click the AutoSum button on the Tables and Borders toolbar.
    The result appears as in **Figure 8.54**.

To enter a formula:

1. If you aren't currently editing the table in Word, double-click the embedded table. Microsoft Word opens.

2. Click the cell where you want the calculation to appear.

3. Choose Table > Formula.

   The Formula dialog box opens.

4. Enter the formula in the Formula box (**Figure 8.55**).

   For example, type =**AVERAGE(left)** to average a row of numbers or =**AVERAGE (above)** to average a column.

5. Click OK.

   The result appears in the cell.

✔ Tip

■ If you need even more functionality in your table—for example, currency ($) cell formatting or advanced functions—try Insert > Object > Excel Spreadsheet.

To learn more about using Excel spreadsheets in PowerPoint, see "Linking Data" in Chapter 4.

Click here to see a list of available functions

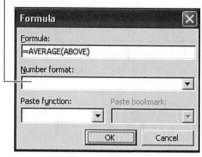

Figure 8.55 To average a row, enter a formula in the Formula dialog box.

ENTERING FORMULAS

ADDING GRAPHICAL OBJECTS

9

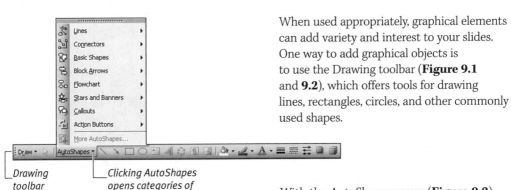

Drawing toolbar

Clicking AutoShapes opens categories of shapes you can insert

Figure 9.1 The Drawing toolbar appears near the bottom of the PowerPoint window.

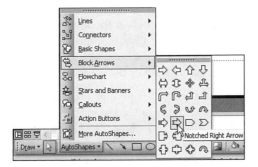

Notched Right Arrow

Figure 9.2 The AutoShapes menu can reveal sublevels of shapes and arrows.

When used appropriately, graphical elements can add variety and interest to your slides. One way to add graphical objects is to use the Drawing toolbar (**Figure 9.1** and **9.2**), which offers tools for drawing lines, rectangles, circles, and other commonly used shapes.

With the AutoShapes menu (**Figure 9.2**) on the Drawing toolbar, you can easily insert predefined objects such as arrows, stars, hearts, and triangles.

✔ Tips

- If the Drawing toolbar is not visible, choose View > Toolbars > Drawing. Generally, the Drawing toolbar is at the bottom of the screen, but you can drag and dock it wherever you prefer.

- You can also import graphics from other applications, such as Adobe Illustrator or CorelDRAW.

  See Chapter 10, "Importing Graphics," for details.

Drawing Lines

Figure 9.3 illustrates how lines can become a graphical element on a slide.

To draw a line:

1. On the Drawing toolbar, click the Line tool.

2. Place the crosshair pointer where you want to begin the line.

3. Hold down the mouse button as you drag in the direction you want the line to follow.

4. Release the mouse button when the line is the desired length.

✔ Tips

- While drawing a line, if you press and hold Shift, the line will constrain to 15-degree angles. This makes it easy to draw perfectly straight lines (horizontally or vertically).

- To draw several lines, double-click the Line tool. It will stay selected until you press Esc or click the Select Objects tool.

- To change the length or angle of the line, click the line to select it (**Figure 9.4**) and drag a selection handle. To change the length without changing the angle, hold down Shift as you drag a handle.

- To reposition a line, select it and drag it into position. The cursor becomes a four-headed arrow while you drag. (Make sure you don't drag a selection handle, or you will change the length of the line.)

- To duplicate a line, press and hold Ctrl as you drag.
  To change the line color, style, or thickness, see "Formatting Lines," next.

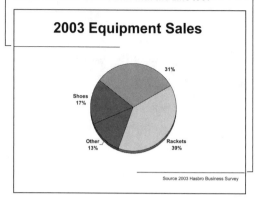

These two lines were drawn with the Line tool

Figure 9.3 Two simple lines, drawn with the Line tool, can provide nice accents and help frame slide elements.

Selection handles

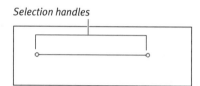

Figure 9.4 When a line is selected, selection handles appear at each end.

- Click Ctrl and Shift at the same time while dragging a line to duplicate it and constrain it to the same horizontal or vertical position as the original line.

- To change the length and angle of a line, right-click the line, go to Format > Autoshape, and adjust the values in the Size tab. This is handy when precision is needed.

- When you just need a quick duplicate, and you don't care about precision placemet, just press Ctrl+D.

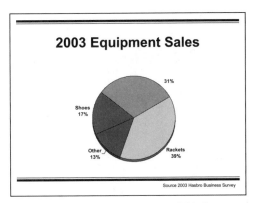

2003 Equipment Sales

Figure 9.5 This slide has both thick and thin lines drawn on it.

Choose a line color here   *Select from a list of nine line weights and four styles of double lines*

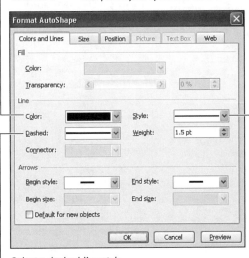

Select a dashed-line style

Figure 9.6 Format your lines on the Colors and Lines tab of the Format AutoShape dialog box.

Formatting Lines

You can format lines and object borders in a variety of ways. For instance, you can change the line thickness (**Figure 9.5**), choose a double-line style, or create a dashed line.

To format lines:

1. Select the line or shape to be formatted and choose Format >

   or

   Double-click the line or shape.

   The Format AutoShape dialog box appears, with the Colors and Lines tab on top (**Figure 9.6**).

2. In the Line section of the dialog box, choose a color in the Color field.

3. In the Style field, click the style and weight of line that you want. If necessary, fine-tune the weight with the Weight field.

4. If desired, click one of the sample lines on the Dashed list.

5. Click OK.

✔ Tips

■ The Style field offers a variety of styles and weights. If the list doesn't include the precise line thickness you need, make the line thicker or thinner in the Weight field.

■ To select more than one line, hold down Shift as you click each one.

■ You can also format lines with the Line Color, Line Style, and Dash Style tools on the Drawing toolbar (**Figure 9.7**).

■ To turn a line into an arrow, use the Arrow Style tool (**Figure 9.8**).

See "Formatting Arrows" later in this chapter.

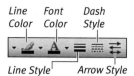

Figure 9.7 Use tools on the Drawing toolbar to format lines.

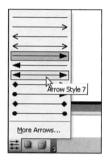

Figure 9.8 Choose an arrow style from this list.

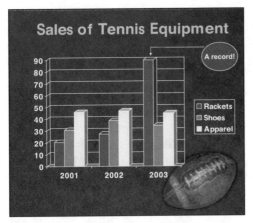

Figure 9.9 The 90-degree line is actually two separate lines and the arrow was created with the Arrow tool.

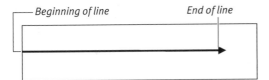

Figure 9.10 The arrowhead appears at the end of the line.

Drawing Arrows

Arrows are helpful for pointing out important areas on a slide (**Figure 9.9**).

To draw an arrow:

1. On the Drawing toolbar, click the Arrow tool.

2. Place the crosshair pointer where you want to begin the arrow.

   This point will be the beginning of the line—it will not have an arrowhead.

3. Hold down the mouse button as you drag in the direction you want the arrow to point.

4. Release the mouse button when the line is the desired length.

   The arrowhead appears at the end of the line (**Figure 9.10**).

✔ Tips

■ While drawing a line, if you press and hold Shift, the line will constrain to 15-degree angles. This makes it easy to draw perfectly straight lines (horizontally or vertically).

■ To draw several arrows, double-click the Arrow tool. When you're finished drawing arrows, press Esc, click the Select Objects button, or click the Arrow tool again to toggle off.

■ After drawing an arrow, you can change the arrowhead's shape, size, and position.
   See "Formatting Arrows" in the next section.

■ Another way to create an arrow is by drawing a connector line.
   See "Adding Connector Lines" later in this chapter.

Formatting Arrows

PowerPoint offers a variety of ways to format arrows. For example, you can choose different arrowhead shapes and sizes for the beginning and/or end of the line.

To format an arrow:

1. Select the arrow or line to be formatted.

2. Click the Arrow Style button on the Drawing toolbar.

   The Arrow Style drop-down list appears (**Figure 9.8**).

3. Click the arrow with the thickness, direction, or style you prefer.

   or

   Click More Arrows to open the Colors and Lines tab of the Format AutoShape dialog box (**Figure 9.11**).

4. Choose the appropriate beginning and ending styles and sizes from the bottom section of the dialog box.

✔ Tips

- To select more than one arrow on your slide, hold down Shift as you click each one.

- You can also open the Format AutoShape dialog box by double-clicking the arrow.

  To change the line weight or color, see "Formatting Lines" earlier in this chapter.

- To convert an arrow to a line, click the Arrow Style tool and choose the first style in the list (the line without arrowheads).

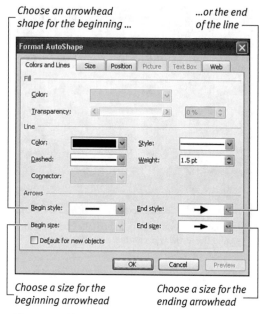

Choose an arrowhead shape for the beginning ...   *...or the end of the line*

Choose a size for the beginning arrowhead   *Choose a size for the ending arrowhead*

Figure 9.11 When you click More Arrows at the end of the arrow style list, this dialog box appears.

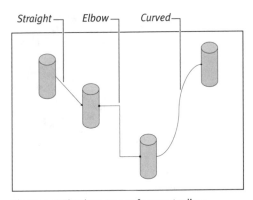

Figure 9.12 The three types of connector lines.

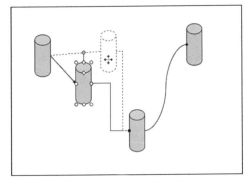

Figure 9.13 When you move an object, the connector lines automatically move with it.

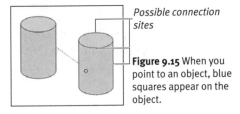

Figure 9.14 Choose the type of connector line you want.

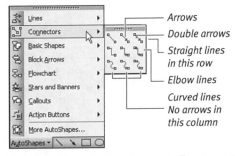

Possible connection sites

Figure 9.15 When you point to an object, blue squares appear on the object.

Adding Connector Lines

A connector line extends between two objects (**Figure 9.12**). The advantages of using a connector line rather than a regular line or arrow are that the line automatically snaps to each object when you create it and when you move or resize one of the connected objects, the line moves with the object and automatically adjusts (**Figure 9.13**).

To add a connector line:

1. Create or open a slide containing two objects that you want to connect.

2. On the Drawing toolbar, click AutoShapes to display the menu.

3. Choose Connectors.

4. Choose the desired style of connector line (**Figure 9.14**).

5. Point to the first object that you want to connect.

   Possible connection sites appear as blue squares on the object (**Figure 9.15**).

6. Click the blue square that you want to use as the connection point on the first object.

7. Point to the second object you want to connect.

8. Click the blue square that you want to use as the connection point on the second object.

   The connector line is drawn between the two objects.

✔ Tips

- Red squares at the ends of a connector line indicate that the line is locked onto an object. A green square indicates that the connector is unlocked—this happens after you move the line away from a connection site.

- You can connect to a different point by dragging the connected end of the line to a different blue square on the object.

Drawing Rectangles and Ovals

Using the Rectangle tool, you can create rectangles and squares. The Oval tool works identically for creating ellipses and circles. **Figure 9.16** shows an example of all four.

To draw a rectangle:

1. On the Drawing toolbar, click the Rectangle tool.

2. Place the crosshair pointer where you want to begin the rectangle.

3. Hold down the mouse button as you drag toward the opposite corner of the box (**Figure 9.17**).

4. Release the mouse button when the box is the desired size.

To draw an ellipse:

◆ Repeat the preceding steps 1 through 4 for drawing a rectangle, but using the Oval tool instead.

✔ Tips

■ To create a perfect square or circle, hold down Shift as you draw the object.

■ To create several objects, double-click the Rectangle or Oval tool. When you are finished drawing your objects, press Esc.

■ To change the size or shape of an object, click it and drag a selection handle.

■ To reposition a rectangle or oval, just drag it into position. (Make sure you don't drag a selection handle, or you will change the object's size or shape.)

■ To type centered text inside a selected object, just start typing. The text is actually part of the object.

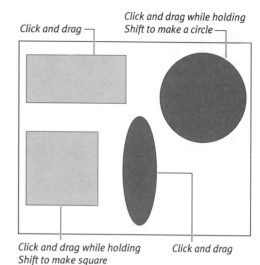

Click and drag — *Click and drag while holding Shift to make a circle* —

Click and drag while holding Shift to make square — *Click and drag*

Figure 9.16 The Rectangle tool created the rectangle and square; the ellipse and circle are courtesy of the Oval tool.

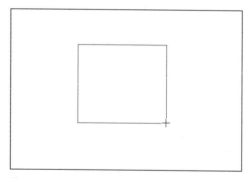

Figure 9.17 Creating rectangles and ovals requires a simple click-and-drag maneuver.

■ To change the border or fill color, use the Format > Autoshape command and choose the Color and Lines tab.

■ Pressing Ctrl while dragging to draw the oval or rectangle draws it from the center as opposed to the top left point of origin.

Figure 9.18 This mountain range at night sketch features a geometric effort with the Freeform tool and a star from the Stars and Banners menu.

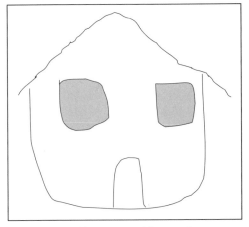

Figure 9.19 It's either a very sad face or a house. A very sad house...

Scribble

Curve   *Freeform*

Figure 9.20 To select one of the special Line tools, click the AutoShapes button and then choose Lines.

Creating Polygons and Freehand Drawings

The Freeform tool lets you create open or closed shapes, such as the ones in **Figure 9.18**. If you are artistically inclined, you can use the Scribble tool to create freehand drawings. **Figure 9.19** proves conclusively that if you are not artistically inclined, you should not use Scribble.

To create a polygon:

1. On the Drawing toolbar, click AutoShapes > Lines.

2. In the set of line choices, click the Freeform tool (**Figure 9.20**).

3. Click at each point of the shape you want to draw—PowerPoint draws a line segment between each point.

4. To finish the drawing, double-click the final point. If your ending double-click is at the same point as your first click, PowerPoint automatically closes the shape. (If you are creating a closed shape, you can finish your shape with a single click instead of a double-click.)

To create a freehand drawing:

1. Click the Scribble tool from AutoShapes > Lines.

2. Click on the slide and press and hold the mouse.
   The cursor becomes a pencil.

3. While continuing to hold the mouse button, start drawing on the slide.

4. To finish the drawing, release the mouse button.

✔ Tips

- Closed shapes are automatically filled with the default color; open shapes are not (**Figure 9.21**). Use the Fill Color tool on the Drawing toolbar to add, remove, or change the fill of a selected object.

- To edit a drawing, click the Draw button on the Drawing toolbar and choose Edit Points from the drop-down menu. Drag any of the points that appear.

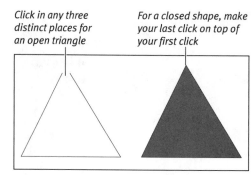

Click in any three distinct places for an open triangle

For a closed shape, make your last click on top of your first click

Figure 9.21 You can create open or closed shapes.

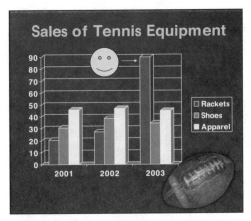

Figure 9.22 This chart was annotated with AutoShape > Basic Shapes.

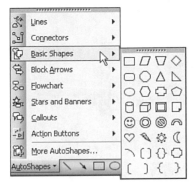

Figure 9.23 The basic set of AutoShapes contains a variety of symbols and icons.

■ To create a shape whose height is equal to its width, hold Shift as you draw the object. Release the mouse first, then Shift, to ensure that you maintain the correct aspect ratio.

■ If you know you will be sizing the shape later, use the shortcut of clicking once (instead of dragging) to create the shape in the default size.

Using AutoShapes

PowerPoint comes with a set of built-in AutoShapes that you can add to any slide. The chart in **Figure 9.22** owes its smiley face not only to strong third-quarter sales but also to the AutoShapes menu of Basic Shapes. **Figure 9.23** shows the rest of the Basic Shapes.

To create an AutoShape:

1. On the Drawing toolbar, click the AutoShapes button to display the menu. The AutoShapes drop-down menu appears, as in **Figure 9.23**.

2. Choose a shape category (such as Basic Shapes) and then a desired shape.

3. Place the crosshair pointer on your slide where you want to begin the object.

4. Drag the pointer diagonally to create the object, and release when the object is the desired size.

   or

   Click the slide once in the desired position to create an object of the default size.

✔ Tips

■ To type centered text inside a selected AutoShape, just start typing. The text becomes part of the AutoShape object. The text does not wrap—you must press Enter or Return after each line.

■ To replace a selected AutoShape with another, use Change AutoShape, which is accessed from the Draw drop-down menu. The new shape will have the same size, text (if any), line, and fill attributes as the shape it replaces.

Customizing AutoShapes

You can customize many of the AutoShapes by dragging the diamond-shaped adjustment handle (**Figure 9.24**). **Figure 9.25** shows a few of the countless changes you can make to an AutoShape.

To customize an AutoShape:

1. Select the object.

2. Look for the yellow diamond inside or near the selected object (**Figure 9.24**). This diamond is an adjustment handle.

3. Drag the diamond in the direction you want to change the AutoShape.

✔ Tips

■ Not all AutoShapes have a diamond adjustment handle, and some have more than one.

■ When you see a rotational lever in an AutoShape, you can turn the object at an angle by hovering your mouse over the end and moving the lever in either direction (**Figure 9.26**).

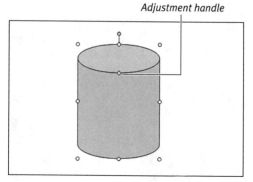

Adjustment handle

Figure 9.24 When you select an AutoShape, a diamond-shaped adjustment handle appears.

Figure 9.25 The first column shows several AutoShapes in their default condition; the second column shows these same shapes after they were adjusted.

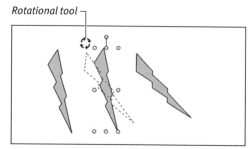

Rotational tool

Figure 9.26 Drawing objects may also have a rotational tool to enable them to be turned to different angles.

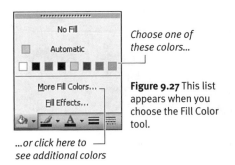

Choose one of these colors...

Figure 9.27 This list appears when you choose the Fill Color tool.

...or click here to see additional colors

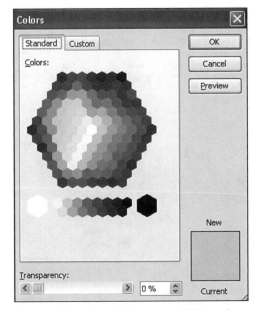

Figure 9.28 Hundreds of colors are available on the Standard and Custom tabs.

Filling an Object with Color

You can add, change, or remove the fill color for the shapes you create in PowerPoint.

To add or change a fill color:

1. Select the object you want to fill and click the arrow next to the Fill Color tool on the Drawing toolbar.

   A small color palette appears (**Figure 9.27**).

2. Choose a color from the palette.

   or

   Click More Fill Colors and choose a color from the Standard or Custom tab of the Colors dialog box that appears (**Figure 9.28**).

3. Click OK.

✔ Tips

- To remove the fill from a selected object, click the arrow next to the Fill Color tool and choose No Fill.

- To reapply the last fill color you used, select the object and click the Fill Color tool itself (not the arrow next it).

- You can also modify the fill color by double-clicking the object to open the Format AutoShape dialog box.

- Select an autoshape or textbox and go to Format > Autoshape (or textbox) on the menu bar; on the Colors and Lines tab, there's a section for Fill. Pull that arrow down where you'd change the fill color, and one of the options is "Background." This is also available when you double-click the object to open the Format AutoShape dialog box as you described.

Filling an Object with a Pattern

You can fill an object with a gradient, texture, or pattern. **Figure 9.29** shows examples of these types of fills.

To fill an object with a gradient, texture, or pattern:

1. Select the object you want to fill and click the arrow next to the Fill Color tool on the Drawing toolbar.

2. Click Fill Effects.

   The Fill Effects dialog box appears.

3. Select the Gradient tab and choose the gradient colors and shading style (**Figure 9.30**).

   or

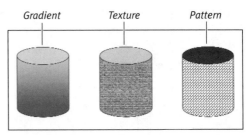

Figure 9.29 You can fill your shapes with any of several types of fill.

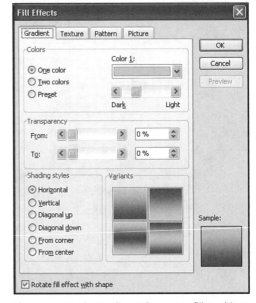

Figure 9.30 On the Gradient tab, you can fill an object with graduating shades of color.

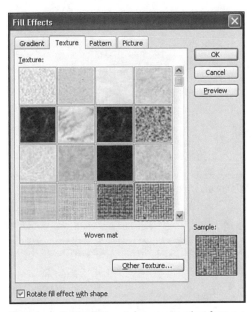

Figure 9.31 On the Texture tab, you can select from a variety of textures, such as granite, canvas, and sand.

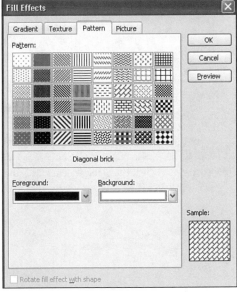

Figure 9.32 The Pattern tab offers simple geometric shapes of two-color contrast.

Select the Texture tab and click a texture (**Figure 9.31**).

or

Select the Pattern tab and click a pattern (**Figure 9.32**).

4. Click OK.

For information on creating gradients, refer to "Creating a Gradient Background" in Chapter 12.

✔ Tip

- To remove the border around an object, click the arrow next to the Line Color button and choose No Line.

Filling an Object with a Graphics File

Figure 9.33 shows an object that is filled with a graphics file.

To fill an object with a graphics file:

1. Select the object you want to fill and click the arrow next to the Fill Color tool on the Drawing toolbar.

2. Click Fill Effects.
   The Fill Effects dialog box appears.

3. Select the Picture tab.

4. Click Select Picture to open the Select Picture dialog box.

5. Navigate to the drive and folder containing the graphics file.

6. Choose the filename and click Insert.

7. Click OK in the Fill Effects dialog box when you're finished (**Figure 9.34**).

✔ Tip

- If you aren't sure where your graphics files are, choose Tools > Search in the Select Picture dialog box.

Figure 9.33 The sun shape is filled with a photo of a sunset.

Figure 9.34 Select the name of the graphics file in the Select Picture dialog box.

Figure 9.35 Three objects that can benefit from a shadow.

Figure 9.36 This list of shadow styles appears after you click the Shadow button on the Drawing toolbar.

Shadow On/Off   *Shadow Color*

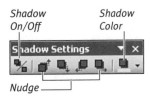

Nudge

Figure 9.37 Use the Shadow Settings toolbar to format a shadow.

Adding a Shadow

A shadow can add a feeling of depth to an object or just provide a nice accent. When applied to text, it can help with contrast against a background that is not uniform in terms of color or pattern. **Figure 9.35** offers an example of all three effects (depth, accent, and contrast).

To add a shadow:

1. Select the object you want to shadow.

2. On the Drawing toolbar, click the Shadow button.

   The set of shadow choices appears.

3. Choose a shadow style (**Figure 9.36**).

To adjust the color and offset of a shadow:

1. Select the shadowed object.

2. Click the Shadow button on the Drawing toolbar and choose Shadow Settings.

   The Shadow Settings toolbar appears (**Figure 9.37**).

3. To adjust the shadow position, click the appropriate Nudge buttons on the Shadow Settings toolbar.

4. To adjust the shadow color, click the arrow next to the Shadow Color button.

   continues on next page

ADDING A SHADOW

5. Choose a color from the palette (**Figure 9.38**), or click More Shadow Colors and choose a color from the Standard or Custom tab.

6. When you finish using the Shadow Settings toolbar, click its close button.

✔ Tips

■ A semitransparent shadow allows you to see what's behind it.

■ To remove a shadow from a selected object, click the Shadow button on the Drawing toolbar and choose No Shadow.

■ To put a shadow on text within an object, select the text, right-click, and select Font from the shortcut menu. Select the Shadow check box in the Font dialog box to apply a shadow to the text. You can also use the shadow settings on the Drawing toolbar to add shadows to text. This lets you control the color of the shadow.

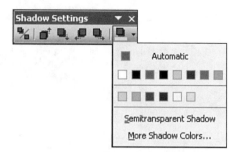

Figure 9.38 The Shadow Color box gives you access to a full color palette from which to choose a color.

No 3D   *Default 3D, lower-
right direction* —   *Tilted up*   *Tilted left*

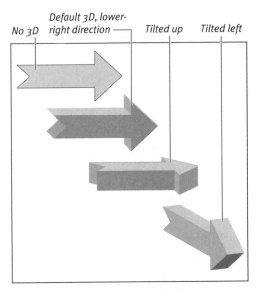

Figure 9.39 The original arrow (top-left) has no 3D setting; the other three have various 3D settings applied to them.

Figure 9.40 Select one of the 3D styles from this list.

3D On/Off   Depth —   Lighting 3D Color

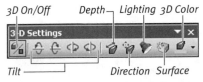

Tilt ——————   Direction Surface

Figure 9.41 Use the 3D Settings toolbar to format a three-dimensional object.

Adding 3D Effects

You can add a 3D effect to objects you have drawn in PowerPoint. After adding a 3D effect, you can tilt the object or change its depth and direction (**Figure 9.39**).

To add a 3D effect:

1. Select the object.

2. On the Drawing toolbar, click the 3D button.

    The set of 3D effects appears.

3. Choose a 3D style (**Figure 9.40**).

To adjust the settings of a 3D object:

1. Select the 3D object.

2. Click the 3D button on the Drawing toolbar and choose 3D Settings.

    The 3D Settings toolbar appears (**Figure 9.41**).

3. To tilt the object, click the appropriate Tilt buttons on the 3D Settings toolbar.

continues on next page

4. To adjust the depth of the object, click the Depth button and choose an amount (**Figure 9.42**).

5. To select the perspective of the 3D effect, click the Direction button and choose a direction (**Figure 9.43**).

6. To adjust the color of the 3D portion of the object, click the arrow next to the 3D Color button. You can choose a color from the small color palette, or you can click More 3D Colors and choose a color from the Standard or Custom tab.

7. When you are finished using the 3D Settings toolbar, click its close button.

✔ Tips

■ To select the angle at which you want light to hit the object, click the Lighting button and choose the desired lighting angle (**Figure 9.44**).

■ To change the reflective tone of the object, click the Surface button and choose the desired surface type (such as Matte or Metal) (**Figure 9.45**).

Depth button

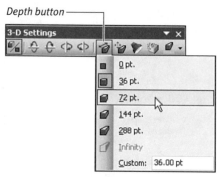

Figure 9.42 Click the Depth button on the 3D Settings toolbar to adjust the amount of the 3D effect.

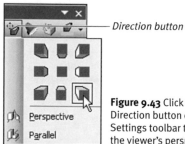

Direction button

Figure 9.43 Click the Direction button on the 3D Settings toolbar to adjust the viewer's perspective.

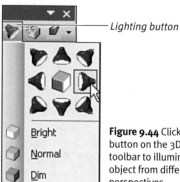

Lighting button

Figure 9.44 Click the Lighting button on the 3D Settings toolbar to illuminate the object from different perspectives.

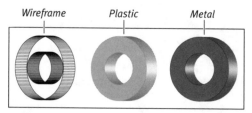

Figure 9.45 Click the Surface button on the 3D Settings toolbar to give the object different reflective attributes.

IMPORTING GRAPHICS

PowerPoint offers decent graphic drawing tools for simple work, but in many cases, you will just need a bit more. You might need the help of an image-editing program to fix up a photo, or the more robust drawing environment of a program like Adobe Illustrator or CorelDRAW. Happily, you can import graphics from other applications—just about anything that an Adobe or Corel program can produce—and you can import photos directly from a digital camera or scanner.

Using the Clip Organizer

Think of the Clip Organizer as a big database and cataloging system. Any graphic or image file that you can see from your computer can be added to the Clip Organizer for quick import into PowerPoint, and any other Office 2003 application.

You can add files to the Clip Organizer anytime, either by searching for them yourself, asking the Clip Organizer to do it for you, or by acquiring them from a scanner or digital camera.

You open the Clip Organizer by clicking Organize Clips from the Clip Art task pane. When you first open the Clip Organizer, it can automatically compile files on your whole computer, or just selected folders.

Figure 10.1 The front door of the Clip Organizer.

To search with Clip Organizer:

1. Click Organize Clips from the bottom of the Insert Clip Art task pane.

   The Clip Organizer opens (**Figure 10.1**). The Collection List box shows the three main categories for cataloging content:

   ▲ My Collections is for files that you have throughout your hard drive and network drives

   ▲ Office Collections is for files that come with Office 2003

   ▲ Web Collections is for artwork that resides on Microsoft's Office Online gallery

2. Use the View menu to see the collections as thumbnails, lists of files, or detailed lists (with dates and file sizes).

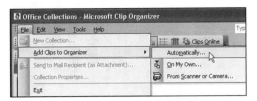

Figure 10.2 Add clip art to the Clip Organizer.

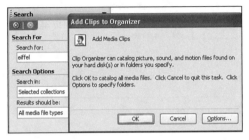

Figure 10.3 Send Organizer on an automatic search.

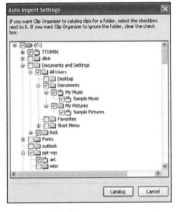

Figure 10.4 Tell it where to search.

To add files to the Clip Organizer:

1. In the Clip Organizer, choose File > Add Clips to Organizer (**Figure 10.2**).

2. Choose Automatically to have the Clip Organizer look for media files in designated folders.

   or

   Choose On My Own to add your files manually from selected folders.

   or

   Choose From a Scanner or Camera to acquire images from compatible peripherals.

3. Click Automatically to send the Clip Organizer on a search of your entire computer (**Figure 10.3**).

4. Click Options to specify where Clip Organizer should and should not search (**Figure 10.4**).

   After the search is done, all clip art that the Organizer finds is displayed. **Figure 10.5** shows that it found all the artwork for this book, contained in a folder called PPT VQS.

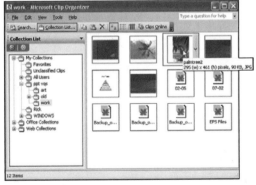

Figure 10.5 All of this book's screen images and graphics are now in Clip Organizer's catalog.

USING THE CLIP ORGANIZER

✔ Tips

- Right-clicking or clicking the arrow next to an image provides a wealth of controls for file management, including adding keywords to aid in future searches (**Figure 10.6**).

- Deleting files from a collection does not delete the files from your computer. There are two deletion options in **Figure 10.6**; make sure you know which one you are choosing! If you delete the file from the name of the folder (in this case "work"), you are removing the file from your hard drive altogether. Deleting the file from the Clip Organizer simply removes the file from its catalog.

- Your collections can be used across all Office 2003 applications, and the more keywords you enter, the more powerful the utility becomes.

- You can also add your own shapes and drawings by dragging them from the PPT slide onto the Clip Organizer button on the taskbar. They will be stored in a standard graphic file format (WMF), which you can then easily reuse in other presentations and applications.

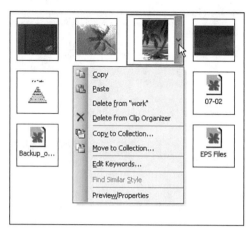

Figure 10.6 The shortcut menu provides many options for organization.

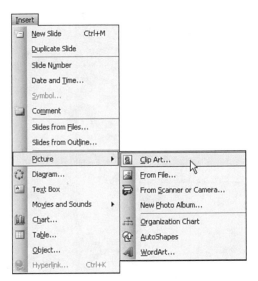

Figure 10.7 You can access clip art included with PowerPoint or files that are anywhere on your hard drive or network drives.

Enter keyword here

Filter the results to specific media types

Click to add image to slide

Organize clip art into categories

Find clip art on the Internet

Figure 10.8 If the clip art contains keywords (as do all that come with Office 2003), you can search for specific topics.

Using Clip Art

One way to add graphical objects is to insert a clip art image from the library of art that comes with PowerPoint. These images are no different from ones you can import from other applications (in fact, most of them were created with Adobe and Corel software), but they are organized for you with a handy import engine called the Clip Organizer.

Choose Insert > Picture > Clip Art (**Figure 10.7**) to display the Clip Art task pane. (You can also click the Insert Clip Art icon on the Drawing toolbar.) From here, you can survey artwork that comes with Office 2003, is already on your computer, is available on your LAN, or exists out on the Web.

In **Figure 10.8**, we are using the Clip Art task pane to search for any artwork that has "food" as one of its keywords. Of the four graphics that turned up, one of them is an animated file, as evidenced by the little star icon in the lower-right corner. During a slide show, the candle flickers and the confetti twirls.

To insert a clip art image:

1. Create or open a slide on which you want to place clip art.

2. If it is not already visible, choose Insert > Picture > Clip Art to open the Clip Art task pane.

continues on next page

3. Use the Search features in the task pane to locate clip art that came with Microsoft Office or resides on your computer. In **Figure 10.9**, we searched for, and found, a graphic of the Eiffel Tower.

4. After you've found the image you want, choose Insert from the task pane's drop-down menu, or just click on the image in the task pane to insert it into your slide (**Figure 10.9**).

✔ Tips

■ When adding a new slide, you can choose a content layout in the Slide Layout task pane. Then, you can click the Clip Art icon in the Content box (**Figure 10.10**), or you can import a picture directly from a file by clicking the picture icon.

■ Although the window may not be visible, the Clip Organizer is a separate application that remains open. To switch back to it, press Alt+Tab until you find it.

■ To maintain an image's original proportions as you resize it, select the image and drag a corner selection handle. If you drag a middle handle, the image will stretch out of proportion.

■ The Clip Organizer can take a while to tabulate thumbnails from a new folder. If you know where a specific image is located, choose Insert > Picture > From File.

Figure 10.9 The Insert Clip Art task pane lets you search by filename or keyword. We found the Eiffel Tower by searching on its name; we could also have searched for "building," "tower," or "landmark."

Figure 10.10 Click the Clip Art icon in the Content box.

Enter the search word here

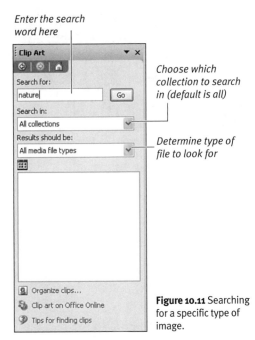

Choose which collection to search in (default is all)

Determine type of file to look for

Figure 10.11 Searching for a specific type of image.

Figure 10.12 The results of searching on the keyword "nature."

Searching for Clip Art

An easy way to locate a particular clip art image is to have PowerPoint search for it in the Clip Art task pane. If the image has one or more keywords associated with it, you can find it when you search for one of those words. Otherwise, you will need to enter its filename to find it. Therefore, there are really two levels of search: Searching through collections in the Clip Organizer, and searching your hard drive for filenames.

To search for clip art:

1. Create or open a slide on which you want to place clip art.

2. Choose Insert > Picture > Clip Art, or on the Drawing toolbar, click the Insert Clip Art button.

   The Insert Clip Art task pane appears.

3. If you want to access the Clip Organizer directly, click Organize Clips (**Figure 10.1**).

4. To add a file directly from the Clip Organizer, locate it within a collection, click it, and use the drop-down menu to copy it to the clipboard (**Figure 10.6**). Then paste it into your slide. Otherwise, return to PowerPoint and the Insert Clip Art task pane.

5. In the Insert Clip Art task pane, in the Search For field, type the keywords you want to search for (**Figure 10.11**).

6. To refine the search, choose the type of files you are seeking in the Results Should Be box.

7. Click Search.

   The task pane now displays pictures that match your specifications from images in your Clip Organizer (**Figure 10.12**).

   continues on next page

8. When you find an image you like, open the drop-down menu in the task pane to insert the image, open it for editing, or remove it from the Clip Organizer (**Figure 10.9**).

or

Click the image to add it to your slide.

✔ Tips

■ Click the Expand Results button in the task pane to view more images at once (**Figure 10.13**).

■ If you don't get satisfactory search results, try different keywords in the Search For field (or use File > Add Clips to Organizer).

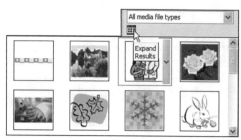

Figure 10.13 Expand the results to view more images.

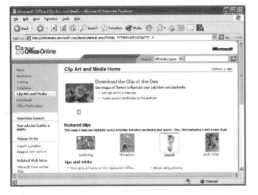

Figure 10.14 Find artwork on Microsoft's Web site and add it to your own.

Figure 10.15 You might enjoy a visit to the Office Online Web site.

Finding Clip Art on the Web

If you can't find the right image in PowerPoint's built-in collections, you can search Microsoft's Design Gallery Online. It contains thousands of images that you can download free of charge.

To find clip art online:

1. On the Drawing toolbar, click the Insert Clip Art button.

2. Enter your search keywords in the Clip Art task pane.

3. In the Search In list of collections, select Web Collections.

4. Click Go.

   PowerPoint will head to the Office Online database of images at the Microsoft Web site and treat all of those images as if they are clip art in your own collection.

5. Click an image to add it to your slide or click the arrow for other options, such as adding it to your own collection. (**Figure 10.14**)

✔ Tips

- Make sure you are connected to the Internet before browsing Office Online.

- Ambitious users can click the Clip Art on Office Online button near the bottom of the Clip Art task pane to visit the Office Online Web site, with many features, images, and a full search-and-download engine (**Figure 10.15**).

FINDING CLIP ART ON THE WEB

Inserting Graphics Files

If you want to import a picture from your computer and you know where it is and what it's called, the Clip Art task pane might be overkill. Issuing the simple Insert Picture command is the better way to go.

To insert a graphics file:

1. Display the slide on which you want to insert the graphics file.

2. Choose Insert > Picture > From File. The Insert Picture dialog box appears.

3. Navigate to the drive and folder that contains the graphics file (**Figure 10.16**).

4. Click the name of the graphics file.

5. Click Insert.

✔ Tips

■ To quickly insert the desired file, double-click it.

■ To insert more than one image, hold Ctrl and click them both. Then press Insert.

■ If you aren't sure where your graphics files are, choose Tools > in the Insert Picture dialog box.

Figure 10.16 Navigate to the desired location and pick a file to insert.

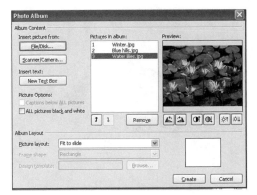

Figure 10.17 Decide how to place them on the slides.

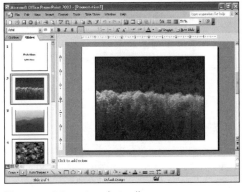

Figure 10.18 One-stop photo albums.

Inserting Multiple Graphics Files

Photo Album, an impressive feature introduced in PowerPoint 2002, gives you the ability to simultaneously import multiple graphics files from specific folders.

To use the Photo Album feature:

1. Open a new presentation with a blank slide.

2. Choose Insert > Picture > New Photo Album.

   The Photo Album dialog box appears.

3. Click the File/Disk button.

4. From the Insert New Pictures dialog box, select multiple pictures by holding Ctrl while clicking them.

5. Click Insert. You see the files you've selected in the Pictures in Album box (**Figure 10.17**).

   The Photo Album options let you configure slides for up to four pictures per slide. You can also search for a design template with the Browse button.

6. Click Create.

   A complete presentation is created with your images inserted (**Figure 10.18**).

✔ Tips

- You can add a Photo Album within another Photo Album (with different numbers of photos per slide) or into any presentation.

- Notice that Scanner/Camera is available under Album Content.

INSERTING MULTIPLE GRAPHICS FILES

Embedding Graphics

If you have created a graphical image in another program, you may want to use Windows' Object Linking and Embedding to bring it into PowerPoint.

When you convert a graphic into an embedded object, you can open it for editing and modification just by double-clicking it. You don't have to go through the effort of launching that application, opening the drawing, and then re-inserting it into PowerPoint.

To embed a graphic:

1. Select the graphic in the source application (**Figure 10.19**) and then choose Edit > Copy to copy the graphic to the clipboard.

2. In PowerPoint, display the slide on which you want to insert the graphic.

3. Choose Edit > Paste Special (**Figure 10.20**).

4. Look for the name of the editing software in the Paste Special dialog box, and select it. It is usually the first one on the list.

    This will make the graphic an embedded object. The graphic now appears on the current PowerPoint slide (**Figure 10.21**).

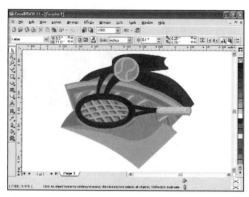

Figure 10.19 Copy the object in the source application.

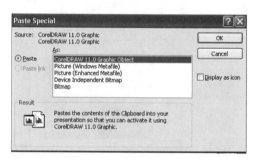

Figure 10.20 Choosing Paste Special gives you all the choices of pasting, including the one that keeps track of the application that created the graphic.

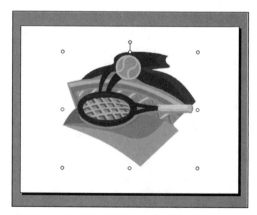

Figure 10.21 This graphic is smarter than the average curve, because it knows the program that created it and can launch that program for editing.

✔ Tips

- Edit > Paste Special is not necessarily any different from Edit > Paste. The first choice on the list is the one that would be performed if you just chose Edit > Paste, so in this case, they would be the same. The value of using Paste Special is that you see all of your choices and know exactly what you are getting when you paste. We recommend that you use Paste Special for all of your clipboard activity that involves receiving data from another application.

- If you do place a graphic as an object from another application (the usual result if you just issue the Edit > Paste command), you have the convenience of being able to double-click the graphic to have the original application launch and open it for editing. However, we think the tradeoff is too high. Embedded objects are often very large in size and often crash-prone. We would rather see you return to the program manually, edit the graphic, and then reimport it or repeat the copy-and-paste command, using Paste Special and selecting one of the Picture or Bitmap choices.

MANIPULATING GRAPHICAL OBJECTS

11

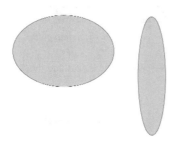

Figure 11.1 The ellipse on the right was scaled and distorted.

PowerPoint offers a number of ways to manipulate graphics you create within PowerPoint, as well as images you import from other applications. **Figures 11.1**, **11.2**, and **11.3** show some of the techniques you can use to manipulate graphical objects. You can size and skew graphics created within PowerPoint (**Figure 11.1**), crop imported photos (**Figure 11.2**), and even disassemble graphics created in other applications (**Figure 11.3**).

In this chapter, you will learn how to use PowerPoint's rulers, guides, and snap feature to place objects; copy graphical attributes; group a set of objects; and change the stacking order of objects.

Figure 11.2 The photo on the right was cropped.

Figure 11.3 This graphic was created in CorelDRAW and completely dismantled in PowerPoint.

Using Rulers and Guides

To help you precisely position graphical objects, you can use rulers and guides (**Figure 11.4**). For example, in **Figure 11.5**, the grid lines were used to position the squares exactly one inch apart and align along their baselines.

To display the rulers:

◆ Choose View > Ruler.

The horizontal ruler appears above the slide; the vertical ruler appears to the left. Notice that the zero point is at the center of each ruler. This enables you to measure distances from the center of the slide.

To display the guides:

1. Choose View > Grid and Guides to enable display.

2. The Grid and Guides dialog box appears (**Figure 11.6**).

3. Click the check box to Display Drawing Guides on Screen.

   Horizontal and vertical guides appear at the zero points in the rulers.

4. Drag the individual guides to place them at any position on the slide.

✔ Tips

■ You can press Ctrl+G to quickly access the Grid and Guides dialog box (**Figure 11.6**).

■ As you drag the guides, a measurement appears (**Figure 11.4**); this measurement represents the distance from the zero point. Thus, if you want to place objects exactly 1.25 inches down from the center of the slide, you can easily drag the horizontal guide to this position (with or without the ruler displayed).

■ Need more guides? Press Ctrl while dragging on a guideline, and another will appear on your slide. You can have up to eight horizontal and eight vertical guides.

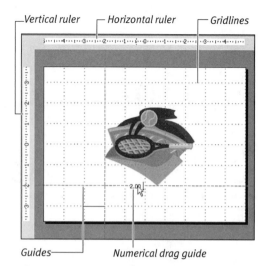

Vertical ruler — Horizontal ruler — Gridlines

Guides — Numerical drag guide

Figure 11.4 Rulers and guides can be displayed by selecting View > Grids and Guides and choosing the appropriate options.

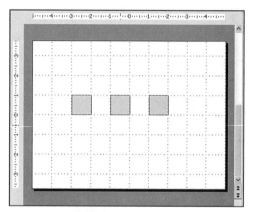

Figure 11.5 You can also use the grid to help position objects on your slides.

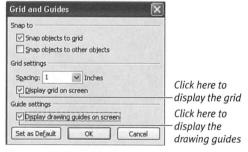

Click here to display the grid

Click here to display the drawing guides

Figure 11.6 Rulers and guides are displayed by checking the boxes.

Using Grid Snap

Another tool that helps position objects is the grid, a series of invisible horizontal and vertical lines with a default setting of about 1/12 inch apart. Whenever you draw, size, or move an object, the object borders snap to the lines along the invisible grid, as though they were magnetized.

You can display or hide the grid, whichever you prefer. You can also set the grid spacing to your specifications. And finally, you can enable or disable grid snap at any time.

To enable grid snap:

1. Press Ctrl+G to reach Grid and Guides (**Figure 11.6**).

2. Enable Snap Objects to Grid.

✔ Tips

- You may want to disable grid snap if you're trying to position several objects precisely and grid snap is interfering. To temporarily disable grid snap when positioning an object, press and hold Alt as you drag.

- You can also override the grid by moving an object with your arrow keys. Press Left, Right, Up, and Down to move an object by a small amount in each of those directions. This is called "nudging."

- The effect of snapping from one gridline to the next is more apparent in zoomed-in views.
  See "Zooming In and Out" later in this chapter.

Snapping to Shapes

PowerPoint offers a way to easily place shapes so their edges are touching: using the snap-to-shape feature. This feature is useful when you want to align objects to one another, irrespective of the grid. In **Figure 11.7**, the line is snapped precisely to corners of two rectangles, and each of the shapes on the left are snapped to one another, even though they are odd sizes that do not conform to any grid.

To enable snap to shape:

1. Press Ctrl+G to open Grid and Guides.

2. Enable Snap Objects to Other Objects.

✔ Tip

■ To temporarily disable shape snap when positioning an object, press and hold Alt as you drag.

■ If you have Snap Objects to Grid turned on, you might want to turn it off when you enable Snap Objects to Other Objects. That way you won't have conflicting controls in place.

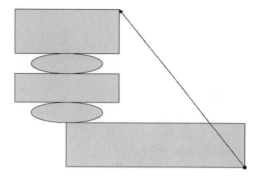

Figure 11.7 The Snap Objects To Other Objects command offers another level of precision placement.

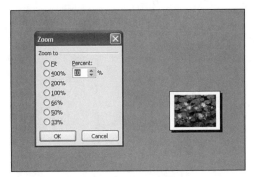

Figure 11.8 This slide is zoomed out to 10 percent.

Figure 11.9 And here is the mega-zoom-in setting.

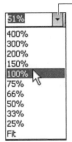

Click here to display a list

Figure 11.10 You can zoom in or out by selecting one of the percentages in the Zoom field.

Zooming In and Out

As you are drawing, sizing, and moving objects, there will be times when you will want or need to change the zoom setting to make sure that objects are positioned properly. **Figure 11.8** shows the minimum zoom setting and **Figure 11.9** shows a zoom setting that gets you as close to the slide content as possible.

To zoom in and out:

◆ Click the arrow in the Zoom field to display a list of zoom percentages (**Figure 11.10**). Then click the desired number.

or

Click the percentage in the Zoom field, type a number between 10 and 400, and press Enter.

or

Choose View > Zoom and choose the desired zoom percentage in the Zoom dialog box (**Figures 11.8** and **11.9**).

✔ Tips

■ Use the Fit zoom option to fit the whole slide in the window; and if it's easier, you can simply type **Fit** in the drop-down.

■ If you have a scroll mouse, you can hold Ctrl and zoom in and out of a slide or other view (Outline or Thumbnails).

■ To zoom in on a particular area of the slide, click an object in the area before choosing a zoom percentage; the selected object will be centered in the window.

Displaying a Slide Miniature

When you are zoomed in, it's helpful to use a slide miniature so you can see the complete slide as you are working on the detail (**Figure 11.11**).

To display a slide miniature:

1. Select one of the zoomed-in views (such as 200%).

   Unless you manually closed the slide thumbnails pane, a slide miniature of the current slide is available.

2. If the slide miniature doesn't appear, choose View > Normal and click the Slides tab to view miniatures of your presentation slides.

Figure 11.11 Displaying a slide thumbnail when you are zoomed in helps you see how your changes affect the entire slide.

Figure 11.12 Choose Align or Distribute from the Draw menu.

Figure 11.13 The star is centered horizontally and vertically inside the circle.

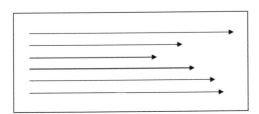

Figure 11.14 The lines are aligned on the left.

Aligning Objects

As explained earlier in the chapter, you can use guides and rulers to help line up several objects. Sometimes, however, you'll need more control, and you have it with the Draw > Align or Distribute command (**Figure 11.12**). For example, you can center one object inside another (**Figure 11.13**) or align a group of objects on the left (**Figure 11.14**).

To align two or more objects:

1. Click to select the first object you want to align and hold down Shift as you click additional objects to be aligned.

   or

   Drag to draw a marquee around the objects to be selected.

2. On the Drawing toolbar, click Draw > Align or Distribute.

3. To align the objects horizontally, choose Align Left, Align Center, or Align Right.

   or

   To align the objects vertically, choose Align Top, Align Middle, or Align Bottom.

✔ Tips

- To center one object inside another, you need to issue two alignment commands: one to align the objects horizontally (Align Center), and the other to align the objects vertically (Align Middle).

- For multiple align operations, pull the menu off the Drawing toolbar by clicking and dragging the top of the menu. When you float it onscreen, it is much easier to issue commands.

ALIGNING OBJECTS

Spacing Objects Equally

You can evenly space three or more objects, such as the rectangles in **Figure 11.15.** The rectangles on the top row are not distributed evenly while the ones on the bottom row are, thanks to Draw > Distribute Horizontally.

When you distribute objects, the top and bottom objects (or left and right objects in a horizontal distribution) remain stationary, and the objects in between them are repositioned so that they are spaced evenly.

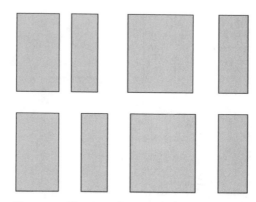

Figure 11.15 The rectangles at the bottom are evenly spaced.

To space objects equally:

1. Click to select the first object you want to distribute and then hold down Shift as you click additional objects to be distributed.

   or

   With your mouse, drag a marquee around the objects to be selected.

2. From the Draw menu on the Drawing toolbar, choose Align or Distribute.

3. Choose Distribute Horizontally or Distribute Vertically.

✔ Tips

- By default, PowerPoint distributes objects relative to the first and last object in the group. If you want to evenly space objects across the slide, choose Draw > Align or Distribute > Relative to Slide before you choose the Distribute Horizontally or Distribute Vertically command.

- You can also use Draw > Align or Distribute > Relative to Slide to distribute two objects on a slide.

- To quickly select all of the objects on a slide, press Ctrl+A.

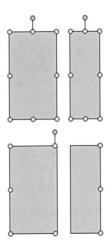

Figure 11.16 After the objects are grouped, one set of selection handles surrounds the design, as in the lower objects

Grouping Objects

To manipulate several objects as a single unit, you need to group them. After the objects are grouped, you can move, resize, scale, flip, rotate, and color the group as if it were a single object.

To group objects:

1. Click to select the first object you want in the group and then hold down Shift as you click additional objects to be grouped.

   or

   Drag a marquee around the objects to select them.

2. From the Draw menu on the Drawing toolbar, choose Group.

   A single set of selection handles appears, and the group is now considered a single object. In **Figure 11.16**, the top objects are ungrouped, and therefore have separate selection handles. The lower objects are grouped and share one set of selection handles.

✔ Tips

■ You can also group objects by pressing Ctrl+Shift+G.

■ To disassemble the group and modify the objects separately, choose the Draw > Ungroup command or press Ctrl+Shift+H.

■ To re-create a disassembled group, you do not need to reselect the objects. Just press Esc to deselect and then choose Draw > Regroup.

■ For more complex drawings, you can create groups within groups.

■ Text placeholders cannot be grouped. PowerPoint 2002 introduced individually selectable objects within a group. Click the group, then click again inside the group to select just one object. You'll see gray handles; those tell you which object you've selected. You can now change the attributes (color, line width, text) of that one object without affecting the entire group.

Copying Object Attributes

Use the Format Painter button to copy attributes from one object to another. You can copy all formatting characteristics, including color, pattern, shadow, and line thickness.

To copy object attributes:

1. Select the object whose formatting attributes you want to copy (**Figure 11.17**).

2. Click the Format Painter button on the Standard toolbar.

   The pointer changes to an arrow with a paintbrush.

3. Click the object you want to format (**Figure 11.18**).

✔ Tips

- If you don't see the Format Painter button on the Standard toolbar, click the More Buttons button to see other buttons.

- To copy attributes to more than one object, select the object with the desired format to be copied and double-click the Format Painter button. Click as many objects as you want to format and press Esc when you are done.

- Format Painter can copy formatting attributes that were applied within PowerPoint only. You cannot use it to copy attributes of images imported or pasted from other applications.

Figure 11.17 Select the object (the star, in this example) with the formatting attributes you want to copy.

The heart now has a pattern fill

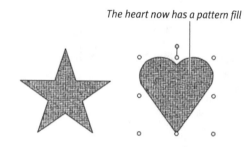

Figure 11.18 After selecting the Format Painter tool, click the heart to paste the star's attributes.

Picture tab ─┐　　　┌─ Click here

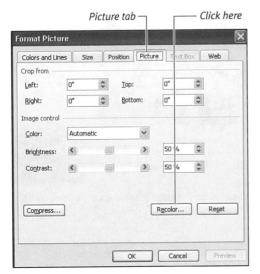

Figure 11.19 On the Picture tab, click Recolor.

Click here to reselect　　Click here to choose
the original color　　　　a new color

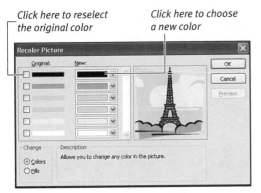

Figure 11.20 Look up the color you want to replace in the Original column and select the replacement color in the New column.

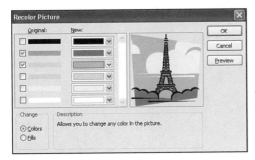

Figure 11.21 If you don't like the new colors, you can revert to the original ones.

Recoloring a Picture

Recoloring a picture involves replacing one color with another in a graphic or piece of clip art you have inserted into PowerPoint.

Working with objects or shapes created in PowerPoint requires different techniques, and you can only recolor vector artwork, not bitmap images or photos. Chapter 9 discusses how to create and color objects directly in PowerPoint.

To replace a color in a picture:

1. Select the picture or object to be recolored.
2. Choose Format > Picture.
   The Format Picture dialog box appears.
3. If necessary, select the Picture tab (**Figure 11.19**).
4. Click Recolor.
   The Recolor Picture dialog box appears (**Figure 11.20**).
5. Choose whether you want to change the colors of all fills and lines (Colors) or just the fills (Fills).
6. In the Original column, locate the color you want to replace. This column lists all the original colors used in the picture.
7. Click the arrow in the adjacent New field to display the small palette.
8. Choose a color from the palette or click More Colors and choose a color from the Standard or Custom tab of the Colors dialog box.
9. Repeat steps 6 through 8 for any other colors you want to change.
10. Click OK.

✔ Tip

- If you want to return a changed color to the original color, select the appropriate check box in the Original column (**Figure 11.21**).

203

Scaling an Object

Scaling resizes the height and width of an object by a designated percentage. This feature works like the Enlarge and Reduce buttons on a copy machine.

If you can select it, you can scale it—this means that you can scale pretty much anything in PowerPoint: objects you create using the drawing tools, groups of objects, clip art from the Clip Organizer or Office Online, photos from your digital camera or scanner, images you download from the Web. **Figure 11.22** is a variation on **Figure 11.2**, in which a photo of a flowerbed has been scaled down significantly—50% to be precise.

To scale an object:

1. Select the object or group to be scaled.
2. Choose Format > AutoShape.

   or

   Double-click the object.

   The Format AutoShape dialog box appears.
3. Select the Size tab (**Figure 11.23**).
4. In the Height field of the Scale section, specify a scaling percentage for the height.

   A number greater than 100 enlarges the object; a number less than 100 reduces it.
5. In the Width field of the Scale section, specify a scaling percentage for the width.

   To scale the object proportionally, make sure that the Lock Aspect Ratio box remains checked.
6. To see how the object looks with the new scale factors, click Preview.

   You may need to drag the Format dialog box out of the way so that you can see the preview.
7. If necessary, adjust the Height and Width values.
8. When you're satisfied with your scale values, click OK.

Figure 11.22 The smaller photo is 50% of the size of the larger one.

Make sure the Size tab is selected   Enter scaling percentages here

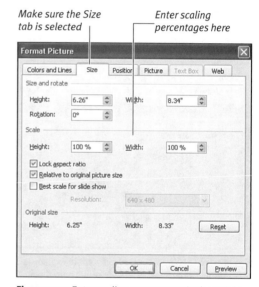

Figure 11.23 Enter scaling percentages in the Height and Width fields.

✔ Tips

- To scale a bitmap image, use the Format > Picture command (or just double-click it).

- Depending on what type of object you have selected, the Format name will change on the menu. You might see Format > Picture, Format > Autoshape, Format > WordArt, Format > Diagram, Format > Text Box, and so on.

- To scale an object manually, use the selection handles and drag in or out. If the object is a bitmap, it will scale proportionally automatically; if the object is a vector, like clip art, press and hold Shift while scaling to maintain its shape and proportion.

- Photos and other bitmap images could become blurry if you start with a small one and scale it way up. Whenever possible, inspect them by playing the slide show on the computer that will ultimately run the show. Vector graphics can be enlarged without losing clarity, but you can still change their proportions if you aren't careful to use the Shift key on a corner handle as you resize them.

SCALING AN OBJECT

Cropping a Picture

Cropping refers to trimming away an unwanted section of a picture. For example, if a graphic displays a person's full body, you can crop it so that only the person's face appears. **Figure 11.24** is a summer rerun of **Figure 11.2**, in which the photo of the flower has been cropped and then scaled. You can crop only the edges of the picture—you cannot crop out anything in the middle without resorting to an image-editing program, such as Adobe Photoshop or Corel PHOTO-PAINT.

Figure 11.24 After inserting a photo, you can crop out unwanted portions.

To crop a picture:

1. Select the picture to be cropped.

2. If the Picture toolbar doesn't appear, right-click the picture and choose Show Picture Toolbar from the shortcut menu. The Picture toolbar appears.

3. Click the Crop tool on the Picture toolbar (**Figure 11.25**). As you do, notice that the selection handles around the photo change.

4. Place the cropping pointer on a selection handle (**Figure 11.26**) and drag toward the middle of the picture until you have trimmed away the unwanted portion.

5. If necessary, drag other selection handles to crop other portions.

6. When you are finished cropping (**Figure 11.27**), click an empty area of the slide or press Esc to deselect the Crop tool. To create the enlarged image shown in **Figure 11.24**, you would increase the scale of the cropped photo.

Crop ⎯⎯⎯ Selection handles

Figure 11.25 The Crop tool is on the Picture toolbar.

Drag this handle to the left

Figure 11.26 After selecting the Crop tool, drag a selection handle to crop the image.

Figure 11.27 The finished crop.

Compress Pictures button

Figure 11.28 Use the Compress Pictures dialog box to delete cropped areas of an image.

✔ Tips

■ When you crop, you are simply temporarily hiding part of the picture. At any time, you can move the selection handle outward to redisplay the hidden portion. *You are not scaling the image.*

■ If you want to actually delete the cropped areas of the picture, use the Compress Picture feature. Turn on the Picture toolbar using View > Toolbars > Picture, and click the Compress Pictures button (**Figure 11.28**). You will then have the option to delete the cropped areas of pictures in your presentation.

■ If you crop an image in another program, you will need to return to that program to "uncrop" it.

Changing the Stacking Order

As you draw objects or place pictures on a slide, PowerPoint layers the new ones on top of the old ones. In **Figure 11.29**, the airplane is emerging from one cloud and flying atop another. The top cloud is in front of the plane; the lower one is behind it.

To change the order in which objects are stacked:

1. Select one of several objects on a slide. The effect will be more noticeable if the objects are overlapping partially.

2. From the Draw menu on the Drawing toolbar, choose Order (**Figure 11.30**).

3. Choose one of the following:
   ▲ Bring to Front to place an object at the top of the stack.
   ▲ Send to Back to place an object at the bottom of the stack.
   ▲ Bring Forward to bring an object one layer up in the stack.
   ▲ Send Backward to send an object one layer back in the stack.

✔ Tips

■ You can also change the stacking order by right-clicking an object and making a selection from the Order submenu.

■ Instead of sending an object all the way to the front or the back, you can use the Send Forward and Send Backward commands to move an object step by step through the layers. If the item you are trying to bring to the front is hidden in the back and difficult to select, click the slide so that nothing is selected and then press the Tab key until you see the selection squares for the hidden object.

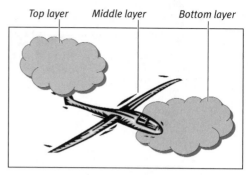

Top layer   Middle layer   Bottom layer

Figure 11.29 Overlapping objects are layered.

Figure 11.30 Choose Order from the Draw menu and use the menu to shift the selected object from layer to layer.

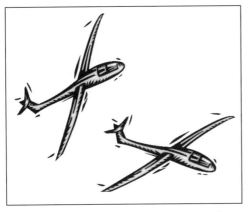

Figure 11.31 The plane on the top left was rotated.

Rotating Objects

Figure 11.31 shows an example of an object before and after it was rotated; the plane on top has changed its course and is ascending instead of descending. You can rotate any object that you can select in PowerPoint.

To rotate an object:

1. Hover your cursor over the rotation tool, as shown in **Figure 11.32**. When you do, the cursor changes shape.

2. Click and drag the rotation handle (**Figure 11.33**).

3. Release the mouse.

   You can tell that an object has been rotated because its rotation handle is no longer at the top—it rotates with the image (**Figure 11.34**).

— Rotation tool

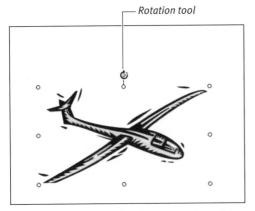

Figure 11.32 The rotation handle appears above the top-middle selection handle.

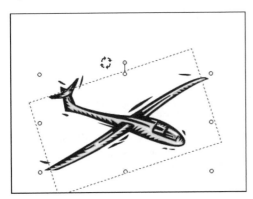

Figure 11.33 Drag it to one side.

Figure 11.34 Release to see the result.

Flipping Objects

You can flip any object in PowerPoint vertically, or in the case of the airplanes in **Figure 11.35**, horizontally. As with rotation, if you can select it, you can flip it.

To flip an object:

1. Select the object to be flipped.

2. On the Drawing toolbar, click Draw to display the menu.

3. Choose Rotate or Flip.

4. Choose Flip Horizontal or Flip Vertical (**Figure 11.36**).

✔ Tip

■ You can also flip an object with its selection handles by clicking a side handle and dragging it across the image to the other side, as in **Figure 11.37**. This has two drawbacks, however: It is very difficult to get a perfect 100% flip, and the object moves on the slide.

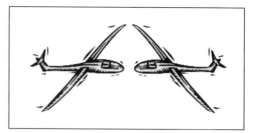

Figure 11.35 Uh oh...

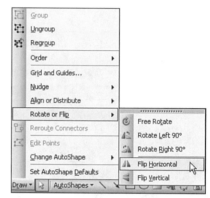

Figure 11.36 Use the Flip Horizontal or Flip Vertical command to flip the selected object.

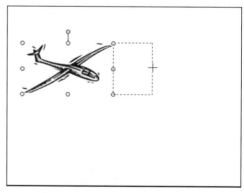

Figure 11.37 To flip interactively, drag a side handle across the object to the other side.

FLIPPING OBJECTS

MAKING GLOBAL CHANGES

Soccer League Proposal

- Number of uniforms
- Number of goals
- Balls to be purchased
- How many teams to have
- Players on each team

Figure 12.1 This bulleted list uses the default settings.

Soccer League Proposal

- Number of uniforms
- Number of goals
- Balls to be purchased
- How many teams to have
- Players on each team

Figure 12.2 After the Slide Master has been modified, all slides in the presentation are formatted with the same changes—in this case, a typeface change and the insertion of clip art.

Soccer League Proposal

- Number of uniforms
- Number of goals
- Balls to be purchased
- How many teams to have
- Players on each team

Figure 12.3 Applying a template is a quick way to format an entire presentation.

This chapter shows you how to quickly format an entire presentation, without having to change each slide.

You make some global changes, such as replacing fonts and changing colors or backgrounds, with the Format menu.

You can make other changes, such as formatting slide titles and adding logos or footers, by editing the Slide Master. This lets you easily customize a presentation for a particular client or event.

The Slide Master contains default formatting as well as any background items that you want repeated on each slide. **Figures 12.1** and **12.2** show a slide before and after modifying the Slide Master. Notice in **Figure 12.2** how a logo like the soccer ball can be added to the Slide Master so that it shows on every slide in the same position.

Perhaps the most dramatic global change you can make to your presentation is to apply a template. A template controls the color scheme, text formatting, and repeating graphical elements—and you apply it with a single command. **Figure 12.3** shows the same slide after applying a template.

Although these figures show just one slide, if the presentation has 30 slides, they can all be made to look this way with one command.

Changing the Default Colors

Your presentation's color scheme includes color assignments for the slide background, slide titles, text and lines, shadows, object fills, and accents. After you change the default colors, any new slides you create will automatically use the new color scheme.

To create a color scheme:

1. Choose Format > Slide Design to open the Slide Design task pane.

2. Click Color Schemes (**Figure 12.4**).

3. Click Edit Color Schemes at the bottom of the task pane.
   The Edit Color Scheme dialog box opens.

4. Click the Custom tab (**Figure 12.5**).

5. On the Custom tab, choose colors for the various slide elements.

6. When you're finished assigning colors, click Add as Standard Scheme.
   Add as Standard Scheme will become available once you've changed a color in the color scheme.

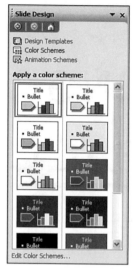

Figure 12.4 Use the Color Scheme task pane to make global color changes in your presentation.

...then click here to choose a color   *Click here to apply the change to all slides*   *First choose a slide element...*

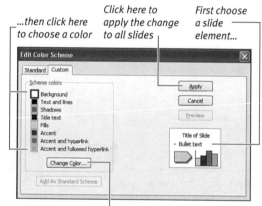

Click here to create your own color scheme

Figure 12.5 Use this dialog box to create your own color schemes.

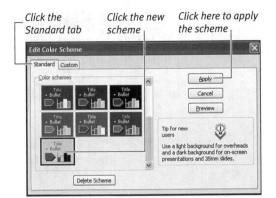

Click the Standard tab   *Click the new scheme*   *Click here to apply the scheme*

Figure 12.6 The new color scheme is now listed on the Standard tab.

7. Click the Standard tab.

Your new color scheme is now listed on the Standard tab (**Figure 12.6**). The scheme is also added to the Slide Design task pane.

8. To apply the new scheme, select it and then click Apply.

✔ Tips

- If you're not happy with the colors after you apply a new color scheme, you can immediately choose Edit > Undo to restore your previous color scheme.

- The color schemes on the Slide Design task pane have a drop-down menu that quickly lets you apply them to selected slides or to all slides (**Figure 12.7**).

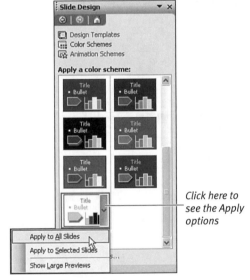

Click here to see the Apply options

Figure 12.7 The color schemes are listed on the Slide Design task pane. When you create a custom scheme, it is added to the selections.

Creating a Gradient Background

A gradient is a gradual progression from one color to another. A black-and-white printout is not the ideal place to see an example of this, but **Figure 12.8** should give you some idea of how a gradient background could be used. Gradient fills can be a blend of one color with varying amounts of white or black added, or can be a blend of two different colors. In **Figure 12.8**, we have blended black with a deep red.

Gradients can be striking. Just be sure to avoid using text colors that blend in too much with the gradient colors, as this can compromise the readability of your slides.

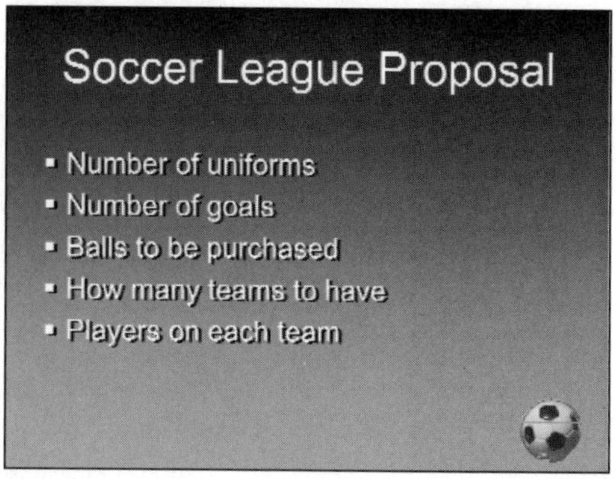

To create a gradient background:

1. Choose Format > Background.
    The Background dialog box appears.

2. Click the arrow beneath the image (**Figure 12.9**) and choose Fill Effects.
    The Fill Effects dialog box appears.

3. Select the Gradient tab.

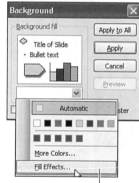

Figure 12.8 When applied intelligently, gradients can be an attractive slide background.

Figure 12.9 To choose a fill effect for the background, click the arrow next to the color field.

Click here and choose Fill Effects

One Color   Drag here to adjust the blended color

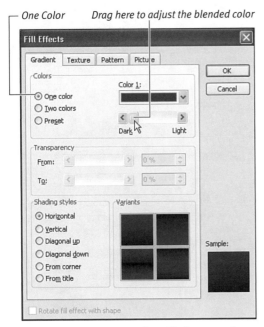

Figure 12.10 To create a gradient fill, choose a color, a shade, shading style, and variant.

4. Select the One Color radio button (**Figure 12.10**).

5. To choose the gradient's primary color, click the Color 1 field.

   The small color palette appears.

6. Choose a color from the palette, either from the current color scheme, any colors added, or from the Standard or Custom tabs. In this example, we have chosen a deep blue.

7. To make the gradient darker or lighter, move the slider below the Color 1 box to be either a bit darker or a bit lighter than your primary color. In **Figure 12.10**, we have chosen a darker blend, the result of which shows up in the Sample display.

8. Choose a shading style to determine the angle of the gradient (diagonal, from the corner, to the corner, and so on).

9. Click one of the four Variants boxes to determine the direction in which the gradient will flow.

10. Click OK and then click either Apply or Apply to All.

✔ Tip

■ As you darken the blended color, you are adding more black. As you lighten it, you are adding more white.

Creating a Two-Color Gradient

In PowerPoint, you can blend two different colors to create vibrant backgrounds for your presentations.

To create a two-color gradient:

1. Choose Format > Background.

2. In the Background dialog box, click the arrow and choose Fill Effects.

   The Fill Effects dialog box appears.

3. Select the Gradient tab and click the Two Colors radio button (**Figure 12.11**).

4. To choose the gradient's first color, click the Color 1 field.

   The small color palette appears.

5. Choose a color from the palette.

   or

   Click More Colors and choose a color from the Standard or Custom tab.

6. To choose the shade's second color, click the Color 2 field and select a color.

7. Choose one of the Shading Styles options (Horizontal, Vertical, and so on).

8. Click one of the Variants options (these are variations of the style you selected in step 8).

9. Click OK.

10. Click Apply or Apply to All.

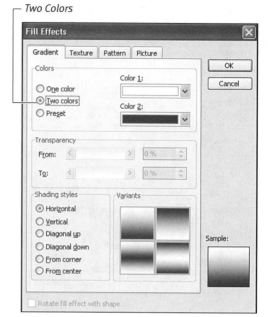

Two Colors

Figure 12.11 Choose Two Colors to create a blend of two different colors.

Preset Colors — Preset Colors list —

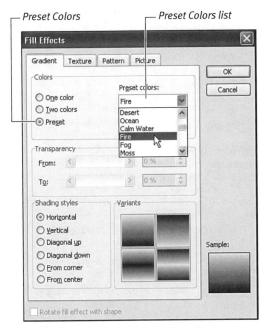

Figure 12.12 PowerPoint ships with a collection of preset gradients: some of them striking...and some of them not.

✔ Tips

■ You can also create a multicolor shade with the Preset option. Choose Preset instead of Two Colors and then choose one of the samples from the Preset Colors list (**Figure 12.12**).

■ If you routinely click Apply to All after creating backgrounds, it might be a sign that you are not taking advantage of PowerPoint's global formatting controls. Most of the time, it would be better to apply the background to the Slide Master than to apply it to a slide and choose Apply to All. For more on Slide Masters, see "Editing the Slide Master," later in this chapter.

■ Again, make sure that your gradients do not span too great of a color distance; otherwise, they will become distracting and create unreadable slides. In fact, the preset color we show in **Figure 12.12** represents a problematic gradient, because it goes from very light to very dark (and perhaps back again, depending upon the variant). Use that if you are creating a picture, but not if you are laying down charts or bullets.

CREATING A TWO-COLOR GRADIENT

Replacing a Font

Suppose you want all of your slide text to be in Verdana instead of Arial as in **Figures 12.13** and **12.14**. You can change fonts easily with the Format > Replace Fonts command.

To globally replace one font with another:

1. Choose Format > Replace Fonts.

2. The Replace Font dialog box appears (**Figure 12.15**).

3. In the With field, choose the new font.

4. Click Replace.

5. Repeat steps 2 through 4 to replace other fonts used in the presentation.

6. When you're finished replacing fonts, click Close.

✔ Tips

- The Replace Fonts command does not substitute typefaces in charts or embedded Word tables.

- Notice that the Arial Bold headline in **Figure 12.13** is Verdana Bold in **Figure 12.14**. Replace Fonts maintains style variations within a typeface.

- To replace the font in only the slide titles or the bullet text, you need to edit the Slide Master.

  See "Changing the Default Format for Text" later in this chapter.

Soccer League Proposal

- Number of uniforms
- Number of goals
- Balls to be purchased
- How many fields to reserve
- Length of season

- How many teams to have
- Players on each team
- Division of age groups
- How many coaches per team

Figure 12.13 In this presentation, the font for text in the text and title placeholders is Arial.

Soccer League Proposal

- Number of uniforms
- Number of goals
- Balls to be purchased
- How many fields to reserve
- Length of season

- How many teams to have
- Players on each team
- Division of age groups
- How many coaches per team

Figure 12.14 After replacing fonts, the text on all slides is Verdana.

Click here to list all fonts used in the presentation   *Click here to list all fonts available on your system*

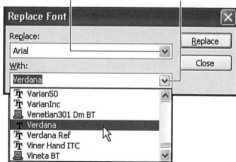

Figure 12.15 Globally replace one font with another using the Format > Replace Fonts command.

REPLACING A FONT

Slide miniature | Master toolbar | Title area placeholder | Object area placeholder

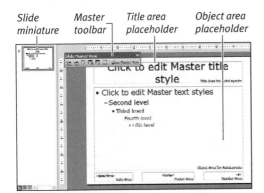

Figure 12.16 Edit the Slide Master to make global changes to your presentation.

Bullet shapes changed | Title reformatted | Graphical object added

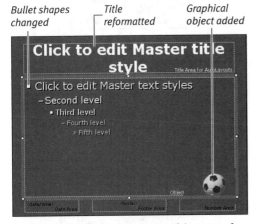

Figure 12.17 This figure shows some of the types of changes you can make on a Slide Master.

Insert New Slide Master | Delete Master | Rename Master | Close Master View

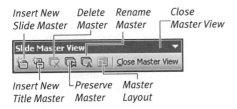

Insert New Title Master | Preserve Master | Master Layout

Figure 12.18 The essential controls needed for working in Slide Master view.

Editing the Slide Master

The Slide Master (**Figure 12.16**) contains the default formatting for your presentation, background color or pattern, and any other objects you would like to appear on each slide of a presentation. Any changes you make on the Slide Master automatically affect all slides in your presentation that use that master.

When you format the Master title and Master text, you are actually formatting all of the titles and text in your presentation (except in embedded Word tables, charts, and org charts). **Figure 12.17** shows a Slide Master after formatting.

To edit the Slide Master:

1. Choose View > Master > Slide Master. The Slide Master appears (**Figure 12.16**).

2. Make your desired changes on the Master, including the following:
   - Adjusting the font and size of the text in the title and bulleted text placeholders
   - Changing the color and style of the bullets
   - Adding and removing graphical objects
   - Formatting the background
   - Adding animation (covered in Chapter 14)

3. Click the Close button on the Slide Master View toolbar (**Figure 12.18**).

   All slides now have the formatting and background items you added on the Master.

   See "Changing the Default Format for Text," "Adding Background Items," and "Inserting Footers," later in this chapter. Also see "Choosing Bullet Shapes," "Adjusting Bullet Placement," and "Formatting a Text Placeholder" in Chapter 3.

Inserting a Title Master

One of the most common actions taken when working in Slide Master view is that of adding a Title Master to control the look of title slides in a presentation. This is different from adding a second set of masters (and Microsoft could have done a better job with its naming system), because the Title Master is considered a companion to the Slide Master. You'll read about creating new masters in the next section.

Figure 12.19 shows the Slide Master and Title Master together in slide miniatures view. While still sharing the same basic design scheme, you can see the obvious differences.

To insert a Title Master:

1. If you are not there already, choose View > Master > Slide Master.

    The Slide Master appears.

2. Choose Insert > New Title Master from the main menu or on the Slide Master View toolbar.

    PowerPoint inserts the Title Master. You will notice in the slide miniature view (**Figure 12.19**) that the Title and Slide Masters are shown linked, indicating that they are a single set of masters.

3. Make your desired changes on the Title Master.

4. Click the Close button on the Slide Master View Master toolbar.

    Now, any slide that you designate as a title slide will take on this new formatting.

    See "Changing the Default Format for Text" later in this chapter.

The Slide Master and Title Master are linked

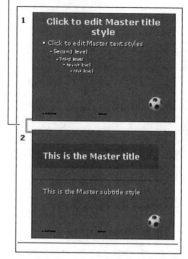

Figure 12.19 With two distinct masters controlling formatting, your title slides can have their own distinctive look, apart from (and yet still related to) your other slides.

✔ Tips

■ To switch between the Title Master and the Slide Master, while you're in the Master view, press the Page Up and Page Down keys or just click the slide in the Slides miniatures pane to select the desired one.

■ The status bar indicates which master is currently displayed.

Figure 12.20 The typical example of a second set of masters—one for showing the presentation and one for printing it.

Using More Than One Master

A long-awaited feature was finally added in PowerPoint 2002, and it remains popular in PowerPoint 2003—that of being able to add more than one Slide Master to a presentation. This is invaluable for those who need to experiment with many possible designs, and for those who need to create their presentations in multiple forms (for example, one design for show and one for print).

To use more than one Master:

◆ While in Master view, Choose Insert > New Slide Master.

◆ Select a Master in the Slides miniature task pane, and use Ctrl+C to copy the slide, then Ctrl+V to paste the copy into the task pane.

✔ Tips

■ The advantage of performing the copy-paste creation of a new master is that the new master inherits the formatting of the existing master, including the presence of a Title Master. Typically, you would create a second master as a variation on the design of the first one, so this is a much better starting point than Insert > New Master, which creates a completely plain master without a Title Master.

■ When you create a new master, immediately right-click it and choose Preserve Master. This will ensure that PowerPoint doesn't remove the master if it is not being used by a slide.

■ Remember, just because you can, doesn't mean you should. A presentation which uses a different master for each slide is not usually a good presentation.

■ **Figure 12.20** shows the classic example of using a second set of masters—one for the presentation and one for the printouts. Printing slides with colored backgrounds consumes a lot of toner or ink and is generally not as readable. It's better to print your handouts with no background and black text. With a second set of masters, this is easily done.

Changing the Default Format for Text

Suppose you want all of your slide titles to be in a larger type size and aligned on the left, all first-level bullets to be squares, and all bullet text to be anchored in the middle. By making these changes on the Slide Master, you need to format the text only once—all new and existing slides will conform to the modified format.

Figures 12.21 and **12.22** show a slide before and after modifying the text formatting on the Slide Master. **Figure 12.23** shows the modified Slide Master.

To change the default format for text in placeholders:

1. Choose View > Master > Slide Master.

2. To format slide titles, click "Click to edit Master title style" and make your changes.

3. To format first-level text in bulleted list slides, click the line "Click to edit Master text styles" and make your changes.

4. To format other text levels, click the appropriate line (such as "Second level") and make your desired changes.

5. When you're finished, click the Close Master View button on the Slide Master View toolbar.

    See "Choosing Bullet Shapes," "Adjusting Bullet Placement," and "Formatting a Text Placeholder" in Chapter 3.

✔ Tips

- When you format text on the Slide Master, only slide text with default formatting is affected. Any formatting that has been directly applied to text overrides the formatting on the Slide Master. So for consistency, apply formatting to the Slide Master.

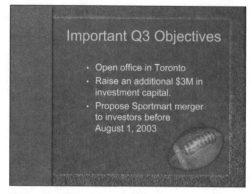

Figure 12.21 This slide uses default text formatting.

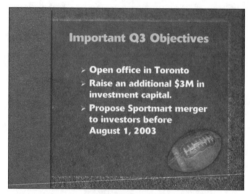

Figure 12.22 This slide illustrates what the text looks like after formatting the text on the Slide Master; all slides are formatted the same way.

Figure 12.23 The slide shown in Figure 12.22 was created by this Slide Master.

Adding Graphics

When graphics are placed on the Slide Master, they are repeated on every slide in the presentation.

Common items are company names and logos, borders, rules, and graphics like the football in **Figures 12.21** and **12.22**.

To add graphic items to all your slides:

1. Choose View > Master >Slide Master. The Slide Master appears.

2. Add background items in any of the following ways:

▲ Use tools on the Drawing toolbar to create graphical objects on the Master.

▲ Use the Text Box tool to insert text on the Master.

▲ Choose the Insert > Picture command or click the Insert Clip Art button to add graphics on the Master.

3. When you're finished, click the Close Master View button on the Slide Master View toolbar.

✔ Tip

■ If you've inserted a Title Master, add items to it that you want to appear only on title slides.

Inserting Footers

With a single command, you can place a footer on each slide containing the date, customizable text (such as the presentation title), and/or the slide number (**Figure 12.24**). Footer text is formatted on the Slide Master (**Figure 12.25**) and defined in the Header and Footer dialog box.

To insert footers:

1. From any view, choose View > Header and Footer.

    The Header and Footer dialog box appears (**Figure 12.26**).

2. Select the check boxes for the items you want: Date and Time, Slide Number, and/or Footer.

3. If you select Date and Time, click Update Automatically to use the current date or click Fixed to use a date that you type in.

4. If you select Footer, type your footer text in the text box.

5. To prevent the footer from appearing on title slides, select the check box for Don't Show on Title Slide.

6. Click Apply to All.

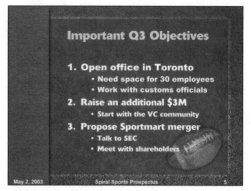

Figure 12.24 This slide—and all other slides in the presentation—contain footers with the date, presentation title, and slide number.

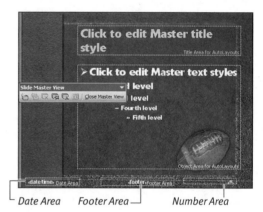

Date Area   Footer Area   Number Area

Figure 12.25 Date Area, Footer Area, and Number Area are placeholders on the Slide Master.

Dates can either update automatically...   *...or be fixed (enter a date here)*

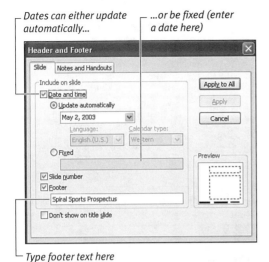

Type footer text here

Figure 12.26 Use the Header and Footer dialog box to specify which elements to include in the footer.

✔ Tips

- To format the footer text, format each footer placeholder on the Slide Master.

- To change the starting slide number, choose File > Page Setup and specify a new number for Number Slides From.

- It might seem like a misnomer to call the dialog box Headers and Footers instead of just Footers, but note that you can move the placeholders anywhere on the master slide, including to the top to act like a header.

- Most of the time, headers and footers are used on printouts, not the presentation itself. To use it for a presentation, you would have to format the text to be much larger than the default so it could be seen by the audience.

- If you accidentally delete any of the date/footer/number placeholders on the Master, you can get them back by going to Format > Master Layout and clicking the appropriate box. If you're having trouble getting any of the text specified in the View > Header and Footer dialog to show up, check your Slide Master to make sure you actually have a placeholder for that text.

Applying a Template

PowerPoint comes with built-in templates that include predesigned formats and color schemes. Applying a specific template to a presentation gives it a particular look that you can easily copy to other presentations.

By applying a template, you can instantly change the format of the text, the background color and any background items, the colors used in the presentation, and animation schemes. PowerPoint includes a number of professionally designed templates, and you can create your own.

Figure 12.27 shows a slide before applying a template and **Figure 12.28** shows the same slide after applying a template. One command did all that!

To apply a template to a presentation:

1. Choose Format > Slide Design to open the Slide Design task pane (**Figure 12.29**).

   There you will see three sections of choices:

   ▲ Designs in use by slides in the presentation

   ▲ Design templates you have recently used

   ▲ Designs available to be used, residing in the Templates section of Documents and Settings on your computer

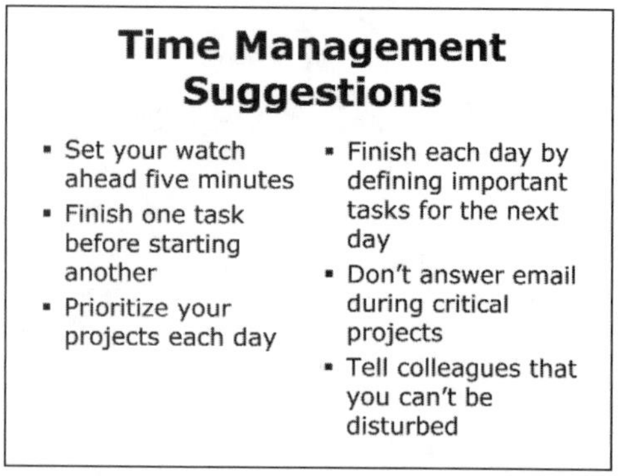

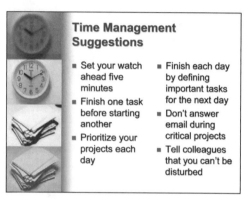

Figure 12.27 This slide uses the plain, default design.

Figure 12.28 Five seconds later, it gets a complete facelift, thanks to a new design template.

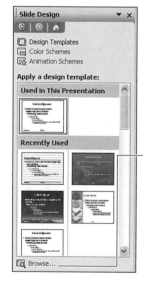

Browse for more templates

Figure 12.29 On the Slide Design task pane, you can browse design templates to apply to your current presentation.

Figure 12.30 After you have chosen a design template, you decide whether to apply it to the current slide or to all slides.

Figure 12.31 If you have more than one master in your presentation, you can switch between them from the Slide Design task view.

2. Pick a design from any of the three sections and click its drop-down arrow.

3. Choose to apply the design to either the selected slide or to all slides (**Figure 12.30**).

✔ Tips

- Be careful with clicking the design preview thumbnail itself—the default for applying designs is to apply it to every slide in your presentation. If you don't want to do that, you can always choose Edit > Undo.

- You can use any PowerPoint presentation file as a template. Click Browse to find it on your hard drive or on a network drive.

- If you have more than one set of masters in your current presentation, you can switch between them using the Slide Design task pane. In **Figure 12.31**, you can see that there are two designs in the first section "Used in This Presentation," one of them dark and one of them light. We are about to apply the Dark Slide design to the slide.

- You can turn any existing presentation into a template by renaming it to have an extension of .pot.

  When you choose File > Save As and change the file type to Design Template, PowerPoint automatically opens the appropriate folder.

WORKING IN OUTLINE VIEW

Although many of PowerPoint's tools are built for representing ideas and concepts graphically, there is no denying that words are a vital component of any presentation. Sometimes, charts, pictures, and clip art can become a distraction, making it hard to focus on the ideas you need to convey with text.

The PowerPoint development team understands that. The program offers a customizable Outline view, which displays text much more prominently than other views. Outline view is ideal for seeing the structure of your presentation, reorganizing bulleted points, and reordering slides. It also offers a quick way to type a series of bulleted lists. In this chapter, you will see how easy it is to type lists, insert new slides, and move slides around using Outline view.

Using Outline View

PowerPoint's Normal view displays an outline of your presentation. You can toggle between Outline view and Slide Thumbnails view (**Figure 13.1**).

The Outline pane in Normal view displays each slide's title and bulleted items, in classic outline form (**Figure 13.2**).

While you are working in Outline view, you can edit any slide title or group of bullets.

To use Outline view:

1. Go to View > Normal and select the Outline tab to display the Outline pane (**Figure 13.1**).

2. Use the scroll bar in the Outline pane to view additional slides in your presentation.

    Changes you make to title or bulleted text in the outline (**Figure 13.3**) are reflected on the slide itself. Similarly, editing the title or bullets of a slide is reflected in the outline.

Toggle between Outline and Slide Thumbnails views   *Click here to display slide thumbnails*

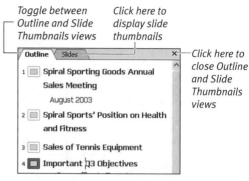

Click here to close Outline and Slide Thumbnails views

Figure 13.1 Normal view displays a pane that toggles between Outline view and Slide Thumbnails view.

Outline pane   *Scrollbar*   *Slide pane*

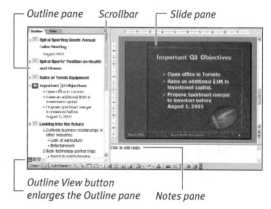

Outline View button enlarges the Outline pane   *Notes pane*

Figure 13.2 Normal view has three panes; drag the pane borders to adjust the amount of space allocated to each area.

Changes you make to text in the outline....   *...are reflected within the slide, and vice versa*

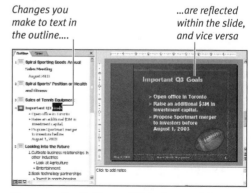

Figure 13.3 The Outline and Slide views work in harmony with one another.

USING OUTLINE VIEW

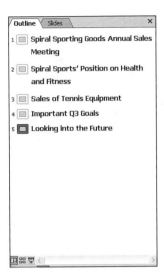

Figure 13.4 You can type your slide titles in Outline view and fill in the details later.

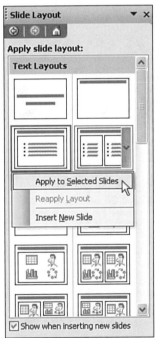

Figure 13.5 Choose a layout from the Slide Layout task pane for the current slide.

Outlining a Presentation

When initially creating a presentation, you may want to focus on developing the overall text content and structure rather than the details—images, fonts, colors—of individual slides. You can do this by typing slide titles in Outline view (**Figure 13.4**).

After you have typed your outline, you can go back to Slide view and complete each slide by adding graphics, inserting charts, changing the slide layout, applying a design template, and more.

To create a new outline:

1. Create a new presentation.

2. Make sure you are in Normal view, then choose the Outline tab in the Slides miniature/Outline pane.

3. For each slide, type the title and press Enter.

4. When you're finished, press Ctrl+Home to move the cursor to the first slide.

5. To change the layout for a particular slide, choose Format > Slide Layout and choose a layout from the Slide Layout task pane (**Figure 13.5**).

✔ Tip

■ While creating your outline, you may find it convenient to type bulleted lists as you go.

  See the next section, "Creating Bulleted Lists."

■ Only placeholder text such as slide titles and bulleted text can be added (or will display) in Outline view. If you have text in manually added text boxes, it will not show in Outline view.

Creating Bulleted Lists

Outline view offers a quick way to create and type bulleted lists. It is so easy, you might be suspicious: You press Tab.

To create a new bulleted list slide:

1. Click at the beginning of a slide title in the outline where you want to insert a slide.

2. Press Enter.

   A new slide appears in both parts of the view (**Figure 13.6**).

3. Type the slide title and press Ctrl+Enter. A blank bulleted line is inserted.

4. Type the bulleted item and press Enter.

5. Continue typing bulleted items, following the same rules as in Slide view:

   ▲ Press Enter to type another line of the same level as the previous one.

   ▲ Press Tab to demote the current line (**Figure 13.7**).

   ▲ Press Shift+Tab to promote the current line.

6. To create another slide, press Ctrl+Enter after the last bullet in the list.

✔ Tips

■ Ctrl+Enter is a handy keystroke for toggling between title and bullet. With it, you can essentially create your entire presentation structure.

■ To create a two-line title and designate where the break should occur (such as the one used in Slide 4 in **Figure 13.7**), press Shift+Enter after the first line

.■ To change the level of a line, use the Promote or Demote button on the Outlining toolbar. Or press Tab to demote and Shift+Tab to promote (**Figure 13.8**).

New slide

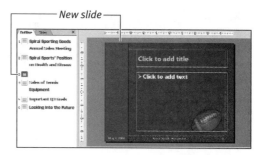

Figure 13.6 Press Enter, and a new slide appears.

Line Break
Press Ctrl+Enter to insert a bullet   *Press Tab to demote the bullet*

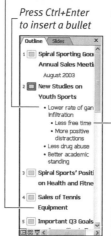

Figure 13.7 Type your bulleted lists in Outline view just as you do in Slide view.

Promote

Demote

Figure 13.8 The Outlining toolbar.

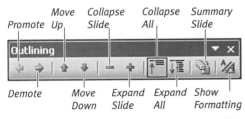

Expand All

Outline Slides ×

1 Spiral Sporting Goods
Annual Sales Meeting

2 New Studies on
Youth Sports

3 Spiral Sports' Positio
on Health and Fitnes:

4 Sales of Tennis
Equipment

5 Important Q3 Goals

6 Looking into the Futu

Collapse All

Figure 13.9 In this outline, only the slide titles are displayed.

Outline Slides ×

1 Spiral Sporting Goods
Annual Sales Meeting

2 Spiral Sports' Position on Health
and Fitness

3 New Studies on Youth Sports
• Lower rate of gang infiltration
• Less drug abuse
• Better academic standing

4 Sales of Tennis Equipment

5 Important Q3 Goals
• Open office in Toronto
• Raise an additional $3M in
investment capital.
• Propose Sportmart merger
to investors before
August 1, 2003

6 Looking into the Future

Figure 13.10 The text in Slides 3 and 5 is expanded; the text in other slides is collapsed.

Promote *Move* *Collapse* *Collapse* *Summary*
Up *Slide* *All* *Slide*

Outlining ▼ ×

Demote *Move* *Expand* *Expand* *Show*
Down *Slide* *All* *Formatting*

Figure 13.11 Click the Move buttons to relocate a slide title in the outline.

Collapsing and Expanding the Outline

You can get a better idea of your presentation's structure by hiding the main text on your slides and displaying only the slide titles (**Figure 13.9**). This way, you can see how the information flows. Furthermore, when text is hidden, you can see more slides in the window.

When you hide text, you are collapsing the outline. When you redisplay hidden text, you are expanding the outline. **Figure 13.10** shows an outline in which some text is collapsed and some is expanded. You can collapse and expand the outline using the Outlining toolbar.

To collapse outline text:

1. If the Outlining toolbar isn't displayed, choose View > Toolbars > Outlining.

   The Outlining toolbar appears (**Figure 13.11**).

2. To collapse the entire outline, make sure your cursor is in the text on the Outline pane, and then click the Collapse All button on the Outlining toolbar (**Figure 13.11**).

   or

   Choose Edit > Select All, and then click Collapse.

3. To collapse the currently selected slide(s), click the Collapse button.

✔ Tips

■ To select a single slide in Outline view, just place your cursor in any of the text for that slide.

■ To select more than one slide in Outline view, click and drag with the mouse. You can also use Shift+click in Outline view: Click on a slide's title text, hold down the Shift button, and then click in the text of another slide.

To expand outline text:

◆ To expand the entire outline, click the Expand All button on the Outlining toolbar.

◆ To expand the currently selected slide(s), click the Expand All button (**Figure 13.9**).

✔ Tips

■ Another way to collapse or expand the text in a single slide is to double-click the slide's icon.

■ You can also right-click the slide text and choose Expand or Collapse from the shortcut menu.

Move Down
Move Up

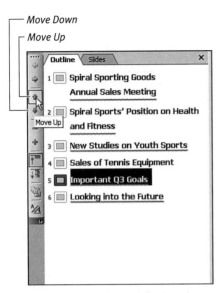

Figure 13.12 Reordering slides is easier if only the slide titles are displayed.

Drag slide icon to this horizontal line.

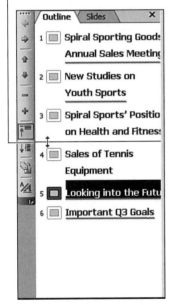

Figure 13.13 You can drag a slide icon to reposition a slide.

Rearranging and Deleting Slides

Because the outline shows many slides at once, the Outline pane is ideal for repositioning slides in a presentation. You can use either the Move buttons on the Outlining toolbar or the drag-and-drop technique. **Figure 13.12** shows the Move buttons on the Outlining toolbar, which has been docked to the left side of the task pane, for convenience.

To reposition a slide with the Move buttons:

1. If the Outlining toolbar isn't displayed, choose View > Toolbars > Outlining.

2. Click the Collapse All button on the Outlining toolbar so that only slide titles are displayed (**Figure 13.12**). This is not required, just recommended.

3. Click anywhere in the title of the slide you want to move.

4. Click the Move Up or Move Down button (**Figure 13.12**) until the slide is in the position you want.

To reposition a slide with the drag-and-drop technique:

1. Click the Collapse All button so that only slide titles are displayed (not required).

2. Drag the slide icon for the slide you want to move.

   A horizontal line indicates where the slide will be inserted (**Figure 13.13**).

3. When the horizontal line is in the desired location, release the mouse button.

✔ Tips

- When the target location cannot be seen on the screen, you may find it easier to move slides by cutting and pasting them.

- Be careful to use the slide icon when dragging and dropping slides to rearrange them in the Outline pane. Selecting the text instead makes it very easy to drag and drop text from one slide into another instead of simply moving the entire slide.

To delete a slide from the outline:

- Click anywhere on the slide in the Outline pane and choose Edit > Delete Slide.

  or

  Using the Outline pane, select all text on a slide and press Del. PowerPoint will ask you if you're sure (**Figure 13.14**).

Figure 13.14 You can remove a slide by deleting all of its text in Outline view.

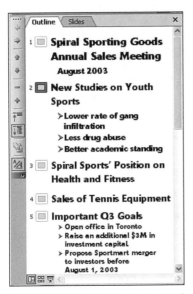

Figure 13.15 Text formatting is displayed in this outline.

Hiding and Displaying Formatting

As you can see in **Figure 13.15**, Outline view can show text formatting and display the actual bullet symbols for bulleted list slides. At times, it might be distracting to show the formatting, so it is helpful to know about the Show Formatting toggle button on the Outlining toolbar.

To hide or display text formatting:

◆ On the Outlining toolbar, click the Show Formatting button (**Figure 13.11**) to toggle the formatting on and off.

✔ Tip

■ When formatting is hidden, you will probably see more slides in the outline, because standard formatting for slides calls for text that is larger than the default font used in unformatted outline view.

Importing an Outline

If you have created an outline in your word processor (**Figure 13.16**), you can bring it into PowerPoint by importing the outline into an existing presentation or by opening the outline as its own stand-alone presentation.

If you intend to create an outline in your word processor and then import it into PowerPoint, make sure it conforms to the following rules:

♦ Each title must be in its own paragraph.

♦ Two-line slide titles must use a line break (not a paragraph break) between the lines. Most word processors use Shift+Enter to create this.

♦ If you are importing an outline from Word, it's best to represent the titles and bulleted text with styles: Heading 1 for a slide title, Heading 2 for primary bullets, Heading 3 for secondary bullets.

♦ If you are importing an outline from a *.TXT file, it is best to represent bulleted items with simple tabs (no tabs for a title, one tab for a first-level bullet, two tabs for a second level, and so on).

Note how plain the outline is in **Figure 13.16**—PowerPoint doesn't need much to discern the levels of an outline.

To insert an outline into an existing presentation:

1. In PowerPoint, choose Insert > Slides from Outline.

   The Insert Outline dialog box appears (**Figure 13.17**).

2. Navigate to the folder in which your outline is stored.

3. Double-click the name of the outline file.

   The outline will be imported into Power-Point. Slides will automatically be created with titles that match the outline titles.

Figure 13.16 You can type an outline in your word processor and then import or open it in PowerPoint.

Figure 13.17 Use the Insert > Slides from Outline command and choose an outline to insert into a presentation.

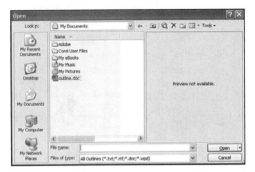

Figure 13.18 When an outline file is opened, Power-Point automatically creates a new presentation from the outline.

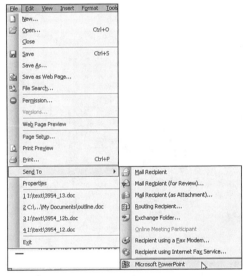

Figure 13.19 You can send a Microsoft Word outline directly to PowerPoint with the File > Send To command.

To create a new presentation by opening an outline:

1. In PowerPoint, choose File > Open (Ctrl+O).

   The Open dialog box appears.

2. In the Files of Type field, choose All Outlines (**Figure 13.18**).

3. Navigate to the folder in which your outline is stored.

4. Select the name of the outline file and click Open.

   PowerPoint opens the outline file as a PowerPoint slide show, with titles and bullets imported in the correct hierarchy.

✔ Tips

- Make sure that the file you are opening as a PowerPoint presentation is not also open in your word processor. PowerPoint will fail with a generic message about not being able to open the file, leaving it to you to figure out why!

- PowerPoint can import outlines from a variety of programs; your choices depend on which import filters you selected during installation of PowerPoint.

- Microsoft Word can send an outline directly to PowerPoint. In Word, choose File > Send To > Microsoft PowerPoint (**Figure 13.19**), and the presentation will open as slides. Note that the bullets and formatting will be determined by your PowerPoint slide masters and design templates, so don't waste time formatting the outline in Word.

Creating a Summary Slide

You can quickly summarize the slides in your presentation by creating a summary slide. A summary slide is a bulleted list that PowerPoint automatically creates from your slide titles.

A great way to use a summary slide is to create links from bullets to the slides they represent so you can click and go directly to the full slide (for example, if you get a question from the audience during a presentation). These are called actions or hyperlinks, and they are discussed in Chapter 15.

To create a summary slide:

1. Select all of the slides that you want included in the summary slide (**Figure 13.20**).

   If you select slides that have no title, the summary slide will display them as Topic 1, Topic 2, and so on.

2. If the Outlining toolbar isn't displayed, choose View > Toolbars > Outlining.

3. Click the Summary Slide button on the Outlining toolbar.

   The summary slide appears at the beginning of the selected set (**Figure 13.21**). Depending on the number of slides you select, the summary may be continued on additional slides.

4. Select and delete any bulleted lines you don't want in the summary.

5. If you like, change the title of the summary slide.

6. Move the summary slide where you want it to appear in the presentation.

Summary Slide button

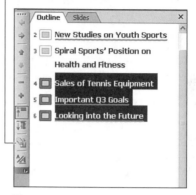

Figure 13.20 To create a summary slide, select all of the slides you want in the summary and then click the Summary Slide button.

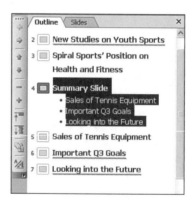

Figure 13.21 The summary slide lists the titles of all the slides you selected in the presentation.

✔ Tips

- You can also create a summary slide in Slide Sorter view. The advantage to using this view is that you can choose which slides you want to include based on their visual elements rather than just the text in them. Slide Sorter view is covered in Chapter 14.

- Slides must have title placeholders (even if there is no text in them) in order to create a summary slide. If you've used a blank slide layout in one of the slides you've selected to use in a summary slide, the summary slide command will be unavailable.

- If PowerPoint created a second summary slide and you want to consolidate the summary on a single slide, select the bullets on the second slide and click the Move Up button until the bullet points from the second summary slide are part of the first summary slide's list.

- To fit more items on your summary slide, you may need to choose a smaller font size. (But make sure that the text is still legible.) You can also spread a summary slide out to more than one slide.

WORKING IN SLIDE SORTER VIEW

Slide Sorter toolbar

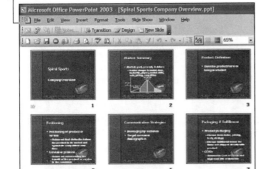

Slide Sorter view button

Figure 14.1 In Slide Sorter view, you can see many slides at once.

Slide Sorter view shows miniatures of each slide in your presentation (**Figure 14.1**). This view is similar to the Slide Thumbnails view in that you see many slides at once.

However, in Slide Sorter view, you have the advantage of being able to see the objects in your slide (charts, tables, and so forth) more clearly. This view is better for observing the flow of your presentation, and it allows you to reorder your slides by copying and moving slides within your presentation—or even to and from other presentations.

This view is also useful for instantly seeing the effects of global changes to your presentation, such as applying a template, changing the color scheme, and adding a background (see Chapter 12 for more on global changes). Slide Sorter view is also useful when adding slide show effects; see Chapter 15 for details.

Using Slide Sorter View

Slide Sorter view gives you the best overall look at the flow of your presentation and its graphical elements. You can easily delete and reorder slides in this view, and if you decide to modify a particular slide, you can easily switch to a view that allows editing.

To use Slide Sorter view:

1. Choose View > Slide Sorter.

   or

   Click the Slide Sorter View button—the middle button of those three small ones at the lower-left of the application window.

2. If necessary, use the scroll bar to view additional slides.

3. To modify a slide, double-click the slide.

   The slide now appears in Normal view, and you can make any changes you like to the slide.

Zoom field

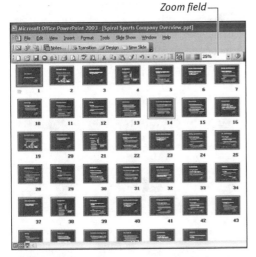

Figure 14.2 When you zoom out to 25 percent, you can see more slides.

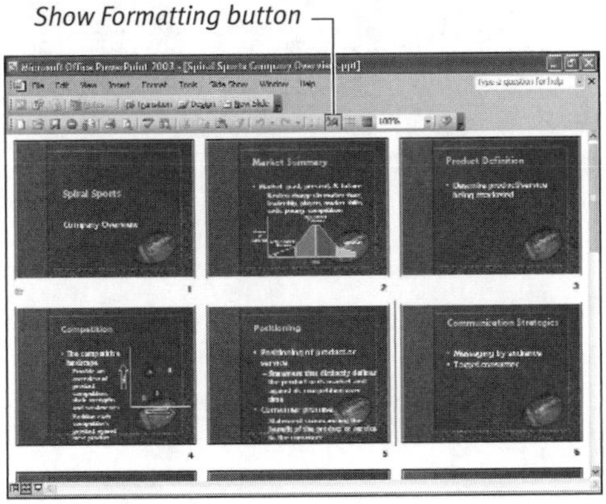

Show Formatting button

Figure 14.3 When you zoom in to 100 percent, you can see more detail on each slide.

Figure 14.4 Choose a zoom percentage or enter any value between 20 and 100 in the Percent field.

Zooming In and Out

You can control the number of slides you see in Slide Sorter view, as well as the level of detail, by zooming in and out. To see more slides, zoom out (**Figure 14.2**). To see more detail, zoom in (**Figure 14.3**).

To zoom in and out:

◆ Click the arrow in the Zoom field in the Standard toolbar (**Figures 14.2** and **14.3**) to display a list of zoom percentages. Then click the desired number.

or

Click the percentage in the Zoom field, type a number between 20 and 100, and press Enter.

or

Choose View > Zoom and choose the desired zoom percentage in the Zoom dialog box (**Figure 14.4**).

✔ Tips

■ If you have a scroll mouse, you can zoom in and out by turning the wheel as you hold the Ctrl key.

■ If your computer seems to redraw the slides too slowly when zooming in and out, try it with Show Formatting toggled off. This will display only the titles on the slides, allowing your computer to render the Slide Sorter view more quickly.

■ In Slide Sorter view, the slide content cannot be changed. You can edit text in the Outline pane or double-click a slide to edit its content in Normal view, but only slide order, appearance, and slide transitions can be changed in Slide Sorter view.

■ You cannot zoom closer than 100% in Slide Sorter view.

ZOOMING IN AND OUT

Creating a Summary Slide

As mentioned in Chapter 13, a summary slide lists the topics covered in your presentation. Creating a summary slide in Slide Sorter view offers one main advantage over Outline view: you can more easily pick and choose which slides to include in the summary. Instead of remembering where you click to select the slide and whether you should collapse the outline first, in Slide Sorter view, just select the slides you want included in the summary.

See "Creating a Summary Slide" in Chapter 13.

To create a summary slide:

1. Hold down Ctrl and click each slide you want in the summary.

2. Click the Summary Slide button on the Slide Sorter toolbar (**Figure 14.5**).

   The summary slide appears before the first slide in your selection (**Figure 14.6**).

3. To edit the summary slide, double-click the slide to switch to Normal view.

✔ Tips

■ After you have created a summary slide, you can move it to any location in the presentation.

   See the next section, "Reordering the Slides."

■ If PowerPoint needs to create your summary on several slides and you prefer to fit it on one, you may need to choose a smaller font size (but make sure that the text is still legible). You can then move the text onto the first slide to consolidate it.

■ If you select slides for a summary that don't have a title, the summary slide will list them as Topic 1, Topic 2, and so on.

Figure 14.5 Select only the slides whose titles you want to appear on the summary slide.

Summary slide

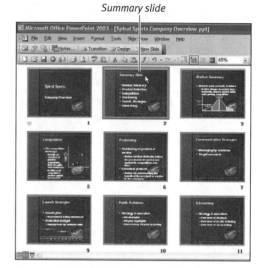

Figure 14.6 Slide 2 is the summary slide.

■ If you select slides for a summary that don't have a title *placeholder*, the summary slide option will not be available. To correct this, change any Blank slide layouts to Title Only. In Normal view, you can drag the title placeholder off the edge of the slide to hide it.

■ To learn how to create navigation links from the bullets on the summary slide to the slides they reference, see "Creating Action Buttons" in Chapter 15.

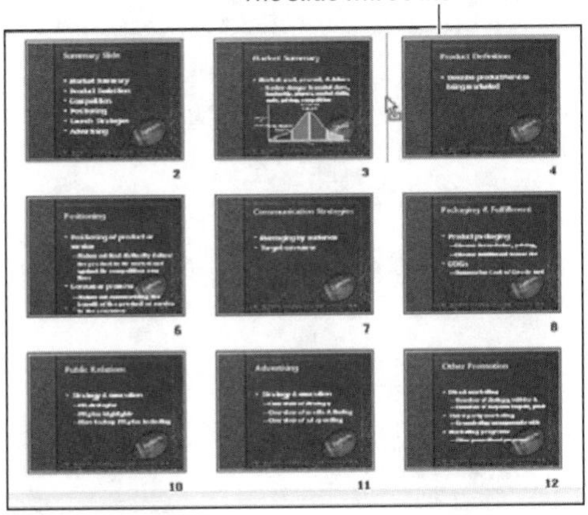

The slide will be moved here

Figure 14.7 When you are dragging a slide, a vertical line indicates where PowerPoint will insert the slide when you release the mouse button.

Reordering the Slides

Because you can see many slides at once in Slide Sorter view, it is the ideal view for rearranging your presentation. PowerPoint offers two ways to move slides in this view.

To move slides with the drag-and-drop technique:

1. Zoom out until you can see the slide you want to move as well as the destination (if possible).

2. Drag the slide you want to move.

   A vertical line follows the mouse pointer to indicate where the slide will be inserted. In **Figure 14.7**, slide 5 is being moved ahead of slide 4.

3. When the vertical line is in the correct position, release the mouse button.

✔ Tips

■ You can also move a slide with cut and paste. Select the slide to move and press Ctrl+X to cut it to the Clipboard. Then, select the slide that precedes your desired location and press Ctrl+V.

■ When you rearrange slides, they are renumbered automatically.

REORDERING THE SLIDES

Copying Slides

Sometimes, you may want to create a slide that is similar to an existing one. Rather than creating the new slide from scratch, you can create a copy of the existing slide and then make any necessary revisions.

PowerPoint offers three ways to copy a slide: You can duplicate it as you drag it (sometimes known as "drag and dupe"), use the Duplicate command, or copy and paste it.

To copy a slide with "drag and dupe":

1. Zoom out until you can see the slide you want to copy as well as the destination (if possible).

2. Press and hold Ctrl while you drag the slide you want to copy. In **Figure 14.8**, slide 9 is being duplicated between slides 2 and 3.

   A vertical line follows the pointer to indicate where the copy will be inserted, and a plus sign (+) shows that it will be copied rather than moved.

3. When the vertical line is in the correct position, release the mouse button.

   The duplicate slide appears.

✔ Tip

■ Be sure to keep holding the Ctrl key until after you release the mouse button, or you'll simply move the slide instead of duplicating it.

The duplicate will be placed here ⎯

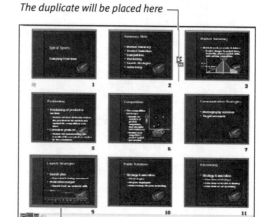

This slide will be duplicated

Figure 14.8 To drag and dupe (duplicate) a slide, hold Ctrl as you drag.

Original   Copy

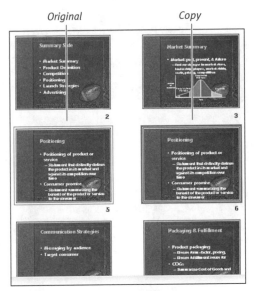

Figure 14.9 When you use the Edit > Duplicate command, the duplicate appears to the right of the original.

To duplicate a slide:

1. Select the slide to be copied.

2. Choose Edit > Duplicate (or press Ctrl+D).

   A copy appears to the right of the original (**Figure 14.9**).

3. Drag the copy into a different place, if necessary.

To copy and paste a slide:

1. Select the slide to copy and press Ctrl+C.

2. Select the slide that precedes your desired location.

3. Press Ctrl+V to paste.

Deleting slides

You can also easily delete a slide in Slide Sorter view.

To delete a slide:

1. Click the slide you want to delete. To select multiple slides, press and hold Ctrl as you click each one (**Figure 14.10**).

2. Press Delete or choose Edit > Delete Slide.

✔ Tips

- You can select a range of slides by clicking one and then holding the Shift key as you click the last one in the selection set.

- You can select all of the slides in the presentation by pressing Ctrl+A.

- If you want to conceal a slide without permanently deleting it, you can select it and choose Hide Slide from either the Slide Sorter toolbar (**Figure 14.11**) or the shortcut menu. Remember, the hidden slide will still show up in Slide Sorter and Normal view, but it won't be shown in the slide show itself.

Show Formatting button

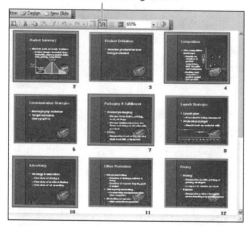

Figure 14.10 Slides 2, 4, 7, and 10 are selected.

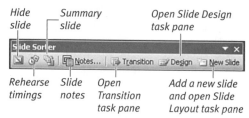

Figure 14.11 The Slide Sorter toolbar gives you quick access to important options and task panes.

DELETING SLIDES

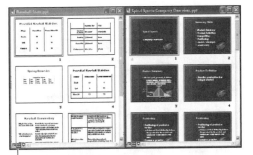

Click in the presentation if necessary
to choose Slide Sorter view

Figure 14.12 It's easy to move slides between
presentations when you can see both presentations'
slides on the screen at the same time.

Select the   Location where slide
slide   will be placed

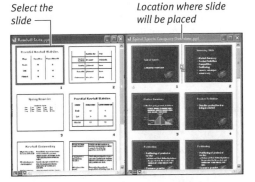

Figure 14.13 Dragging across presentations is no
different from moving a slide within its own
presentation.

Drag slide to the other window

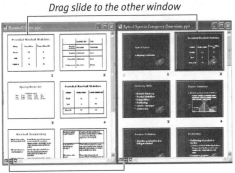

Each presentation has its own
set of View buttons

Figure 14.14 Drag any of the selected slides to the
other window, and all of the slides will move into the
new presentation.

Copying Slides Between Presentations

If a presentation gets so large that it
becomes unwieldy, you may want to divide
it into two or more files, moving some of the
slides into a new presentation. You also may
want to rearrange slides between two existing presentations.

In either case, you can open the presentations beside each other in Slide Sorter view.
By having both presentations open at the
same time (**Figure 14.12**), you can copy
slides from one to the other. You can then
delete the slides from the original presentation, if you want. The first step is to be able
to see both presentations.

To open and view two presentations:

1. Choose File > Open to find and open
   both presentations.

2. Choose View > Slide Sorter for each
   presentation.

3. Choose Windows > Arrange All to see
   both presentations.

   If there is a third presentation open, it
   will be arranged also. You will likely want
   to close it or minimize it and then issue
   the Arrange All command again.

4. Adjust the view as needed.

To copy slides into another presentation:

1. Select the slide to be copied.

2. Drag it across to the other presentation
   and position your cursor where you want
   it to reside (**Figure 14.13**).

3. Release the mouse (**Figure 14.14**).

   or

continues on next page

To copy a series of consecutive slides, hold down Shift as you click one slide and then another.

or

To copy a series of nonconsecutive slides, hold down Ctrl as you click one slide and then another.

✔ Tips

- In **Figure 14.14**, notice that the copied slide took on the look of the design and color scheme of the presentation it now lives in. If it was formatted according to the default of its initial presentation, it takes on the default of its new home.

- If you want the slide to retain its original formatting, you can reapply the design template from its initial presentation. Open the Slide Design task pane and look in the Recently Used section. You'll find the name of the template used there; or if the slide uses the Default Design, you'll find it in the Available for Use section. In **Figure 14.15**, the template that designed the original presentation is called Baseball.pot, and it is being used here to return the slide to its original formatting.

- Another way to retain a slide's original formatting is to click the Paste Smart Tag below the copied slide and select Keep Source Formatting (**Figure 14.16**).

- Before consolidating presentations by moving slides from one to the other, make sure you have backed up your work!

- If you want to remove the slides from the original presentation, just go back and delete them.

Apply the template from the original presentation to the new slides ⌐

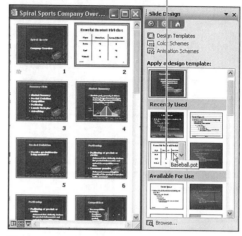

Figure 14.15 To format the new presentation the same as the original, apply the design of the original file from the Slide Design task pane.

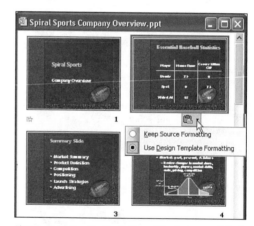

Figure 14.16 Use the Paste Smart Tag to keep original formatting.

Click Browse to select a file

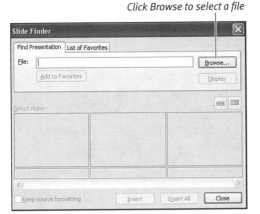

Figure 14.17 The Slide Finder dialog box helps you find the slide you want to copy to another presentation.

Inserting an Entire Presentation

PowerPoint offers another easy way to copy all (or some of) the slides from one presentation into another.

Using the Insert menu, you can insert slides from any presentation into the one that is currently open—or insert an entire existing presentation. This approach is useful when you need to combine the slides created by several individuals into a single presentation.

To insert slides from another presentation:

1. Open the presentation into which you want to insert the slides.
2. In Slide Sorter view, click after the slide where you want the slides to be inserted.
3. Choose Insert > Slides from Files to open the Slide Finder dialog box (**Figure 14.17**).
4. Click Browse to display the Browse dialog box (**Figure 14.18**).
5. Navigate to the folder containing the file with the slides you want to copy.

continues on next page

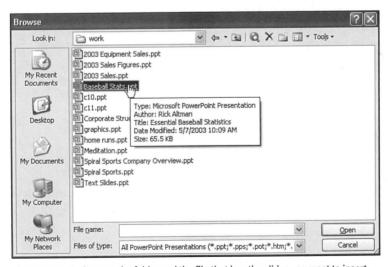

Figure 14.18 Navigate to the folder and the file that has the slides you want to insert.

INSERTING AN ENTIRE PRESENTATION

6. To see the slides, click Open.
Miniatures of the first three slides
appear in the Slide Finder dialog box
(**Figure 14.19**).

7. If you want the whole file inserted,
choose Insert All.

or

Select the slides you want to insert.
When you're finished selecting slides
from this file, click Insert.

8. Navigate to a different presentation to
insert more slides.

9. Click Close when you are finished
inserting slides.

The slides you selected from the other
presentations appear in the current file.

✔ Tips

■ The copied slides use the Slide Master and
color scheme of the target presentation
unless you click Keep Source Formatting
in the Slide Finder dialog box.

■ If you make a mistake, choose Edit >
Undo—this will work even if you just
inserted 200 slides!

■ If you make a really big mistake, close
the file without saving. When you reopen
it, it will be as it was before you began
the insertion process.

■ Of course, you can always copy and paste
slides from one presentation to another
as described in previous sections.

Select a slide

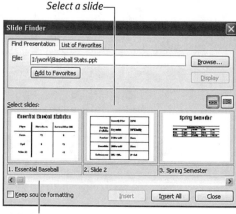

Click the scroll bar to view more slides

Figure 14.19 You can now select the slides you want
to insert into the current presentation.

PRODUCING A SLIDE SHOW

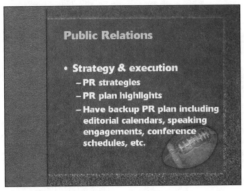

Figure 15.1 Slides are presented at full-screen size during a slide show.

For most PowerPoint users, displaying a slide show onscreen represents final output. Getting there and being there are, of course, two different things, and there are many decisions to make even after you get there! As a result, this will prove to be one of the meatier chapters in this book. For many readers, it will also be the most critical.

PowerPoint's slide show feature displays one slide at a time, full screen (**Figure 15.1**). You can use this feature to show your presentation to an audience or to preview it yourself. In this full-screen view, you can often spot mistakes you may have missed during editing.

You can present your slide show directly on your monitor to a few people, or project the show onto a big screen to a large audience. Rarely does anyone go through the effort of creating 35mm slides—just about every LCD projector on the market today will connect with just about every notebook computer out there. Today, that is how you project your show to a large room full of people.

Organizing a Slide Show

During a slide show, slides are displayed in the order they appear in your presentation, so before presenting your slide show, you should carefully consider the order of your slides and rearrange your slides if necessary.

To change the slide order, move the slides in Slide Sorter view (**Figure 15.2**). You could also use Outline view to reorder slides, but most find that task easier in Slide Sorter view. *See "Reordering Slides" in Chapter 13.*

Suppose that just before a speech you discover that there is less time allotted for your presentation than you anticipated. Instead of panicking or deleting slides, you can omit slides from a slide show by hiding them.

Hidden slides stay in your presentation file in all other views, and you still can show them in response to a question if necessary.

To hide a slide:

1. In Slide Sorter view, click the slide you want to hide.

   or

   To select more than one slide, press and hold Ctrl or Shift while clicking the slides.

2. Click the Hide Slide button on the Slide Sorter toolbar.

   or

   Right-click and choose Hide Slide.

   The number of the hidden slide is displayed with a slash (**Figure 15.3**).

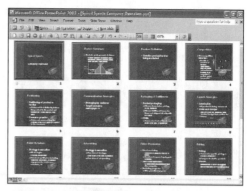

Figure 15.2 Slide Sorter view offers a convenient way to organize your slides for a slide show.

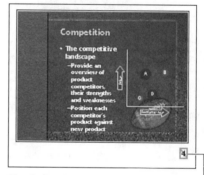

The slash indicates that the slide will be hidden during a slide show

Figure 15.3 Slide 4 will be hidden during a slide show.

Current slide ———— Hidden slide

Figure 15.4 During the show, you can navigate to other slides. The current slide has a check mark; the numbers of hidden slides are in parentheses.

✔ Tips

- To redisplay a hidden slide while editing the presentation, select the slide and click the Hide Slide button to toggle on the display (or right-click and toggle off Hide Slide).

- To redisplay a hidden slide during a slide show, right-click, select Go To Slide, and choose the hidden slide from the list. It will appear in parentheses (**Figure 15.4**).

- You can hide slides in any view using the Slide Show > Hide Slide command. Slide Sorter view and the Slide Miniature pane in Normal view offer the visual indication that a slide is hidden.

- Another way to hide a slide is to right-click the slide in Slide Sorter view and choose Hide Slide from the shortcut menu.

- A hidden slide can still be part of a presentation if you create a hyperlink to it (covered later in this chapter). It just won't appear in the show when you advance slide by slide.

ORGANIZING A SLIDE SHOW

257

Displaying a Slide Show

It's easy to display an onscreen slide show in PowerPoint.

To display a slide show from the beginning:

1. Press F5. That's it!

   or

   Choose View > Slide Show.

   The slide appears at full-screen size.

2. Press Enter or the left mouse button to view the next slide.

3. Press Enter or the left mouse button until you have viewed all of the slides.

   or

   Press Esc to cancel the slide show.

To display a slide show from the current slide:

◆ Click the Slide Show button at the extreme lower-left of the screen (**Figure 15.5**).

✔ Tips

■ Hallelujah! PowerPoint users finally have a hotkey for displaying a slide show from the current slide. New to PowerPoint 2003, pressing Shift+F5 does the trick.

■ You can also display the next slide in the show by pressing the mouse button (the left button on a two-button mouse). See **Table 15.1** for other ways to navigate a slide show.

■ You can make clicking the right mouse button move to the previous slide by going to Tools > Options, and on the View tab, deselecting Popup menu on right mouse click. This will disable the right-click popup menu discussed later in this chapter.

Slide Show button

Figure 15.5 Use the Slide Show button to begin a slide show.

Table 15.1

Slide Show Navigation	
To…	Press…
Advance to the next slide or perform the next animation	N, Enter, Page Down, Right Arrow, Down Arrow, or the Spacebar (or click the mouse)
Return to the previous slide or perform the previous animation	P, Page Up, Left Arrow, Up Arrow, or Backspace
Go to slide [number]	[number]+Enter
End the slide show	Esc, Ctrl+Break, or "–"

■ Pressing the F1 key during a slide show will give you a list of all navigation commands.

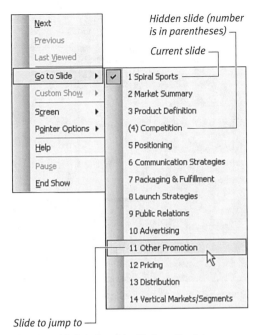

Hidden slide (number is in parentheses)

Current slide

Slide to jump to

Figure 15.6 Select the slide title from the list.

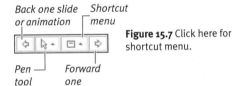

Back one slide or animation

Shortcut menu

Pen tool

Forward one

Figure 15.7 Click here for shortcut menu.

Navigating to a Slide

PowerPoint allows you to jump to any slide during a slide show by choosing the slide title from a list.

To navigate to a slide:

1. Start the slide show.

2. Right-click anywhere on the slide to display the shortcut menu.

3. Choose Go to Slide and choose the desired slide from the list (**Figure 15.6**).

✔ Tips

- Putting titles on slides is essential to locating them during a show. If you want to have an untitled slide, consider hiding the title behind an object (picture), making its font color identical to the background, or reducing the font size to 1 point. Or simply drag the title placeholder off the edge of the slide, and it won't be seen in Slide Show view.

- You can also reach the shortcut menu from one of the icons at the bottom of the screen (**Figure 15.7**). These appear after you move the mouse.

- If you would rather the icons at the bottom of the screen don't show, you can remove them by going to Tools > Options, and on the View tab, deselecting Show Popup menu button. If you do this, you may want to leave Popup menu on right-mouse-click enabled so that you will still be able to access the shortcut menu by right-clicking your mouse.

- The P key (or one of the others mentioned in Table 15.1) is the easiest way to navigate to the previous slide.

Creating Action Buttons

In addition to keyboard shortcuts and navigation by title, PowerPoint offers another way to jump to a slide in a slide show— by the use of buttons that have been programmed with specific actions.

You can create an action button on any slide and program it to jump to another specific slide during a show. Action buttons can also be used to jump to different slide shows, run other programs, and even visit websites.

This branching is faster and more seamless than navigating by title, because the audience sees no menus on the screen.

To create an action button:

1. In Normal view, go to the slide on which you want to create the action button.

2. Click AutoShapes on the Drawing toolbar and choose Action Buttons (**Figure 15.8**).

   or

   Choose Slide Show > Action Button.

3. Choose the Forward button (the triangle pointing to the right).

4. Drag a rectangular shape on the slide where you want the button to appear.

   When you release the mouse button, the Action Settings dialog box appears (**Figure 15.9**).

   Note that the default action for the Forward button is to hyperlink to the next slide.

5. Click OK.

✔ Tip

■ Each different Action Button has its own default setting. For instance, the Forward button defaults to hyperlink to the next slide, and the Home button (graphic of a house) defaults to hyperlink to the first slide in the presentation.

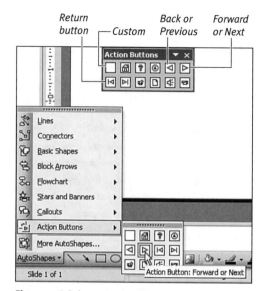

Figure 15.8 Select an action button.

Figure 15.9 PowerPoint fills in this dialog box for you.

■ You can change an Action Button's default action by choosing one of the other options in the Hyperlink to box as described in the next steps.

Figure 15.10 You can hyperlink to practically anything.

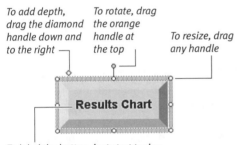

To add depth, drag the diamond handle down and to the right

To rotate, drag the orange handle at the top

To resize, drag any handle

Results Chart

To label the button, just start typing while the button is selected

Figure 15.11 This action button was sized and formatted.

To create a custom button:

1. Click AutoShapes on the Drawing toolbar and choose Action Buttons.

   or

   Choose Slide Show > Action Button.

2. Choose the first button, the empty one called Custom (**Figure 15.8**).

3. Draw a shape onscreen.

   When you release the mouse, the Action Settings dialog box appears again, but this time nothing is filled in for you.

4. Click Hyperlink To, click the drop-down list, and see all of the choices that are available to you (**Figure 15.10**).

5. Choose the slide you want to link to.

6. Click OK to close the Action Settings dialog box.

   The action button appears on the slide.

7. Format, resize, and move the button as needed (**Figure 15.11**).

   To make sure the button works properly, start the slide show and, when you reach the slide with the action button, click it. The presentation should jump directly to the slide you elected.

✔ Tips

- Action buttons function only in a slide show.

- You can also create action buttons that go to the first or last slide, open other files, jump to Web sites, or launch multimedia events.

- To modify an action button's action, select the button, right-click, and choose Action Settings.

- You can make any item an action button—Action Settings is available for any selected object, including text.

Creating a Return Button

If you create an action button that branches to another slide or different slide show, you will probably want an easy way to return to where you were. You can create a Return button that allows you to resume your presentation at the point where you were before your detour.

Figure 15.12 Clicking the Return button in a slide show is like the Back button on your web browser.

To create a Return button:

1. In Normal view, go to the slide on which you want to create the Return button.

2. Click AutoShapes on the Drawing toolbar and choose Action Buttons.
   or
   Choose Slide Show > Action Button.

3. Choose the Return button (usually the lower-left button on the list).

4. Drag a rectangular shape on the slide where you want the button to appear.
   When you release the mouse button, the Action Settings dialog box appears. The Hyperlink To field defaults to Last Slide Viewed, precisely what you want.

5. Click OK to close the dialog box.
   The Return button appears on the slide (**Figure 15.12**).

6. Format and resize the button as needed.
   Double-clicking the button brings up the Format AutoShape dialog box, where you can choose from many formatting options.

✔ Tips

■ There might be times when you want to jump to a particular slide or return to the previous slide without anyone seeing or without cluttering your screen with buttons. You can make your button invisible by creating an object (like a simple rectangle), applying the action setting to it, and removing its outline and its fill. Of course, because the button is hidden, you'll need to remember where it is (make it big!), but your screen will remain nice and clean.

■ You can set an action button to respond to a mouse over so the action will occur when you move your mouse over the button, not just when you click. To do this, follow the same steps as you would to create an action button, but set your hyperlink action on the Mouse Over tab instead of on the Mouse Click tab in the Action Settings dialog box (**Figure 15.9**).

Choose between   Custom show   Reorder
these slides   is built here   them

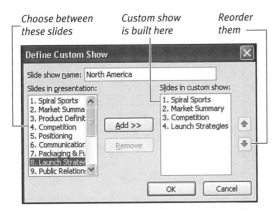

Figure 15.13 Select the slides you want to include in the custom show.

Figure 15.14 This presentation has four custom shows.

Creating Custom Shows

Think of a custom show as a show within a show. You can assign names to the different parts of your presentation and then quickly go to these areas during a slide show.

To create a custom show:

1. Choose Slide Show > Custom Shows.
   The Custom Shows dialog box appears.

2. Click New.
   The Define Custom Show dialog box appears.

3. In the Slide Show Name field, type a descriptive name for the custom show.

4. In the Slides in Presentation list, double-click each slide (or click the slide and then click Add) that is to be part of the custom show (**Figure 15.13**).

5. Click OK.

6. Repeat steps 2 through 5 to define additional custom shows.
   The Custom Shows dialog box lists the custom shows you have created (**Figure 15.14**).

7. When you're finished, click Close.

✔ Tip

■ To modify a custom show, choose Slide Show > Custom Shows, select the show's name, and click Edit.

CREATING CUSTOM SHOWS

Viewing a Custom Show

You can start a custom slide show from any PowerPoint view, or you can jump to the different custom shows while you are giving a presentation.

To view a custom show:

1. Choose Slide Show > Custom Shows.

2. Click the name of the show you want to view (**Figure 15.14**).

3. Click Show.

   The first slide in the custom show is displayed.

4. Press Page Down (or one of the other navigation keys in **Table 15.1**) until you have viewed all of the slides in the custom show.

To jump to a custom show:

1. During a slide show, right-click to display the shortcut menu.

2. Choose Custom Show (**Figure 15.15**) and click on the name of the custom show you want to jump to.

   The first slide in the custom show is displayed.

3. Press Page Down to view other slides in the custom show.

✔ Tips

■ You can hyperlink to a custom show from an action button.

■ It's helpful to display an empty black slide after the last slide in a custom show so that you have the opportunity to immediately select another custom show. To display an empty black slide at the end of a show, choose Tools > Options, select the View tab, and then click the End with Black Slide check box.

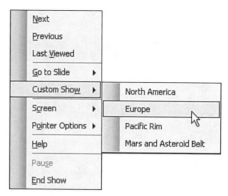

Figure 15.15 You can jump to a custom show during a slide show by using the shortcut menu.

■ You may want to add an action button on the last slide in the Custom Show so that you can easily move back to the main show.

Underlining indicates a hyperlink

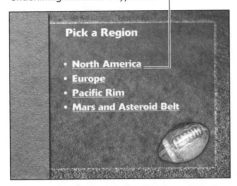

Figure 15.16 An agenda slide offers hyperlinks to custom shows.

Click here to display this list

Figure 15.17 Create a hyperlink to a custom show in the Action Settings dialog box.

Creating an Agenda Slide

An agenda slide (**Figure 15.16**) is a slide with a simple list of hyperlinked topics. Each topic is linked to a custom show pertaining to one area of your presentation.

When you click an item on the agenda slide during a slide show, PowerPoint displays the custom show and then returns to the agenda slide.

Agenda slides are useful for dividing your presentation into logical areas and keeping the audience tuned in to where you are in the presentation.

To create an agenda slide:

1. Create a custom show for each of the sections in your presentation.

   See "Creating Custom Shows" earlier in this chapter.

2. Create a new slide with a bulleted list layout.

3. Enter a title and type bulleted items to describe each of the sections in your presentation.

4. Select the text in one bulleted item.

5. Right-click and choose Action Settings.

6. Click the Hyperlink To radio button and choose Custom Show (**Figure 15.17**).

continues on next page

CREATING AN AGENDA SLIDE

7. In the Link to Custom Show dialog box, select the show to which you want to jump (**Figure 15.18**).

8. Select the Show and Return check box.

This option returns you to this agenda slide after the custom show finishes.

9. Click OK twice to close both dialog boxes.

The bulleted item is now underlined, indicating a hyperlink (**Figure 15.16**).

10. Repeat steps 4 through 9 for each item.

✔ Tips

■ Hyperlinks function only in a slide show.

■ You can shortcut this process by using the Summary Slide function button to create a slide with bullets that reference other slides. Just add hyperlinks to the bullets, and the slide quickly becomes an agenda slide.

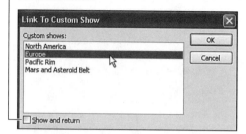
Show and Return

Figure 15.18 Select the name of the custom show you want to link to.

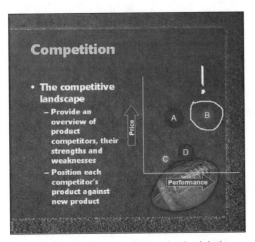

Figure 15.19 B is the goal and is emphasized during the presentation.

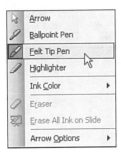

Figure 15.20 Ballpoint, felt tip, or highlighter... your choice.

Annotating a Slide

During a slide show, you may want to mark a slide to emphasize a point. Using the mouse like a marking pen, you can draw circles, lines, arrows, and so forth (**Figure 15.19**). These annotations are normally temporary, and as soon as you move on to the next slide in the show, your freehand drawings disappear. However, PowerPoint 2003 adds the option of saving your annotations as objects on your slide.

To annotate a slide:

1. During a slide show, press Ctrl+P or click the Pointer button (second from left)

   or

   Right-click anywhere on screen and choose Pointer Options to display the pen choices.

2. Choose the type of pen to use (**Figure 15.20**).

   Position the pen where you want to make an annotation and click and drag the mouse.

3. To turn off Annotation mode, press Esc or Ctrl+A.

   or

   Press Ctrl+H to exit Annotation mode and hide the pointer altogether.

✔ Tips

- To erase all annotations on a slide, press E.

- While in Annotation mode, you can't use the mouse button to advance slides. Keyboard navigation keys such as the arrow keys, however, will still operate.

- New to PowerPoint 2003 are the pen choices, including the Highlighter. In **Figure 15.21**, several words have been highlighted.

- In previous versions of PowerPoint, leaving a slide would cause all annotations to disappear. In PowerPoint 2003, annotations remain for the duration of the show, and when you quit the show, PowerPoint offers to make the annotations permanent (**Figure 15.22**). You can always delete the annotations from the slides later if you discover you don't need them.

- To choose a different pen color, right-click during the show, choose Pointer Options > Pen Color, and choose a color (**Figure 15.23**).

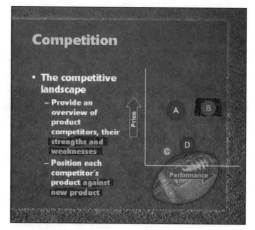

Figure 15.21 New annotations include onscreen highlighting.

Figure 15.22 If you choose Keep, PowerPoint creates objects out of the annotations and makes them part of the slide.

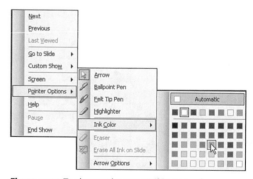

Figure 15.23 To change the annotation pen color, use the shortcut menu and click Pointer Options > Ink Color.

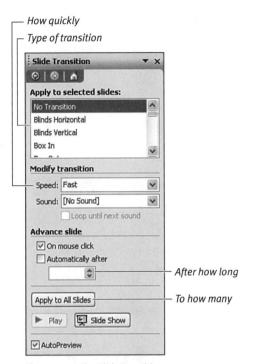

How quickly

Type of transition

After how long

To how many

Figure 15.24 The Slide Transition task pane can control the display of a single slide or all slides.

- You can always advance a slide before the specified time has passed by pressing one of the keys that advance a slide show. (Note: Mouse clicking will work only if the On Mouse Click check box is selected in the Slide Transition task pane or dialog box.)

- If you want to disable both mouse click and keyboard advances and limit your audience to the automatic transition timings and/or any navigation (action setting buttons) you've provided, use Slide Show > Set Up Show and select Browsed At a Kiosk.

Creating a Self-Running Slide Show

There are dozens of reasons why you might need to create a slide show that runs itself, and today's proliferation of CD-based presentations and email-able PowerPoint files add two more to the list. For times when you are not there to click the mouse, or just don't want to, you can tell PowerPoint to advance each slide automatically after a certain number of seconds.

To create a self-running slide show:

1. Choose Slide Show > Slide Transition to reach the Slide Transition task pane (**Figure 15.24**).

2. Choose the type of transition in the list box at the top of the pane.

3. Next, choose the speed.

4. In the Advance Slide section, choose whether to allow a mouse click to advance, and then enter the number of seconds you want each slide to remain on the screen.

5. If you want to change the transition for only the selected slide or slides, you are finished. If you want to make this change for your entire presentation, click Apply to All.

✔ Tips

- The number of seconds that the slide will remain on the screen is indicated beneath each slide when in Slide Sorter view.

- To temporarily suspend a self-running slide show, press S. To continue with the show, press one of the many keys that advances a slide show: Space, Down Arrow, Right Arrow, Page Down, Enter or a left click of the mouse button.

Rehearsing the Slide Show

You may have only a specific length of time to make your presentation. To make sure your slide show fits the allotted time, you can rehearse your slide show and record the timing.

To time your slide show:

1. Choose Slide Show > Rehearse Timings.

   The first slide in the show appears, and the Rehearsal window appears in the corner of the screen (**Figure 15.25**).

2. Rehearse whatever you want to say when the slide is displayed.

3. When you are ready to advance to the next slide, press any of the keys that perform that function or click the Next button in the Rehearsal window.

4. Continue this way through your slide show.

   When you're finished, PowerPoint displays the total time for the slide show (**Figure 15.26**) and asks if you want to save the transition times for each slide and use them when viewing a slide show.

5. Choose Yes to record the slide times and create a self-running slide show.

   or

   Choose No if you don't want to record the slide times.

   If you record the times, they appear underneath each slide.

✔ Tip

- To run a slide show manually but still preserve the timings, choose Slide Show > Set Up Show to open the Set Up Show dialog box, and under Advance Slides, select Manually (**Figure 15.27**).

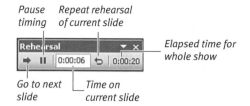

Pause timing   *Repeat rehearsal of current slide*

Elapsed time for whole show

Go to next slide   *Time on current slide*

Figure 15.25 The Rehearsal dialog box.

Figure 15.26 Choosing Yes saves the rehearsal timings to be used for a self-running slide show.

Figure 15.27 Choose to advance slides manually using the timings you've already set up.

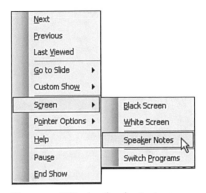

Figure 15.28 Display the shortcut menu during a slide show and choose Speaker Notes.

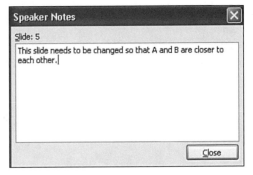

Figure 15.29 Enter your notes here.

Taking Notes During a Slide Show

As you are giving a slide show, you and your audience may come up with ideas that need follow-up, or parts of your presentation that need refinement. Sometimes, there is no time like the present, and if it is appropriate to do so, PowerPoint essentially lets you call a time-out and type a note to yourself.

To make a note to yourself:

1. During a slide show, right-click and choose Screen > Speaker Notes (**Figure 15.28**).

2. Type the note in the Speaker Notes dialog box (**Figure 15.29**).

✔ Tips

- The Speaker Notes box can remain onscreen throughout all the slides. Simply click out of the Speaker Notes dialog box onto the slide itself to move to the next slide.

- You can move the Speaker Notes box by dragging its title bar.

- You can view these notes later by choosing View > Notes Page. If a slide already has notes on it, you would see them in the Speaker Notes dialog box if you invoked it during a slide show.

APPLYING
ANIMATION

16

Applying animation to the elements of a slide or to the slide itself is not difficult to do. Doing it right, however, often proves to be a challenge. That is why this chapter begins on a cautionary note:

Please do not overdo animation!

Few things are more distracting and annoying, not to mention harmful to your reputation as a presenter, than a presentation littered with animations whose content does not warrant them. As we show you all of these impressive-looking animation schemes, please keep this in mind.

Adding a Transition Effect to a Slide

Transition button ─┐

Figure 16.1 Slides 3 and 5 are about to have transitions added to them.

The most basic animation is the one that happens to the entire slide as the show moves from one slide to the next. These are actually known as transitions. You've seen this just about every time you watch television, and you probably don't pay much attention to it. Transition effects can help direct the attention of your audience and add a professional touch (please see our previous admonition, however).

To apply slide transition effects:

1. Switch to Slide Sorter view (recommended, not required).

2. Select the slide for which you want to add a transition effect.

   or

   To apply the same transition effect to multiple slides, Ctrl-click each slide or Shift-click consecutive slides (**Figure 16.1**).

3. Choose Slide Show > Slide Transition to view the Slide Transition task pane (**Figure 16.2**).

4. In the Apply to Selected Slides list, click the desired transition effect.

   Immediately after you choose an effect, selected slides are drawn with that effect to show you what it looks like. In fact, there is no Apply button for selected slides; by choosing the transition, you have applied it to the selected slides.

   Uncheck AutoPreview if you don't need to see the effects or if they take too long.

5. In the Modify Transition area, change the speed of the effects or add sounds.

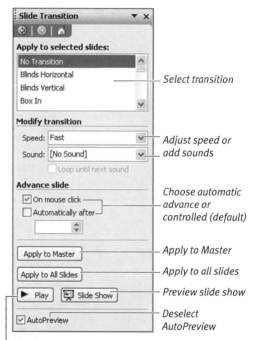

Figure 16.2 The Slide Transition task pane.

6. In the Advance Slide area, decide whether the slide should advance automatically after a time that you specify or under your direct control (default). Or, you can do both—you can instruct PowerPoint to wait for a specified time, and if you haven't clicked for the next slide, to advance it for you.

7. You can apply the same effect to every slide by clicking Apply to All Slides. (The preview will appear for all slides.)

   or

   Repeat steps 4 through 6 to apply transition effects to other individual slides.

8. To preview the effects for the whole slide show, press F5 or click the Slide Show button on the Slide Transition task pane.

✔ Tips

■ You can choose a transition and apply it to the Slide Master, automatically creating a global transition for your entire presentation.

■ Wipe, fade and dissolve are all transitions that are fit for widespread use. Then, if you truly need to highlight one or two slides, you can use a more dramatic transition and its effect will be felt.

■ If you choose Random Transition, you give PowerPoint permission to choose any transition for any slide. Please don't, as this can be very distracting for the audience.

■ Clicking the Play button in the Transition task pane previews the transition, either in Slide Sorter view or in the slide window of Normal view.

■ If your presentation uses only one set of masters, you may not have an Apply to Master button in the Slide Transition or the Slide Design—Animation Schemes task pane. In that case, simply use Apply to All Slides.

ADDING A TRANSITION EFFECT TO A SLIDE

Applying Preset Animations

Whereas a transition effect controls the display of an entire slide during the slide show, an animation controls how a particular object or piece of text appears on a slide.

In other words, you can command a slide to transition a certain way, and when it does, display the elements of that slide according to specific animations. For example, you can create a slide title whose characters appear to be typed, one character at a time, as if they were coming from an old typewriter. (You can even accompany them with typewriter sound effects...please don't.)

Introduced in PowerPoint 2002, you can apply an entire package of animation (called an "animation scheme") to all of the elements of a slide, or to the entire presentation. This is a very quick way to apply animation—one command and you can address the entire presentation. Again, however, it is your job to determine whether that is appropriate to the topic of your slides.

1. Switch to Slide Sorter view (recommended, not required).

2. Choose Format > Slide Design and then click Animation Schemes (**Figure 16.3**).
   If a task pane is already open, it will change to the Animation Schemes task pane. If the task pane isn't already open, the Animation Schemes task pane will open.

3. Select the slide you want to animate.

4. Click the desired animation scheme.
   The series of effects will appear in a preview within the slide. You can select from the most Recently Used schemes or scroll down to see choices categorized as Subtle, Moderate, or Exciting.

Figure 16.3 The Slide Design task pane contains preset animation schemes.

APPLYING PRESET ANIMATIONS

5. AutoPreview is very handy, but you can deselect it if you don't need to see the effects or if they take too long.

6. Repeat steps 3 through 5 to apply preset animation schemes to other slides.

You can also apply one animation to every slide by clicking Apply to All Slides and, as with transition, one click will apply the effect directly to the Slide Master (or Masters, if you have created more than one), controlling every slide in your presentation.

If you apply the animation scheme to the Slide Master, new slides will automatically have the scheme applied to them.

7. To preview the effects during a slide show, press F5 to run the slide show from the beginning or Shift+F5 from the current slide or click the Slide Show button on the Animation Schemes task pane.

✔ Tip

■ Animation schemes might apply a number of animations to various objects on a slide. Furthermore, the schemes often add more than one type of animation to an object—they may apply an entrance, an emphasis, and an exit animation to an object. Always preview and scrutinize the effect, and if your slides contain many objects, do not use preset animation schemes. Instead, apply custom animation yourself, or modify the animation according to the instructions in the next section.

Modifying Animations

Perhaps you've applied an animation scheme to a slide. It's close to what you want, but it's not exactly right. You can modify the preset animation very easily.

1. If the Custom Animation task pane isn't open, right-click an object on your slide and choose Custom Animation.

2. In the Custom Animation task pane, select the object for which you want to change the animation properties by clicking on it in the task pane.

   The Add Effect button will become a Change button (**Figure 16.4**).

3. Modify the Animation Effect by clicking the Change button.

   Select a new Entrance, Emphasis, or Exit animation.

4. To remove the existing animation effect altogether, simply right-click the object in the Custom Animation task pane and choose Remove from the shortcut menu (**Figure 16.5**).

   or

   With the object selected in the Custom Animation task pane, press the Delete key on your keyboard.

✔ Tips

■ When modifying an animation effect, be sure to select the object in the Custom Animation task pane, not in the slide itself. If you select the object in the slide itself, the Change button on the task pane will become an Add Effect button, and you'll be adding more effects instead of changing the existing ones!

■ You can also use these same steps to modify animation effects you've added yourself; they're not used only to modify Animation Schemes.

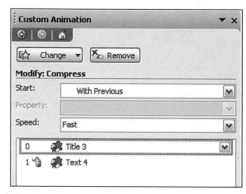

Figure 16.4 Change the animation properties with the Change button.

Figure 16.5 Use Remove in the shortcut menu to remove an animation effect.

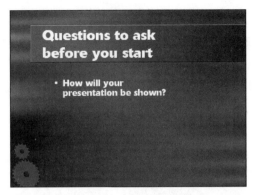

Figure 16.6 The first bullet of a sequence appears onscreen.

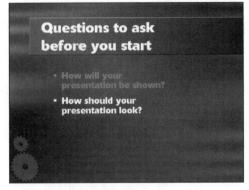

Figure 16.7 When the second one appears, the first one dims...

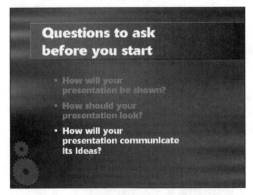

Figure 16.8 And the third bullet makes the second one dim.

Animating a Bulleted List

The prototypical use of animation in a PowerPoint presentation is to present a series of bullets on a slide. During a slide show, you can create an animation that progressively reveals the bulleted items on a slide.

By animating your bulleted lists, you can display each successive bulleted item when you are ready to discuss it. In addition, if the situation calls for it, you can dim previous items so the current item stands out. Do this if you think the audience needs help focusing on the correct bullet of a busy slide. **Figures 16.6** through **16.8** show an animated bulleted list in progress (with bullets dimmed after they are shown). PowerPoint refers to this as Custom Animation, to differentiate it from the preset Animation Schemes just discussed.

To animate a bulleted list:

1. In Normal view, select the bullet area you want to animate. You can select the placeholder or place your cursor into any one of the bullets in the list.

2. Choose Slide Show > Custom Animation. The Custom Animation task pane opens (**Figure 16.9**).

3. Click the Add Effect button and choose between Entrance, Emphasis, or Exit.

   Entrance is the standard effect, whereby an object animates on its way into the slide. An emphasis plays the animation after it has arrived, and an exit animation plays before it or as it leaves the slide. Motion Paths is for advanced users who want complete control over the movement of an object. In **Figure 16.10**, we are applying a Wipe upon the entrance of the bullet. Wipe and peek animations are good to use for normal situations, as they're not terribly distracting to your audience.

4. Choose one of the following:
   ◆ Start: By mouse click, after the previous object has appeared, or at the same time as the previous object.
   ◆ Direction: From top, bottom, left, or right.
   ◆ Speed: From slow to very fast.

5. Click Play to see how your animations behave. **Figure 16.11** captures this slide in mid-animation—note the half-displayed bullet and the timeline in midcourse.

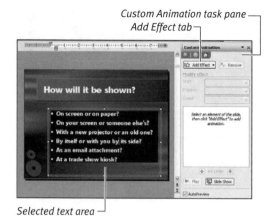

Custom Animation task pane
Add Effect tab

Selected text area

Figure 16.9 The Custom Animation task pane lets you add effects to text and bullets.

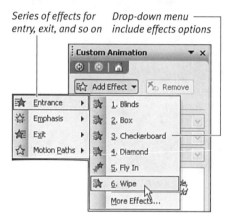

Series of effects for entry, exit, and so on   *Drop-down menu include effects options*

Figure 16.10 This will cause each bullet to Wipe onto the slide.

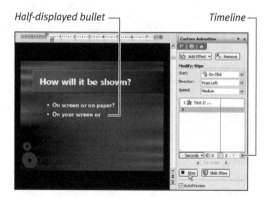

Half-displayed bullet   *Timeline*

Figure 16.11 Click Play to test out an animation from the task pane.

✔ Tips

- Before settling on your animation, click Slide Show to run the Slide Show full-screen. That will give you a better idea of timing and appearance. Also, the Play button will advance each animation automatically, even if each is set to advance On Click.

- Check the speed of your animation on the computer from which the presentation will be shown. PowerPoint's timings may be different on different computers, so you will want to ensure that the animations are not running too slowly or quickly on the show system.

- You can add more than one effect to an object—for instance, an entrance and an exit, or entrance and an emphasis. To do this, select the object on the slide and choose the Add Effect button on the Custom Animation task pane.

- As mentioned in the section on Modifying Animations, it's easy to add more than one animation effect to an object when you really just intend to modify the animation, if you're not careful. To modify an animation effect, be sure to select the object in the Custom Animation task pane, not in the slide itself.

- Dimming the bulleted text is covered in the next section, "Fine-Tuning an Animation."

ANIMATING A BULLETED LIST

Fine-Tuning an Animation

Making further adjustments to an animation is a bit like finding a buried treasure, and we mean that almost literally. **Figure 16.12** shows how many important functions are hiding in the drop-down menu instead of on a button in the task pane. The top half of that drop-down is a repetition of the Start options in the task pane; the others are divided into three categories.

To enhance an animation:

1. Choose Effect Options from the drop-down list.

2. To add a sound to an animation, pick one of the ones included with the program, or choose Other Sound at the bottom of the list and navigate your system for the desired .wav file.

3. To change the color of an object after animation, pick the color from the After Animation drop-down list.

4. To animate bullets in smaller pieces (letter by letter or word by word), set that in the Animate Text drop-down list and then set a delay rate.

   In **Figure 16.13**, the bullets are set to play a chime as they animate, turn yellow afterward, and appear word by word with a 10% delay between each word. (These are for demonstration purposes only; do not try this at home!)

Figure 16.12 The buried treasure of controls for custom animation.

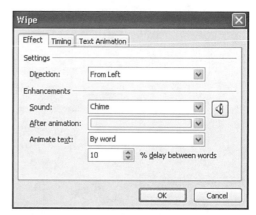

Figure 16.13 Use the Wipe dialog box to attach sound to animations and control how the animations behave.

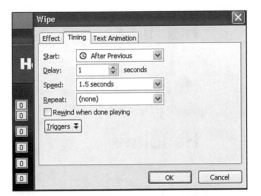

Figure 16.14 These bullets are being meticulously animated.

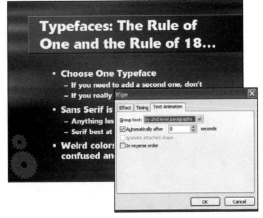

Figure 16.15 Choose how to animate second-level bullets, by themselves, or with their parent bullet.

5. To adjust the timing of your animation, click Timing from the drop-down list in the Custom Animation task pane or the Timing tab of the effect dialog box.

6. Set a Delay value if you want to insert a pause before the object appears.

7. Enter or choose a value for the speed of the animation.

8. Enter or choose a value for Repeat if you want the object to animate more than once.

In **Figure 16.14**, the bullets appear one after the other (without waiting for a mouse click), delay for one second between each one, and appear at a speed of 1.5 seconds per bullet.

9. To adjust animation of text, click the Text Animation tab and experiment with the controls there.

The most significant option here is text grouping—whether to present each list of bullets according to the first level or second level.

In **Figure 16.15**, these bullets are animated in three stages, according to their first-level paragraphs. When the first bullet displayed, the two second-level bullets automatically displayed, as well.

10. To have bullets animate from the bottom up, choose In Reverse Order.

continues on next page

FINE-TUNING AN ANIMATION

✔ Tips

- If you attach a sound file to an animation, it is embedded in the presentation, not referenced externally. This makes the .ppt file larger, but ensures that it is always available, no matter what system the presentation is shown on. Only WAV sound files can be attached to animations.

- When setting the speed of an animation, the drop-down list is handy, but note that you can set any speed. In **Figure 16.14**, we typed in **1.5**, a choice not available on the list. You don't have to type the word "seconds."

- To add an effect for emphasis, click Emphasis in the task pane to see the drop-down menu for fonts, moves, and spins. Typically, you should be careful to not go overboard, but when used correctly, it can be very handy. For instance, **Figure 16.16** shows a headline slowly flying down from the top. It is black as it passes over white space, but it is designed to sit atop a black bar. To accommodate this, its emphasis was set to be a simple color change to white.

- When animating multiple elements on one slide, you can change the animation order in the task pane. Note, however, that this does not change the stacking order; you can have Element A animate after Element B and yet appear behind Element B.

- A set of bullets are animated together by the task pane, but you can expand them and select any one bullet for animation by clicking the double set of downward-facing arrows. More information on this is included in the next section on how to animate bullets using different effects.

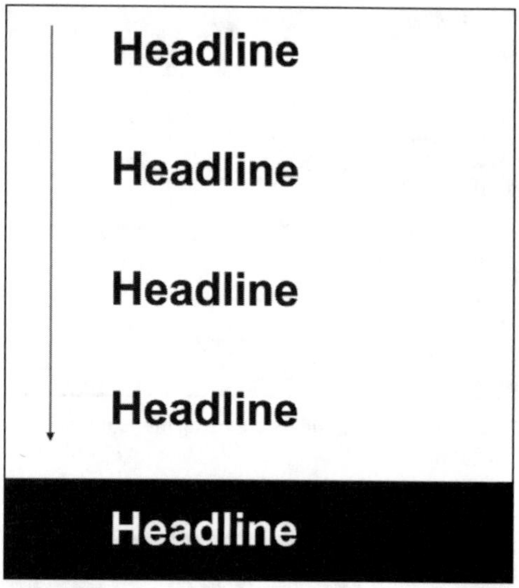

Figure 16.16 Use of Emphasis allows this headline to travel through white space in black and then turn to white as it arrives atop the black bar.

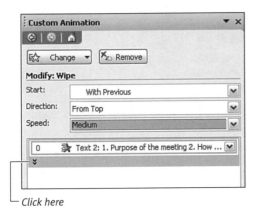

Click here

Figure 16.17 You can expand the contents of the list.

Figure 16.18 You can change the effects for text in bulleted lists.

To animate the bullets using different effects:

1. Add an animation effect to the bulleted placeholder as described in the section, "To animate a bulleted list."

2. Click on the double-downward-pointing arrow in the Custom Animation task pane to expand the contents of the bulleted list (**Figure 16.17**).

3. Select a bulleted text object in the list on the Custom Animation task pane and make changes to the timing, the animation effects, the effect options, and more, as desired (**Figure 16.18**).

✔ Tips

■ You can use this technique to cause the first bullet to come in automatically, and all subsequent bullets to come in on mouse click. Or, by using the timing options on the subsequent bullets, you could have those lines come in automatically after a delay.

■ You can use the Shift and Ctrl buttons when selecting objects in the Custom Animation task pane to select and apply effects to more than one object.

Using Triggers

Animation triggers were introduced in PowerPoint 2002, and they can be very powerful tools. Triggers are used when you need to be able to click an object on a slide and cause something to happen, like trigger another animation.

Let's say you've created a quiz in PowerPoint. You want your viewer to click on the appropriate answer text on the slide. If the person clicks on the correct answer, they'll see an "explosion" autoshape appear.

To create a trigger:

1. Right-click the explosion autoshape which should appear when the correct answer is selected. Select Custom Animation.

2. Add Effect > Entrance Effect

3. Choose an entrance effect. We used Pinwheel in this example.

4. Click the arrow next to the star in the Custom Animation task pane and choose the Timing option (**Figure 16.19**).

   The Timing tab will open in the Pinwheel dialog box (**Figure 16.20**).

5. Click the Triggers button

6. Select Start Effect On Click Of.

Figure 16.19 Choose a timing option for the "explosion" autoshape.

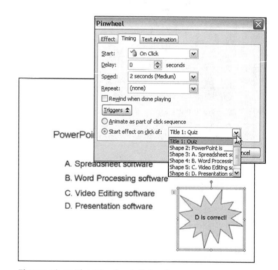

Figure 16.20 The Pinwheel dialog box.

USING TRIGGERS

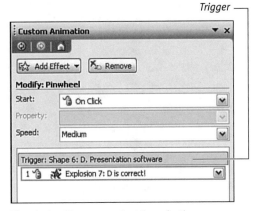

Trigger

Figure 16.21 You can see the trigger for the "explosion" autoshape.

7. In the Start Effect On Click Of box, choose Shape 6: D. Presentation Software.

D. Presentation Software is the one you want to trigger the appearance of the explosion autoshape.

8. Click OK.

The Custom Animation task pane will now show a trigger before the object's animation (**Figure 16.21**).

✔ Tips

■ In the previous example, we'd also want to set the incorrect answers to trigger something. Right now if someone were to click on answers A, B, or C, we'd simply move to the next slide.

■ To prevent simply moving to the next slide when clicking an incorrect answer, we could put the presentation into Kiosk mode using Slide Show > Set Up Show > Browsed at a kiosk. Of course, we'd then want to add action buttons so that we could navigate to the next slide once we've answered the question correctly.

■ You can set any animation effect to happen on a trigger. In fact, triggers are a fantastic way to make an object disappear when you click it. Simply set the animation effect to Exit and the trigger to the object itself.

Animating Charts

Charts are ideal for animation effects. You can progressively display various chart elements, such as categories or series. **Figure 16.22** shows an animated chart in progress.

To animate a chart:

1. In Slide view, select the chart.

2. Select Slide Show > Custom Animation.
   or
   Right-click the chart and choose Custom Animation (Custom Animation is almost always available on your shortcut menu). The Custom Animation task pane opens.

3. Under Add Effect, choose an Entrance effect, such as Box.

4. Set the direction (Out) and the speed (medium) at the top of the Custom Animation task pane (**Figure 16.23**).

5. With the chart object highlighted in the task pane, choose Effect Options from the drop-down menu.

6. Click the Chart Animation tab.

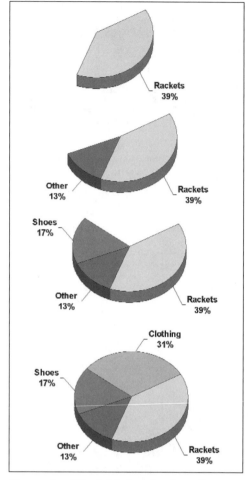

Figures 16.22 This pie is to be enjoyed one slice at a time.

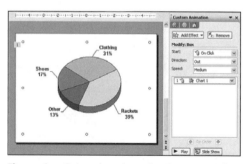

Figure 16.23 Outward-moving animations are good for pie charts, where slices emanate from the center.

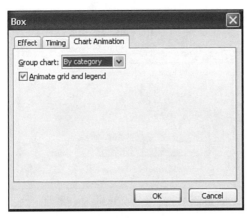

Figure 16.24 Tell PowerPoint to give each category its own animation.

7. At Group Chart, choose By Category to instruct PowerPoint to treat each slice as a separate element (**Figure 16.24**).

8. Click OK.

9. To see the chart animation in action, click the Play button in the task pane.

The effects you selected appear in a preview in the slide. A timeline appears within the task pane, showing the duration of the effects.

10. To see the effects as they will appear in a show, at full-screen size, click the Slide Show button.

If you chose On Click as the start option, you will need to press one of the slide advance keys (Space, Page Up, Page Down, Arrow Down, mouse click) to see each pie slice.

✔ Tip

■ Some animations do not allow you to animate a chart by category or series. If those options are unavailable, choose a different animation effect and see if the options become available.

Animating the Slide Masters

It's all fine and well to animate the bullets on one slide, two slides, or even 30 slides. However, for an important presentation in which everything needs to be right and you need global control over your slides, you need to go the extra step. You need to control animation on your Slide Masters.

Technically speaking, animating your Slide Masters is no more difficult than animating one slide. The difference is in power and control.

To create animation for all bullet slides:

1. Choose View > Master > Slide Master.

2. If necessary, choose which set of masters to work on.

   If you created multiple masters, as discussed in Chapter 12, you would see two or more sets of masters in the Slides pane in Normal view.

3. Select a bullet level (**Figure 16.25**).

   When working on the Slide Master, one click selects the entire bullet and all the bullet points underneath it.

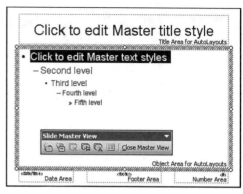

Figure 16.25 Apply animation to the Slide Master bullets and every bullet in your presentation animates.

4. Choose Slide Show > Custom Animation (or right-click > Custom Animation) to open the Custom Animation task pane.

5. Add the desired entrance and exit effects and make all of the desired adjustments of timing, delays, appearance, and so on.

6. If necessary, expand the bullets in the Custom Animation task pane and change the settings for the other bullet levels.

See the section earlier in this chapter, "To animate the bullets using different effects."

7. And if desired, repeat for the title placeholder.

8. Also if desired, repeat on the placeholders in the Title Master.

9. Click Close Master View on the Slide Master View toolbar and test out your animation by pressing F5 to run the slide show or click the Slide Show button on the Custom Animation task pane.

All bullets and titles should now animate according to the settings you just defined for them on the Slide Master.

ANIMATING THE SLIDE MASTERS

Overriding Animation on the Slide Master

To override the animation setting for any particular slide, you need to find a well-hidden command on the Custom Animation task pane. **Figure 16.26** shows how the task pane indicates global formatting—with the animation appearing grayed-out and seemingly unavailable.

To override a slide master's animation:

1. Right-click on the animation in the task pane (Master: Body).

2. Choose Copy Effect to Slide (**Figure 16.27**).

   This "de-globalizes" the animation and lets you override it for just this slide.

3. Edit the animation normally.

✔ Tips

- This chapter has covered animation of bullets and charts; but, any object at all can be animated, from titles to full-page photographs. If you can select it, you can right-click it; and if you can right-click it, you can get to Custom Animation.

- If you copy the Slide Master animation to the slide, it is all too easy to add a second animation instead of changing the original one. (If you select the bullet in the slide, the task pane shows the Add Effect button, and you would be adding a second entrance instead of changing the first one.) After you copy the animation to the slide, select the animation in the task pane (not the bullet on the slide). Then, the Add Effect button becomes a Change button.

- One more time: When you make an animation global by adding it to the Slide Master, its ability to do both good and harm increases significantly. Only use global animation if you know that it is appropriate to your presentation.

Figure 16.26 Animation on the Slide Master appears to be unavailable. It's not...

Figure 16.27 After you copy the effects to the slide, you can edit them.

USING SOUND AND VIDEO

It's a bold new world out there, with standard desktop and notebook computers taking on with ease multimedia tasks that were out of reach just a few years ago. Today, even a casual hobbyist can incorporate sound from a multitude of sources. And capture or obtain video? That's practically kid stuff; today, you can create your own.

All these exciting new capabilities can make their way into PowerPoint presentations. This chapter is relatively short and that's a good thing: As impressive as it is to incorporate new types of multimedia into your slide shows, it's not that difficult. We're happy to report that it doesn't take pages of instructions to work a sound track into your slides or play a movie clip in your intro.

Inserting Movie Clips

PowerPoint can insert and play movies that were recorded in a variety of formats, such as AVI (Audio Video Interleave), WMV, and MPEG (Moving Picture Experts Group) videos. PowerPoint can also accept Macromedia Flash files, but inserting those is not so straightforward and not terribly inviting to new users. Nonetheless, we will cover it in brief later.

For most of the multimedia that you can add to a presentation, you need look no further than **Figure 17.1**. In fact, if you learn nothing else and read no further in this chapter, we will still have done our jobs just by showing you this menu item.

To insert a movie clip:

1. In Slide view, go to the slide on which you want to insert a movie (or insert a blank slide).

2. Choose Insert > Movies and Sounds > Movie from File.

   The Insert Movie dialog box appears (**Figure 17.1**).

3. Navigate to the drive and folder containing your movie file.

4. Select the movie file and click OK.

   PowerPoint asks if you want the movie to play automatically during a slide show (**Figure 17.2**).

5. Choose Automatically if you want the movie to play automatically when the slide appears.

   or

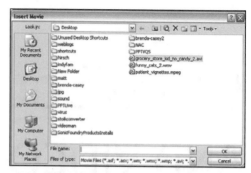

Figure 17.1 The Insert > Movies and Sounds command is your gateway to all things multimedia.

Figure 17.2 Click Automatically for PowerPoint to play the movie when the slide appears.

Drag a corner selection handle to resize the movie, but be sure to check it in Slide Show view to ensure its quality has not been compromised ⎯

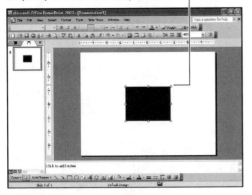

Figure 17.3 After you insert a movie file, the first frame of the movie appears on the slide.

■ If your movie is in the Clip Organizer, you can use a Content layout, from the Slide Layout task pane, to import a media object. It's not recommended that you insert movies and sounds through the Clip Organizer, though, as PowerPoint may not be able to find the multimedia file if you move the presentation to another computer.

Choose When Clicked if you want the movie to start only when you click it during a slide show. **Figure 17.3** is hardly an inspiring image, but it points out an important fact: The first frame of the movie appears in the center of the slide. Many moviemakers intentionally begin with a solid fill like this to not distract or give anything away. Others work hard at that first image, knowing it will be seen longer than any others. That creative decision is left in your creative hands.

6. Your movie won't play while you're in Normal view. To see what it will look like during a slide show, click the Slide Show button in the lower left of the screen, go to View > Slide Show, or click F5. Or you can click Play on the Custom Animation task pane.

If you set the movie to play automatically, it will begin automatically when you come to that slide in Slide Show view. If you didn't set the movie to play automatically, click the movie to play it.

✔ Tips

■ Very important: Only the first frame of your movie is in PowerPoint. Your movies are linked from the source file, so if you move your presentation, the link to the movie may break. The best way to keep this from happening is to copy the movie into the same folder with the PowerPoint presentation file *before* you insert the movie into PowerPoint. Then you can move that entire folder around as needed.

■ You can start and stop the movie during a slide show by clicking it. (If you click outside the movie, you stop the movie and advance the slide or introduce the next object.)

INSERTING MOVIE CLIPS

Playing Back Your Clips

Most of the time, you will play back your clips during a slide show, and the only question is whether the movie plays automatically or when you click it. However, there are several other things to know about playback, which is actually controlled via the Custom Animation task pane.

Figure 17.4 Your movie can have animations attached to it just like other objects.

To control movie playback during a slide show:

1. In Slide view, choose Slide Show > Custom Animation.

   The Custom Animation task pane appears, and you will see many of the same options and settings that were covered in Chapter 16. If desired, you can choose an animation effect to have your movie dissolve in, dim, or hide when another object on the slide appears. Don't confuse those animation effects with the actual playback of your movie.

   Even if you don't add any animation effects to it, when you add a movie to a slide, there will still be a trigger animation in the Custom Animation task pane. This trigger is necessary so that the movie will play when you click the movie, and the trigger will appear even if you opted to have your movie begin playback automatically (**Figure 17.4**).

2. Click the Timing option (**Figure 17.5**).

   The Timing tab on the Pause Movie dialog box will open (**Figure 17.6**).

   You can delay the start of the movie by as long as you want. You can also choose a Start Option from among After Previous, With Previous, and On Click.

   You can also set a trigger so that the movie will begin playback when a different object on the slide is clicked.

   See "Using Triggers" in Chapter 16 for information on start options and triggers.

Figure 17.5 You can control the timing options for your movie.

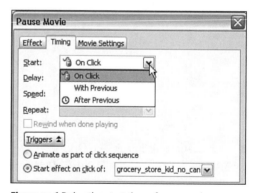

Figure 17.6 Delay the start time of your movie.

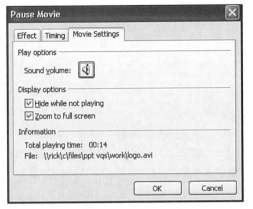

Figure 17.7 A lot of information and control settings can be found on the Movie Settings tab of the Pause Movie dialog box.

3. Click the Movie Settings tab in the Pause Movie dialog box.

With the setting shown in **Figure 17.7**, you can control a movie's volume and determine whether a movie is visible before and after playing, and how much screen to consume during playing. Also, the movie's playing time is displayed here.

4. If you added an animation effect to the movie, click on the Effect tab and add animation effect enhancements such as an entrance sound or an after-animation dim color, if necessary. (Usually this won't be necessary.)

5. Click OK to exit the Pause Movie dialog box.

✔ Tips

■ You can also access the Movie Settings controls by right-clicking the movie in Slide view and choosing Edit Movie Object.

■ To play the movie in Normal view, right-click and choose Play Movie. You can also use the Play button on the Custom Animation task pane.

■ Very important: Only the first frame of your movie is in PowerPoint. Your movies are linked from the source file, so if you move your presentation, the link to the movie may break. The best way to keep this from happening is to copy the movie into the same folder with the PowerPoint presentation file *before* you insert the movie into PowerPoint. Then you can move that entire folder around as needed.

■ Use discretion when attaching animation effects to a movie. By definition, a movie is animation; doing something fancy to a movie's entrance or exit could have the opposite effect, becoming one big distraction. You want to enhance your content, not hit people over the head with it.

PLAYING BACK YOUR CLIPS

Adding Sounds

You can liven up your PowerPoint slide shows by adding sound effects, playing songs, or even playing tracks from a music CD in your CD-ROM drive.

To insert a sound:

1. In Slide view, go to the slide to which you want to add a sound.

2. Choose Insert > Movies and Sounds > Sound from File.

   The Insert Sound dialog box appears

3. Navigate to the drive and folder containing your sound file (**Figure 17.8**).

   Note how much information you can get about your sound clip by hovering the cursor over it.

4. Select the sound file and click OK.

   As with movie clips, you are asked if you want the sound to play automatically during a slide show.

5. Choose Automatically if you want the sound to play automatically when the slide appears.

   or

   Choose When Clicked if you want to play the sound by clicking its icon.

   A sound icon appears on the slide (**Figure 17.9**).

6. Drag the sound icon to an empty area of the slide (such as a corner), or simply drag it off the edge of the slide if you don't want it to show on the slide at all.

7. To play the sound, if you selected When Clicked in step 5, just click the icon when you play the slide in Slide Show view.

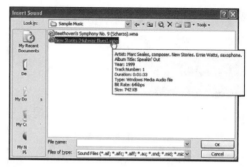

Figure 17.8 Choose a sound file by finding it on your hard drive or network drive.

Sound icon

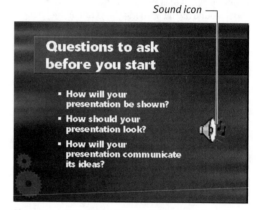

Figure 17.9 This slide will now play beautiful music.

Figure 17.10 You do not have to start from the beginning, nor must the clip stop after the current slide.

To control a sound clip's playback:

1. In Normal view, select the sound icon and choose Slide Show > Custom Animation. The Custom Animation task pane opens.

2. Right-click the sound clip in the animation task pane sequence and choose Effect Options.

3. The Play Sound dialog box appears.

4. Click the Effect tab.

   Here, you can choose to have the sound clip play from the beginning, from where it last left off, or from a specified position. You can also set its duration. In **Figure 17.10**, we have asked the clip to begin playing four seconds into the song and play through the next two slides (including the current one).

5. Click the Timing tab.

   To have the sound play after the previous event, change the Start to After Previous.

6. Click the Sound Settings tab.

   Here, you will find the option to hide the sound icon during the slide show.

7. Click OK.

✔ Tips

- If you hide the sound icon, make sure its setting is to play automatically. Otherwise, you won't be able to click it during a slide show and it will be useless.

- If you need to play consecutive sound (music) throughout your slides, for each sound file, put 999 in the Stop Playing After box of the Play Sound > Effect tab (**Figure 17.10**). The first sound will stop playing when the next sound begins. 999 is not an intuitive setting, but trust us—it works!

- Make sure the volume of the clip is acceptable. If it needs adjustment, you can do so from Sound Settings, although you will usually get better results by increasing the volume in a sound editing program. Try to test the sound in the room where the show will be given to ensure that it's loud enough.

ADDING SOUNDS

Playing CD Sound Tracks

During a slide show, you can play tracks from an audio CD in your computer's CD-ROM drive. You can have the music play while one slide is displayed, for the entire show, or for any range of slides.

To play CD sound tracks:

1. In Slide view, go to the slide on which you want the CD to start playing.

2. Choose Insert > Movies and Sounds > Play CD Audio Track (**Figure 17.11**). The CD Audio Options dialog box appears.

3. Fill in the starting and ending track numbers you want to play.

   Note: Track numbers correspond to the order in which songs play on the CD. In **Figure 17.12**, we have asked just for Track No. 2 to play, resulting in just over three and a half minutes of music.

4. Click OK.

   You are asked if you want the sound to play automatically during a slide show.

5. Choose Automatically if you want the CD to play automatically when the slide appears.

   or

   Choose When Clicked if you want to start playing the CD by clicking the sound icon.

   A CD sound icon appears in the center of the slide.

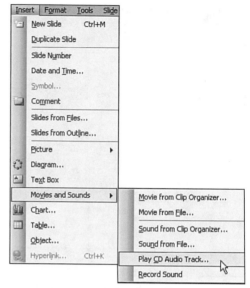

Figure 17.11 Asking for music from a CD.

Figure 17.12 You decide which tracks to play, how many times, and how loud.

PLAYING CD SOUND TRACKS

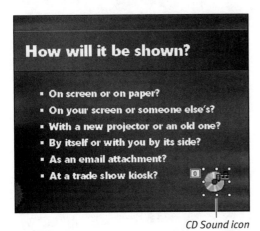

CD Sound icon

Figure 17.13 A slide with a CD track programmed to play.

6. Drag the sound icon to an empty area of the slide (**Figure 17.13**), or drag it off the edge of the slide if you don't want it to show at all.

✔ Tips

■ CD tracks will not play immediately— the CD needs to be accessed, and that is slower than reading from your hard drive. Therefore, it is difficult to stage precise timings of tracks.

■ When you insert a CD track, PowerPoint does not record the title of the CD. If you ask for Track No. 3 to play, it will play that track, no matter what CD is in the drive. So, check your CD-ROM before your presentatiion.

■ All the animation settings for playing a sound clip apply to playing a CD track, including the part about discretion!

■ If you need to play nonconsecutive tracks throughout your slides, insert each track on the appropriate slide. Then, for each sound track, put 999 in the Stop playing After box of the Play Sound > Effect tab (shown in **Figure 17.9**). The first track will stop playing when the next track begins. 999 is not an intuitive setting, but trust us—it works!

■ If the slide contains other animated objects, you'll need to change the animation order so that the music begins playing before the animation starts. To do this, use the Re-Order buttons at the bottom of the Custom Animation task pane. Click the up arrow to move the media (sound) object to the top of the list. You can also simply drag and drop to move the items in the task pane.

PLAYING CD SOUND TRACKS

Using the Clip Organizer to Play Sounds and Movies

Discussed at length in Chapter 10, the Clip Organizer really earns its stripes when tasked with managing multimedia files. You can search the established download and storage locations on your system, the gallery of clips that comes with Office, or the Office Online Internet site.

To use the Clip Organizer:

1. Choose Insert > Movies and Sounds > Movie from Clip Organizer or Sound from Clip Organizer.

   The Clip Art task pane appears and the Results drop-down is pre-assigned to search for either movies or sounds (whichever you chose in step 1).

2. Modify the Search In fields to include the locations in which you typically store your clips.

3. Modify the Results list, if necessary, to refine the search of clips.

   This is especially useful for finding a specific file type that is not WAV or MIDI, because otherwise, a search will return many dozens of files of those two formats.

4. Right-click on a clip in the task pane and choose Preview/Properties.

   The Preview/Properties dialog box (**Figure 7.14**) is especially handy, as it provides useful information about the size, file type, and resolution of video clips, as well as play the movie or sound clip in its window.

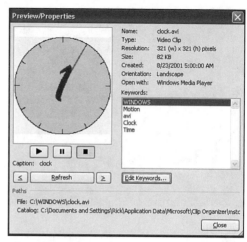

Figure 17.14 The Preview/Properties dialog box for choosing sound and movie clips from the Clip Organizer.

5. Left-click on the clip in the task pane to add the clip to your slide.

You are asked if you want the sound or movie to play automatically during a slide show.

6. Choose Automatically if you want the CD to play automatically when the slide appears.

or

Choose When Clicked if you want to start playing the CD by clicking the sound icon.

✔ Tips

■ If you place a clip into a folder but the Clip Organizer doesn't see it, you might need to refresh its memory (or its cache, to be technical). Click Organize Clips at the bottom of the task pane and navigate once to the folder that contains the newly placed clip. It will not only show up there, but will appear when you return to the Clip Organizer and perform your next search.

■ Multimedia (sound and movie) clips inserted through the Clip Organizer often have convoluted file paths associated with them. Because all multimedia is linked to, not embedded in, your presentation, it is entirely possible that the link to the multimedia will not remain intact. This could happen if you move the presentation elsewhere on the computer, port the presentation and multimedia clips to another computer, or even if someone uses a different profile to log on to the computer! Therefore, adding movies and sounds through the Clip Organizer is not advised. It's best to use the Clip Organizer to locate the multimedia file, copy it, paste it into your "working" folder with the presentation file, then go back to Insert > Movies and Sounds > Movie (or Sound) from File to actually insert it.

■ WAV files are an exception to the linked multimedia rule, as they can actually be embedded—up to 50MB! Before a WAV of this size can be embedded, you need to go to Tools > Options and put 50000 in the box on the General tab where it says, "Link sound files greater than XXX kb." (It would sure make more sense if this box said "Embed WAV files smaller than XXX kb," as that's really what it means.)

TAKING YOUR SHOW ON THE ROAD

There is little more stimulating to the new or seasoned road warrior than preparing a presentation at home or at work, taking it to a remote location, and watching it play perfectly when there.

At the same time, little is more agonizing than watching helplessly as that same procedure fails miserably.

The goal of this chapter is to give you more of the former experiences and fewer of the latter...

Showing Your Presentation on Another Computer

To successfully show your presentation on another computer, there are several important questions you must ask:

◆ What kind of projector will be used to display it?

◆ What computer will be used to run it?

◆ What version of PowerPoint is installed?

◆ What files need to be copied?

◆ What do I do with fonts?

Find out about your projector:

◆ Contact the supplier or the manufacturer of the LCD projector and ask if it is:

SVGA (800 x 600)

or

XGA (1024 x 768)

You will always get the best results if your computer's resolution matches that of the projector.

If you own the traveling computer:

1. Match the projector's resolution by right-clicking on the Desktop, choosing Properties, and then Settings.

2. In the Screen Resolution field, adjust the value to the desired resolution, 800 x 600 or 1024 x 768 (**Figure 18.1**).

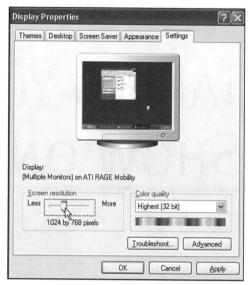

Figure 18.1 Your presentations will look their best and be most compact when you match resolutions between computers and projectors.

3. If you will be creating the presentation on your desktop system and then transferring it to your traveling system, set the resolution on your desktop system to match.

4. Begin work on your presentation.

✔ Tips

■ Working on a system with a different resolution is hardly fatal, and in the case of bullets and titles, it might make no difference at all. However, you will get a better sense of how slides will appear when working in the final resolution.

■ The real savings come if you can prepare external graphics after determining final resolution. You will notice the difference in quality between an 800 x 600 photo and the finer 1024 x 768 photo, and equally important, the reduction in file size by reducing an image to 800 x 600 if that is the resolution of the projector.

SHOWING YOUR PRESENTATION ON ANOTHER COMPUTER

To save in an earlier version:

First let us explain that there's rarely any reason to save a presentation in an earlier version of PowerPoint. In fact, PowerPoint 97, 2000, 2002, and 2003 all use the same file format, and so each can open presentations created in one of those other versions. Just use Save as Presentation, and you'll be in good shape.

The only time you would ever need to "backsave"—save in an earlier version—is if you're working with someone who needs to open the file in PowerPoint 95. And in fact, if that person only needs to *view or show* the file, they would be better off downloading and installing the free PowerPoint Viewer from microsoft.com than they would trying to view it with PowerPoint 95.

Anyway, if you *really must* save as PowerPoint 95, here's how you'd do it:

1. Go to File > Save As.

2. At Save as Type, choose PowerPoint 97 – 11 Beta & 95 Presentation (**Figure 18.2**).

3. Click Save.

4. Click Yes when you're asked if you're sure and warned that you'll lose features.

   Instead of backsaving your "real" presentation, you may want to do this with a copy of it.

✔ Tips

■ To make the change permanent, go to Tools > Options > Save, and make your choice at Save PowerPoint Files As.

■ If you want, you can turn off the new features in PowerPoint 2003 so you're not tempted to use them while you create your presentation. Go to Tools > Options and disable the new features at the bottom of the Edit tab.

Figure 18.2 Saving as an earlier version.

■ If you need to play a presentation on a machine with an older version, make sure to avoid features unique to newer versions, such as import of animated GIF files, new animations, and picture or numbered bullets. PowerPoint 2000 introduced animated GIFs and picture and numbered bullets, so these features won't translate to PowerPoint 97. PowerPoint 2002 introduced a number of new animations and transitions which won't play in PowerPoint 2000 or 97. PowerPoint 2003 is similar to 2002 in that respect.

■ PowerPoint 2002 and 2003 have password protection options. PowerPoint 95, 97 and 2000 will not recognize password protection on presentations and cannot open them.

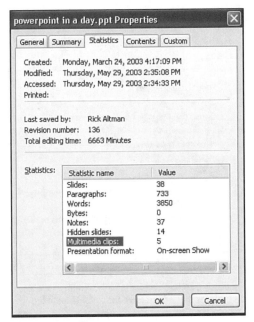

Figure 18.3 Multimedia clips that are externally linked will need to be copied with your presentation.

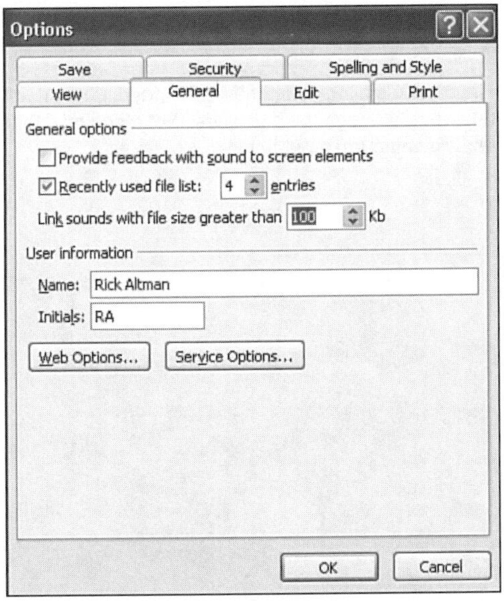

Figure 18.4 You decide which .wav files live within a presentation and which ones live outside.

To gather necessary files:

1. Go to File > Properties > Statistics.

2. Note the number of multimedia clips in the presentation (**Figure 18.3**).

   Those files might be linked externally, instead of embedded within the presentation. If so, you will need to make sure you copy them to the traveling computer.

3. Scroll your presentation and make note of all clips. Choose Edit > Movie Object or Edit > Sound Object to find the location of linked clips. Note that this probably won't show much of the path other than the actual name of the clip, though.

4. Gather them and make sure they are copied to the traveling computer.

   An even better way to gather all the linked files for your presentation is to use the Package for CD function. (See "Packaging Your Presentation on CD" later in this chapter.)

✔ Tips

- To behave correctly on the traveling computer, linked files (including multimedia files as well as other PowerPoint files) need to be in the same relative location on the traveling computer, or else they need to be in same folder as the presentation file itself.

- The easiest way to gather and copy all files is to use the Package for CD command, even if you do not intend to burn a CD. See "Packaging Your Presentation on CD" later in this chapter.

- All files are linked externally except for .wav files that remain below a certain size threshold. You can set that threshold at Tools > Options > General. Set a value for Link Sounds with File Size Greater Than (**Figure 18.4**).

To correctly manage fonts:

If your presentation requires specific fonts be used, and those fonts are TrueType fonts, you can probably embed them in the presentation so that they will display properly on other systems. If the fonts you used in your presentation are not available on the other computer, PowerPoint will substitute the closest font it can find.

1. Choose File > Save As, and click Tools.

2. From the Tools drop-down, choose Save Options.

3. Check Embed TrueType fonts (**Figure 18.5**).

✔ Tips

■ Not all fonts can be embedded, and PowerPoint will tell you so upon saving (**Figure 18.6**).

■ Font embedding is not foolproof. To ensure correct font displays, use the ones that you know are present on all Windows machines: Arial, Times New Roman, Verdana, Tahoma, and Wingdings for accents.

Figure 18.5 Embedding fonts makes them available on systems that do not have those fonts installed.

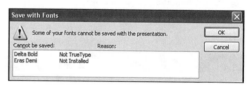

Figure 18.6 If a font cannot be embedded, PowerPoint tells you. Although the box reads "Not Installed," this really means "unembeddable."

Figure 18.7 Saving the file as a Show file means it will automatically show when double-clicked.

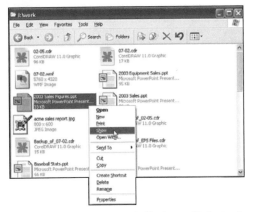

Figure 18.8 You can automatically show a file instead of opening it by using the shortcut menu.

Using PPS Files

Two of the simplest maneuvers in all of PowerPoint can result in the biggest assist to presenters on the go. After you have created your presentation and are ready to show it, isn't it a bit tedious to enter PowerPoint, open the presentation file, and issue the command to show it?

Fortunately, you do not have to do that, thanks to two very simple tips.

To view a show without starting PowerPoint:

1. Choose File > Save As.

2. In the Save As Type drop-down, choose PowerPoint Show (**Figure 18.7**).

3. Click Save.

4. Now open Windows Explorer or My Computer, find the newly saved file, and double-click it.

   Instead of the presentation opening in PowerPoint for editing, it will automatically begin as a slide show.

Or

1. Save the presentation normally as a Presentation (*.PPT) file

2. Open Windows Explorer or a My Computer window and find the PPT file.

3. Right-click the file and choose Show from the shortcut menu (**Figure 18.8**).

USING PPS FILES

✔ Tips

- What is the difference between a regular .ppt file and a .pps show file? One character. That's it! You can make a show file yourself by copying or renaming a presentation file with a .pps extension. PowerPoint does nothing special or magical to a presentation except give it this extension, and that's enough to tell PowerPoint to show the file rather than open it for editing.

- If you need to edit a PPS file, simply open PowerPoint, go to File > Open, and navigate to the PPS file. Opening it in this manner will open the file in Normal view for editing.

- If you show presentations more than edit them on your traveling computer, you can keep the extension as the default .ppt, but tell Windows that the default action for these files should be Show, not Open. To do this, go to Start > Control Panel > Folder Options > File Types. Scroll the list down to .PPT, select it, and click Advanced. Then in the list of Actions, choose Show and click Set Default (**Figure 18.9**). After you do that, everything will be backward: To show a .ppt file, double-click it, and to open it for editing, right-click it and choose Open.

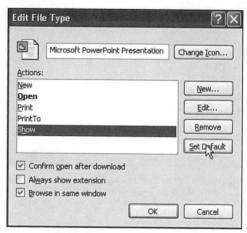

Figure 18.9 A little-known slight of hand with Windows makes it easier to show presentations on machines whose jobs it is to show them.

USING PPS FILES

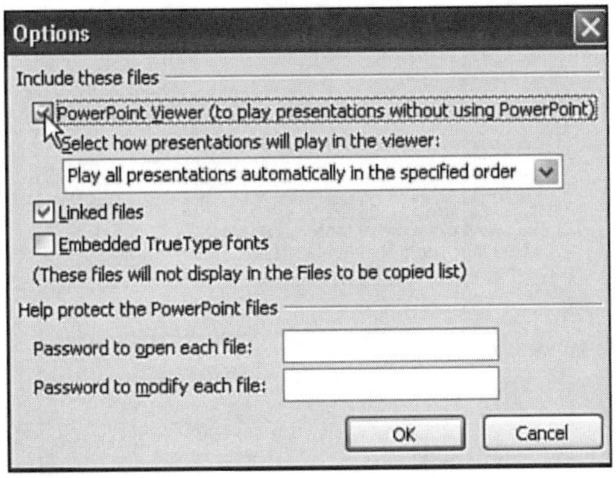

Figure 18.10 You can get the Viewer files with the Package for CD command.

✔ Tips

- The easiest way to copy the necessary files is to use the Package for CD command, which, this chapter is making evident, has been misnamed (you can do much more with it than just burn CDs). Go to File > Package for CD, click the Options button, and then check PowerPoint Viewer (**Figure 18.10**).

- Having the Viewer doesn't guarantee that your presentation will run properly on another machine. You'll still need to address the issues raised earlier in this chapter—namely, matching resolution between projector and computer, making sure the necessary fonts are either installed or embedded, and having external clips available.

Viewing a Slide Show when PowerPoint Is Nowhere to Be Found

It's one thing to bypass PowerPoint's Normal view to show a presentation instead of open it.

It's an altogether different thing to show a presentation on a system that doesn't even have PowerPoint installed. That is what the PowerPoint Viewer is all about.

You might not have heard much about this valuable utility because it has been allowed to wither on the vine for many years, incapable of showing many of the newer features and capabilities of the last two versions. However, PowerPoint 2003 includes a brand new viewer, capable of showing any effect you can create.

Using the Viewer requires the presence of four files, all of which reside in the c:\Program Files\Office03\Office11 folder:

- ◆ pptview.exe
- ◆ gdiplus.dll
- ◆ ppvwintl.dll
- ◆ unicows.dll

If you copy those four files, along with your presentation file, to a different computer, it doesn't matter whether or not that machine has PowerPoint installed. The viewer will ensure that the presentation shows, just as if PowerPoint were there.

Packaging Your Presentation on CD

As we have pointed out, this command really should have just been called Package Presentation, as we have already shown two valuable uses for it that have nothing to do with making CDs.

Nonetheless, this new feature will make its most visible impression when you want to take an entire presentation—fonts, clips, viewer, and all—and have it automatically run when the recipient inserts a CD into their drive.

To create a CD with your presentation on it:

1. With the presentation open, choose Package for CD.

2. Enter a name for the CD (16-character limit, no spaces).

3. Click Options and at Select How Presentations Will Play in the Viewer, choose one of the four options (**Figure 18.11**).

4. Make your other choices about linked files and embedded fonts.

5. If desired, assign passwords to restrict the use of the CD.

   See "Creating Password-Protection" later in this chapter.

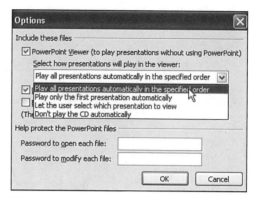

Figure 18.11 This choice will cause the presentation to play automatically.

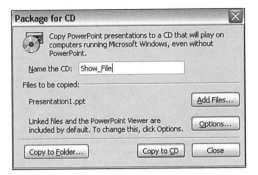

Figure 18.12 The CD being produced.

6. To add any other files (external charts, reference documents, other presentations, and so on), click Add Files and find them on your system.

The Add Files command doesn't refer to files linked to the PPT presentation file (video files, sound files, other presentations). These will automatically be included in the Package for CD. After all, that's the whole point of it!

7. Click Copy to CD to begin (**Figure 18.12**).

✔ Tips

- Don't forget that if you intend to burn your presentation and the Viewer to a CD, you need to have a CD R/RW drive available on your computer.

- Although you can use Package for CD with any operating system that will run Office 2003, the Copy to CD command requires Windows XP.

- You can also use Copy to Folder instead of Copy to CD and then use your own CD writing software to transfer the files to CD. This is especially useful if you're not using Windows XP.

- You can write to a CD-R or a CD-RW, and the CD-RW can be blank or already contain data. However, if data is present, it is erased during the creation process.

- CDs created in this manner (using Package for CD with the Viewer) will run on computers without PowerPoint. Nothing is installed on the recipient machine—it all runs from the CD.

PACKAGING YOUR PRESENTATION ON CD

Sending Out for Review

At this very moment, as this manuscript is being composed, Microsoft Word's Revision Marks is activated, and everything that we type is being recorded as having come from us. Then, a team of editors and technical reviewers will receive copies of this, each making her own comments and edits. Finally, the documents will be merged into one with all comments in tow, and somehow, intelligible prose will be produced as the result.

As of PowerPoint 2002, users can enjoy this same process during the creation stage of a presentation, thanks to the Send for Review feature.

To send a presentation for review:

◆ Choose File > Save As and set the file type to Presentation for Review (**Figure 18.13**), making sure you choose a network location that is accessible by your reviewers.

File > Save As >Presentation for Review is not an available option until the presentation has been saved once. After that, Presentation for Review becomes available in the As Type drop down box.

or

Choose File > Send To > Mail Recipient (for Review) (**Figure 18.14**).

✔ Tips

■ Sending for Review is not a true collaboration—each reviewer must work on his or her own copy. As the author, you will need to manage that flow of traffic.

■ Linked clips and fonts remain an issue. If necessary, you will need to arrange for them to be available to the reviewers.

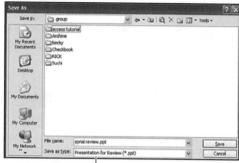

File type

Figure 18.13 Saving a presentation to a network location for review by others.

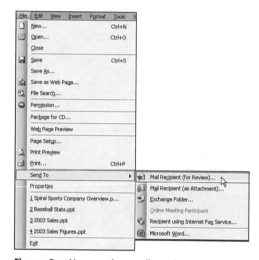

Figure 18.14 You can also email a review copy.

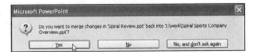

Figure 18.15 Answer Yes to merge comments from reviewers with your original presentation.

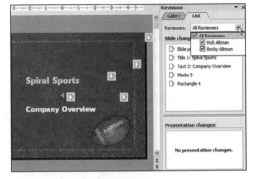

Figure 18.16 Reviews appear like comments on the slide, awaiting your authorization to apply them.

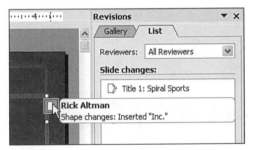

Figure 18.17 Click the item to see what the reviewer suggests.

To review a presentation:

1. Edit it as you normally would.

2. If you never have before, experiment with Insert > Comment to ask questions of or make observations to the author.

3. Save normally.

To merge a presentation:

1. Open the presentations that you receive back from your reviewers.

   When prompted as in **Figure 18.15**, answer Yes.

   Answering Yes here won't merge all the changes, it just merges the presentations so you can review it and either accept or reject those changes.

2. Open as many at one time as you want.

To review the reviews:

Figure 18.16 shows how the reviews appear on the slide, and the Revisions task pane includes a drop-down list of those whose reviews are merged into this presentation. To accept or reject an item:

1. Select the item to see detail on it (**Figure 18.17**).

2. Right-click the item and choose either Apply (to accept it), or Delete Marker (to reject it).

continues on next page

SENDING OUT FOR REVIEW

Figure 18.18 shows what the first slide looks like with revisions accepted or deleted.

✔ Tips

- Animation changes cannot be incorporated into the original presentation, but you can opt to add the entire slide (Figure 18.19).

- Leaving accepted items onscreen is harmless, as they do not appear during a show.

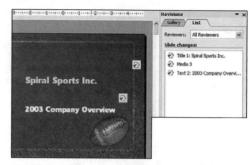

Figure 18.18 Accepted items are still visible onscreen.

Figure 18.19 Changes to animation must be made by copying the entire slide to the presentation.

Figure 18.20 You can set passwords that control who sees the file and who can change it.

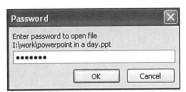

Figure 18.21 Without the password, you don't get past this front door.

Creating Password-Protection

If you are creating presentations of a sensitive nature, you can control who can view them and who can change them. Introduced in PowerPoint 2002, you can assign passwords to a presentation, without which the file cannot be opened and perhaps even modified.

To add a password:

1. Open the presentation.

2. Go to Tools > Options > Security (**Figure 18.20**).

3. Enter passwords for opening and/or modifying.

4. Enter them again when prompted.

5. Close the dialog box and save the presentation.

   Now anyone trying to open this presentation (including its author) must enter the correct password(s) (**Figure 18.21**).

✔ Tips

- If you add a password to the original presentation, you'd better not forget it. If so, you are up the proverbial creek without the proverbial paddle. Better to make copies of presentations, password-protect the copies, and send them to those whose access you want to restrict.

- Passwords can also be added using File > Save As. Open the Tools menu on that dialog box, and passwording is included in Security Options.

FROM SCREEN TO TONER: PRINTING YOUR PRESENTATION

19

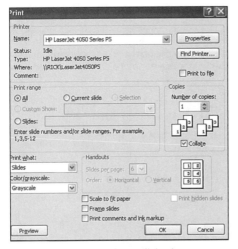

Figure 19.1 The standard Print dialog box.

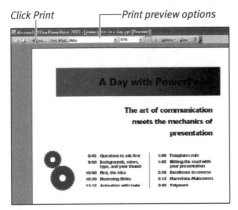

Click Print — Print preview options

Figure 19.2 Print Preview is handy for warning you of impending disaster.

In most cases, the screen is a presentation's final output device. You create your presentation, show it on a computer or projector screen, and then you're done. Often, a presentation never actually makes its way to paper.

Nevertheless, when you need to print a presentation, you need to do it correctly, and that is the focus of this chapter. Little is more frustrating than creating a presentation that looks great onscreen...and watching it come out looking like mud from your laser printer.

You use the Print dialog box (**Figure 19.1**) to send output to a printer or file. Here, you select what to print: slides, handouts, speaker notes, or an outline of the presentation. We'll cover all four types of output in this chapter.

PowerPoint offers a Print Preview option (**Figure 19.2**), which lets you see how different types of output will look when complete. Good thing, too: In this case, we discovered that the dark bar with black text looks pretty awful, and we were able to fix it before printing.

Selecting a Printer

The Print dialog box initially indicates the current printer. If you are connected to more than one printer and want to specify a different one, follow these steps.

To select a different printer:

1. Choose File > Print or press Ctrl+P.

   The Print dialog box appears (**Figure 19.1**).

2. In the Name field, choose the printer you want to use.

3. Choose other options as desired and click OK to begin printing.

✔ Tips

- To set printer-specific options, click Properties in the Print dialog box (**Figure 19.3**).

- If you change any settings in the Properties dialog box, PowerPoint remembers them until you quit the program. If you find yourself changing them often, consider changing them permanently. You do that from Start > Control Panel > Printers and Faxes. Right-click the desired printer and choose Properties. The dialog box will look similar, but now you'll be changing the default permanently.

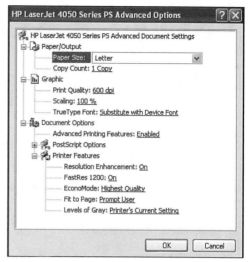

Figure 19.3 You can reach the property sheet for any printer from within the Print dialog box.

Grayscale Preview

Figure 19.4 Use this button to switch between Color and Grayscale previews.

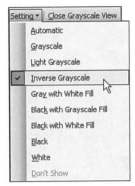

Figure 19.5 Use this menu to adjust grayscale options.

Previewing Slides in Grayscale

If you plan to print your slides on a monochrome printer, you may want to preview them in grayscale beforehand. PowerPoint offers an easy way to do this.

To preview slides in grayscale:

◆ Choose View > Color/Grayscale.

or

Click the Grayscale Preview button on the Standard toolbar (**Figures 19.4**).

In either case, a submenu appears where you can choose between the three main settings: Color, Grayscale, or Pure Black and White. After you are in the preview, a Setting drop-down menu provides several options for grayscale settings (**Figure 19.5**).

✔ Tips

■ You must have an object selected in order to use the Setting drop-down menu on the Grayscale View toolbar.

■ Changing the Settings on the Grayscale View toolbar doesn't affect the color version of the slide; it only affects the black and white for printing. You can see that this is so by leaving the Slide miniature pane open while changing the Grayscale View settings.

Printing Slides

When you print from PowerPoint, you can print a number of ways: one slide per page; two slides per page; or even 3, 4, 6 or 9 slides per page. You can also print slides with speaker notes and outlines.

To print one slide per page:

To print more than one slide per page, see the next sections on formatting and printing handouts.

1. Choose File > Print or press Ctrl+P to display the Print dialog box (**Figure 19.6**).

2. Under Print Range, choose All to print the entire presentation.

   or

   Choose Current Slide to print just the slide that is currently displayed.

   or

   To print specific slides, click Slides and enter the range of slides you want to print. Use a hyphen to indicate a range of slides (such as 1-5) and a comma to indicate nonconsecutive slides (1-5, 7, 10).

3. In the Print What field, choose Slides.

4. At the bottom of the dialog box, click Scale to Fit Paper.

5. Choose Preview if you want to take a last look at the output (**Figure 19.2**). Click Print in the Preview window to return to the Print dialog box.

6. Make sure that your paper or overhead transparencies are loaded in the printer and then click OK.

Choose All...   *...Current Slide...*

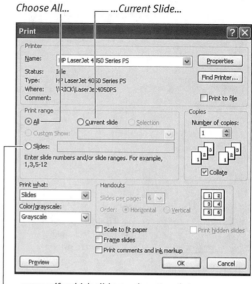

...or specify which slide numbers to print

Figure 19.6 In the Print dialog box, you can choose to print all slides, the slide currently on the screen, or a specific range of slides.

✔ Tips

- Another way to specify a range of slides is to first select them in Slide Sorter view. Then, in the Print dialog box, choose Selection as the print range.

- The Print button on the Standard toolbar bypasses the Print dialog box—clicking it immediately prints whatever options you've specified in PowerPoint's Tools > Options on the Print tab. This is a presentation-specific setting, so be careful that it's not set to print one slide per page before you go printing your 75-slide presentation! This button also prints automatically to your default printer. Because you don't see the Print dialog box, you don't get to choose a printer.

- When you print a color presentation on a monochrome printer, PowerPoint automatically converts the colors to shades of gray.

- If you need to print the last slides first, which helps with collating the presentation on many inkjet printers, input the slide numbers backward in the Slides box. For example, 10, 7, 5-1 will print slides 10, 7, 5, 4, 3, 2, and 1 in that order.

- If you print a color presentation to a black-and-white printer and you want white backgrounds instead of dark ones, check Grayscale or Pure Black and White in the Print dialog.

- Most printers cannot print completely to the edge of the paper. This is a limitation of the printer, not of PowerPoint.

PRINTING SLIDES

Formatting Handout Pages

Handout pages are smaller, printed versions of your slides, used to help your audience follow along in your presentation. They can consist of two, three, four, six, or nine slides per page. Before printing, you may want to add titles, page numbers, or borders. You can perform all of these tasks on the Handout Master.

To format handout pages:

1. Choose View > Master > Handout Master or hold down Shift as you click the Slide Sorter View button.

   The Handout Master appears (**Figure 19.7**).

2. On the Handout Master View toolbar, choose the icon that represents the number of slides you want to appear on each handout page.

3. Make any of the following changes:

   ◆ To add text that you want to appear on each page (such as the presentation title or page number), choose the View > Header and Footer command.

   ◆ Add any desired background graphics.

4. When you are finished, click Close on the Handout Master View toolbar.

✔ Tips

■ The three-per-page layout includes lines on the right half of the page for the audience to take notes next to each slide.

■ Any headers or footers you add do not appear on the Handout Master; you see them only on the printed handout page.

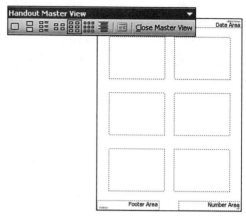

Figure 19.7 To format and lay out your handout pages, edit the Handout Master.

■ If you want to use a word processor to fine-tune handouts or add text, you can choose File > Send To > Microsoft Word.

■ The slide images cannot be resized or moved on the handout master. If this is necessary, use File > Send To > Microsoft Word.

Figure 19.8 This handout page has six slides.

Printing Handouts

After you have formatted the Handout Master, you are ready to print your handouts. **Figure 19.8** shows an example of a printed handout page.

To print handout pages:

1. Choose File > Print.

    The Print dialog box appears.

2. Choose a print range.

    Keep in mind that the number of slides you want printed and the number of pages that will be printed are probably two different things.

3. In the Print What list box, choose Handouts.

4. In the Slides Per Page field, change the number if desired.

5. If you've chosen four or more handouts per page, select Horizontal or Vertical.

6. Choose Preview to review your work. Click Print in the Preview window to return to the Print dialog box.

7. Click OK.

✔ Tip

■ PowerPoint automatically places borders around each slide on the printed handout. To eliminate borders, remove the checkmark from the Frame Slides box in the Print dialog box.

Stopping a Print Job

If you choose the Print command and then decide you want to cancel the print job, you can delete the job from the print queue.

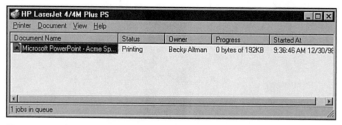

Figure 19.9 To display the print queue, double-click the printer icon on the Windows taskbar.

To stop a print job:

1. Double-click the printer icon on the Windows taskbar (**Figure 19.9**).

   The print queue appears (**Figure 19.10**).

2. Click the document name.

3. Press Delete.

   or

   Choose Document > Cancel Printing.

4. Close the print queue window.

✔ Tips

■ For small print jobs, the printer icon may come and go very quickly. If the icon isn't there, the print job has already been spooled to the printer, and it's too late to cancel the print job.

■ If you're having trouble canceling a print job after you've double-clicked the printer icon on the Windows task pane, try using Document > Pause Printing and then do Document > Cancel Printing.

Figure 19.10 The print queue shows you the job being printed and any others waiting their turns.

STOPPING A PRINT JOB

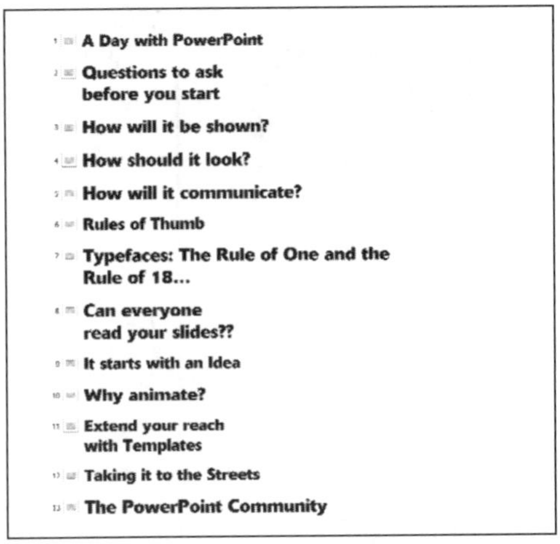

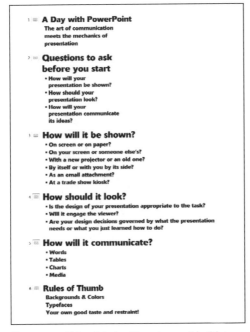

Figure 19.11 This printed outline shows only the slide titles.

Figure 19.12 This printed outline shows slide titles and expanded text.

Figure 19.13 Choose Outline View in the Print What field to print the outline.

Printing the Outline

You can print an outline of your presentation exactly as it appears in Outline view. For instance, if only the slide titles are displayed in Outline view, only the slide titles are printed (**Figure 19.11**). If the outline is completely expanded, all the slide titles and bulleted items are printed (**Figure 19.12**). If formatting is hidden, the text and bullets are not formatted.

Remember that text boxes that were added manually (in other words, not a text placeholder) will not show in Outline view.

To get the results you want, set the options in Outline view before printing your outline.

To print the outline:

1. Switch to Normal view. If the Slide Thumbnails view appears, click the toggle tab to see the outline.

2. Display the Outlining toolbar by selecting View > Toolbars > Outlining.

3. Make any of the following changes:
   - ▲ To hide or display formatting, click the Show Formatting button.
   - ▲ To display only the slide titles, click the Collapse All button.
   - ▲ To display the entire outline, click the Expand All button.

4. Choose File > Print.

5. In the Print What field, choose Outline View (**Figure 19.13**).

6. Click OK to begin printing.

Adding Speaker Notes

To help remind you what to say when you present each slide during a slide show, you can refer to speaker notes saved on notes pages.

When printed, each page of notes consists of the slide on the top half and any speaker notes you have for that slide on the bottom half.

You can enter your speaker notes in Notes Page view (**Figure 19.14**) or in the notes pane in Normal view (**Figure 19.15**).

To enter speaker notes in Notes Page view:

1. Choose View > Notes Page to switch to Notes Page view (**Figure 19.14**).

2. Zoom in if necessary.

3. Click the text placeholder and type your notes.

4. To go to the next slide, use the scroll bar or the Page Down button on your keyboard, and then repeat steps 2 and 3.

✔ Tips

- In PowerPoint 2002 and later, you can set up notes for yourself to appear on a second monitor to prompt you during a slide show. Choose Slide Show > Set Up Show > Show Presenter View (multiple monitors must be enabled).

- If the slide image is taking up too much space on the notes page, you can resize it by dragging the corner. Or you can delete it altogether.

Slide placeholder

Text placeholder for notes

Figure 19.14 Use Notes Page view to enter speaker notes.

Drag these borders to resize the notes pane

Notes pane

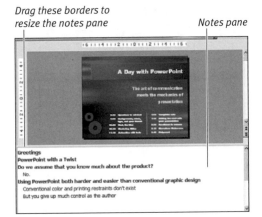

Figure 19.15 You can enter speaker notes in the notes pane in Normal view.

To enter speaker notes in Normal view:

1. Switch to Normal view.

2. Adjust the size of the notes pane (**Figure 19.15**), if desired.

3. Click inside the notes pane and type your notes.

4. To go to the next slide, use the scroll bar or the Page Down button on your keyboard.

5. Repeat steps 3 and 4 for each slide.

✔ Tips

■ The Notes Page view gives you a better idea of how the notes will look as handouts.

■ To return to Normal view, double-click the slide image on the Notes Page view.

■ If you want more than one slide per page plus speaker notes, use File > Send to > Microsoft Word.

ADDING SPEAKER NOTES

Editing the Notes Master

You can perform global formatting of your notes pages on the Notes Master. (It works just like the Slide Master discussed in Chapter 12.)

For instance, if you add bullet symbols to the Notes Master, bullets will automatically appear when you enter text on all notes pages. You can also add page numbers, format the text in a different font, or resize the slide and text placeholders.

To edit the notes master:

1. Choose View > Master > Notes Master. The Notes Master appears (**Figure 19.16**).

2. Zoom in if necessary.

3. Make any of the following changes:

   ◆ Adjust the size and position of the slide or text placeholders.

   ◆ Format the text as desired—add bullet symbols, adjust indents, change the font, and so forth. **Figure 19.17** shows the text placeholders after we decided to apply bullets to the second level, and automatic numbering to the third.

   ◆ To add text that you want to appear on each page (page number or presentation title), use the View > Header and Footer command. You should apply the formatting (bold, font size, italics, color, lines, and so on) to the text placeholders on the notes master, though.

4. When you are finished, click Close Master View on the small floating Notes Master View toolbar.

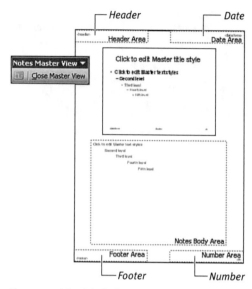

Figure 19.16 To globally format notes pages, make changes to the Notes Master.

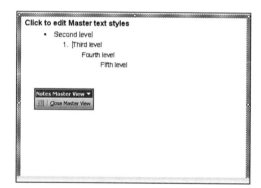

Figure 19.17 In this Notes Master, the second level is bulleted and the third level numbered.

✔ Tip

■ Any headers or footers you add do not appear on the Notes Master; however, you will see them in Notes Page view.

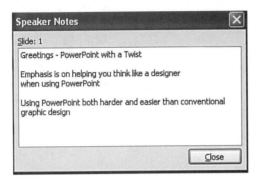

Figure 19.18 During a show, you can access your speaker notes.

Printing Speaker Notes

After you have typed your notes and formatted the Notes Master, you are ready to print the notes pages.

To print speaker notes:

1. Choose File > Print.

2. Choose a print range.

3. From the Print What menu, choose Notes Pages.

4. Click OK.

✔ Tips

- In the Print Options dialog box, you can click the Preview button to see how your notes will look.

- If you want to add information or edit your notes in a word processor, you can choose File > Send To > Microsoft Word.

- You can view your notes pages during a slide show by right-clicking the screen, choosing Screen, and then Speaker Notes (**Figure 19.18**). This is not recommended if your speaker notes remind you to not pick the wax out of your ears while speaking....

  Also see "Taking Notes During a Slide Show" in Chapter 15.

Creating a PDF File

Today, any professional involved in graphics needs to understand the opportunity and the power behind creating Adobe Acrobat or Portable Document Format (PDF) files. When you create a PDF file from a PowerPoint presentation, you make it possible for others to view your slides without owning PowerPoint. You also make it possible for printers to print your slides on high-quality imagesetters and color printers.

Creating PDF files is not a built-in capability of PowerPoint; it requires a separate purchase—of either Adobe Acrobat or the popular alternative, JawsPDF. There are also freeware and shareware PDF creation programs available, but we cannot vouch for their quality.

In either case, after you install one of these programs, an additional printer choice becomes available, as shown in **Figure 19.19**. Printing to Acrobat Distiller or JawsPDF Creator creates a PostScript file that is converted into a PDF file.

Both Acrobat and Jaws offer the option to create a toolbar within Office applications for easy PDF creation (**Figure 19.20**), and this contributes to the popular, albeit mistaken, belief that PowerPoint includes built-in support for PDF file creation.

If you have not yet done it, try using Adobe Acrobat or JawsPDF the next time you need a presentation printed professionally. It has become the official standard method for creating press-ready files.

Additional printer

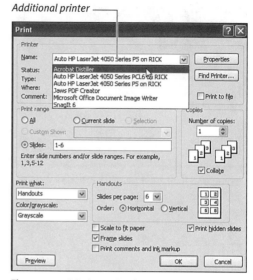

Figure 19.19 Printing to Acrobat Distiller is the most common way to create PDF files.

Figure 19.20 The Acrobat toolbar.

CREATING A PDF FILE

PRESENTING ON THE INTERNET

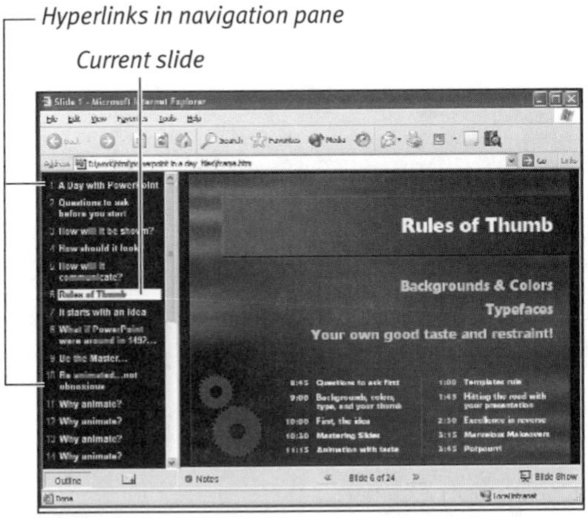

Hyperlinks in navigation pane

Current slide

Figure 20.1 You can produce an HTML file of your PowerPoint presentation so that anyone with a Web browser can view your slide show.

PowerPoint includes a number of built-in features and wizards that use the Internet. For example, you can insert hyperlinks to Web sites, save a PowerPoint presentation directly to an FTP site, and, most salient, produce Web pages from your presentations.

The Web version of your presentation can be viewed in any browser (**Figure 20.1**). From the browser, you can display the slides from frame-based navigation links, similar to using the Outline pane of Normal view, or you can run the show, animation and all. Your browser is unable to render animations as smoothly or accurately as PowerPoint, but it works well enough to give non-PowerPoint users a good idea of what you are trying to communicate.

That's the key: When you publish your presentation to the Web, anyone who has a Web browser can view it, even if PowerPoint is not installed on the local computer.

✔ Tips

- When you publish your slides as a Web page, make sure all of your slides have titles so that there are links to all slides in the navigation pane of the Web browser (**Figure 20.1**). Remember, if you have a slide that uses a blank slide layout, it will appear with no text in the navigation pane. To correct this, change the Blank layout to a Title Only layout, then drag the title placeholder off the edge of the slide so it doesn't show on the slide itself.

- When you publish your slides as a Web page, some of the features (animation and transitions) may be lost on older browsers. Newer versions of Internet Explorer will display these features, but the person viewing the show may need to install the Office Run Time plug-in if they don't have PowerPoint 2002 or 2003. The Run Time plug-in is available at http://office.microsoft.com/downloads/2002/msorun.aspx.

- Test your Web page in as many browsers as possible.

Figure 20.2 Any item that you can select can take a hyperlink, including bullets of text.

 Figure 20.3 The Insert Hyperlink button.

Figure 20.4 Enter the address of the Web page to which you want to link.

Linking to a Web Site

In your presentations, you can create a hyperlink to any Web site so that your audience can view a particular Web page during a slide show. Links to Web sites are useful for slide shows that are published on the Internet as well as those that are presented live to an audience. Any item that can have an action attached to it (that is, practically any object at all) can serve as a hyperlink to a Web page. It doesn't have to be an action button. **Figure 20.2** shows how simple bullets can be used as hyperlinks. See Chapter 15, "Producing a Slide Show," for more information on creating hyperlinks.

To create a link to a Web site:

1. In Normal view, enter the text that will become a hyperlink and then select it.

2. Click the Insert Hyperlink button (**Figure 20.3**) on the Standard toolbar.

   or

   Choose Insert > Hyperlink.

   The Insert Hyperlink dialog box appears (**Figure 20.4**). Note the four choices at the left and choose Existing File or Web Page, if it's not already selected.

3. Enter the URL of the site to which you want to link.

4. Click OK.

   The text is underlined in a different color to show that it's a hyperlink.

✔ Tips

- If you add a hyperlink directly to text on your slide, the color may change. This color, and the color of the hyperlink after it's been followed (clicked), is determined by the Slide Color Scheme.

- Hyperlinks to Web sites are intended to be used during a slide show, but you can make them work in Normal view by right-clicking the hyperlink and choosing Open Hyperlink from the shortcut menu (**Figure 20.5**). However, if you have more than one hyperlink on text in a textbox, this won't work properly; in that case, you'll need to run the slide show in order to test the hyperlink.

- An easy way to create a hyperlink is to type the URL, such as www.acme.com, directly on the slide. PowerPoint immediately recognizes the URL as a hyperlink. Note that you may need to press the spacebar or Enter after typing the text so that PowerPoint recognizes the text as a hyperlink and knows where the address begins and ends.

- To edit or remove a link, right-click it and use the controls on the shortcut menu.

- If you want the text on the screen to be different from the actual link, you can change the text in the Text to Display box shown in **Figure 20.4**.

Figure 20.5 You can open a hyperlink even when not running the show.

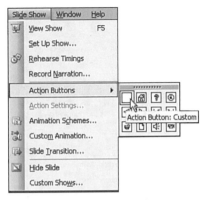

Figure 20.6 To create an action button, choose Slide Show > Action Buttons and then click the Custom button.

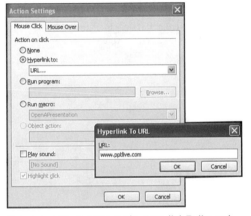

Figure 20.7 Choose URL on the Hyperlink To list and then enter the address.

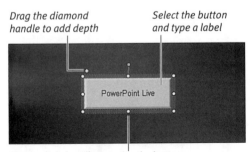

Drag the diamond handle to add depth

Select the button and type a label

Drag a circle handle to resize the button

Figure 20.8 You can format your action button any way you like.

To create an action button that links to a Web site:

1. In Normal view, go to the slide on which you want to create the button.

2. Choose Slide Show > Action Buttons.
   or
   On the Drawing toolbar, click AutoShapes and then choose Action Buttons.

3. Click the Custom button (**Figure 20.6**).

4. Drag a rectangular shape where you want to insert the button.
   When you release the mouse button, the Action Settings dialog box appears.

5. Click Hyperlink To.

6. In the Hyperlink To list, select URL.

7. In the Hyperlink to URL dialog box, type the URL. In **Figure 20.7**, you'll notice that we left off the http:// prefix. If your URL begins with www, you do not need the http prefix.

8. Click OK to close the dialog box.
   The action button appears on the slide.

9. Use the Text Box tool to give your button a label, or simply select the button and begin typing.

10. Format and resize the button as needed (**Figure 20.8**).

See Chapter 15 for more information on creating Action buttons.

LINKING TO A WEB SITE

✔ Tips

- Although action buttons are intended to be used during slide shows, you can activate them in Normal view by right-clicking on them (**Figure 20.9**).

- In addition to linking to other Web sites, action buttons and hyperlinks can link to local Web pages on your hard drive, other points in a presentation, or to other files (Excel spreadsheets, Word documents, and so on). See Chapter 15 for more on action buttons.

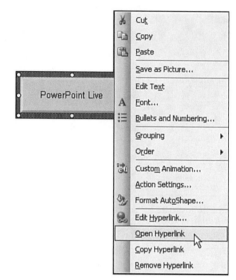

Figure 20.9 Action buttons can be tested from the shortcut menu and the Open Hyperlink command.

Click to display the list...

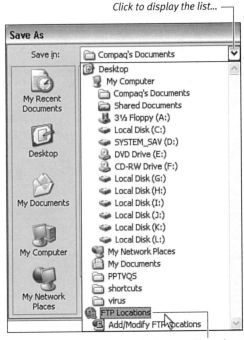

...and choose FTP Locations

Figure 20.10 You can save directly to an FTP site.

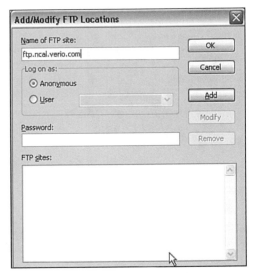

Figure 20.11 To create an FTP location where you can save your presentation, enter the address of the FTP site and click Add.

Saving a Presentation to an FTP Site

It's almost scary how fast you can make a presentation available today. Instead of saving your presentation to your hard drive or network drive, you can save it directly to an FTP site. That way, anyone with access to the FTP site can download the file and open it in PowerPoint.

Before you start, you may need to contact your Internet Service Provider to get the address of your FTP site, the location where you can store files, and a user name and password.

To save a presentation to an FTP site:

1. Connect to the Internet.

2. In PowerPoint, choose File > Save As.

3. Change the filename, if desired.

4. Click the arrow in the Save in field and choose FTP Locations (**Figure 20.10**).

5. If you haven't yet created any FTP locations, click Add/Modify FTP Locations. If you have already set up an FTP location, skip to step 9.

6. In the Add/Modify FTP Locations dialog box (**Figure 20.11**), in the Name of FTP Site field, enter the address of the FTP site.

7. If a password is required, select the User radio button and then enter your user name and password.

continues on next page

SAVING A PRESENTATION TO AN FTP SITE

8. Click Add and then click OK.

The FTP location now appears in the Save As dialog box (**Figure 20.12**).

9. Double-click the name of the FTP site to connect to it.

10. After PowerPoint has found the site, navigate to the folder to which you want to save the presentation. Click Save.

✔ Tip

■ Before saving to an FTP site, make sure you save locally. You do not want your only current copy of a presentation to be on an FTP site. So get in the habit of saving twice when finishing your edits: Save once normally and then do a Save As to place it on the FTP site.

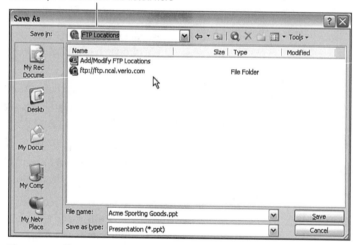

Names of FTP locations are listed here

Figure 20.12 You can save your presentation to an FTP site in the Save As dialog box.

Figure 20.13 This slide has good contrast between the background and slide elements.

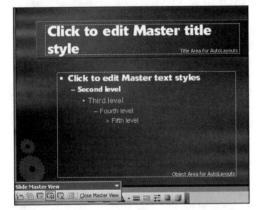

Figure 20.14 Edit the Slide Master to give your Web page consistent formatting.

Creating a Web Page

Designing a Web page is similar to designing a presentation for onscreen slide shows. That means, all of the standard admonishments are in order:

◆ Give careful thought to your color scheme. Be sure that there is sufficient contrast between the slide background and the text and other objects on the slide (**Figure 20.13**).

◆ Whenever possible, format the Slide Master instead of individual slides (**Figure 20.14**). This way, your presentation will be formatted consistently throughout.

See Chapter 12 for information on editing the Slide Master.

◆ Resist the temptation to get too fancy; for best viewability, be conservative with your typefaces, background fills, and special effects. Many of the templates included with PowerPoint will produce attractive and consistently formatted Web pages.

See "Applying a Template" in Chapter 12 for more information about applying templates.

◆ And finally, just because you *can*, doesn't mean you *should*. PowerPoint is about the worst program you can use to design a Web site or Web page and should be used only if absolutely nothing else is available.

Saving a PowerPoint File for the Web

If you would like to post a PowerPoint presentation on the Internet or email a slide show to someone who doesn't have PowerPoint, you can easily create an HTML file of your presentation. When PowerPoint converts your presentation, the HTML file will use the same color scheme, fonts, background, transition effects, animations, and links as your PowerPoint presentation.

To save a presentation as a Web page:

1. Choose File > Save as Web Page.

2. Click Publish.

   The Publish as Web Page dialog box appears (**Figure 20.15**).

3. In the Publish What area, choose what you want to publish.

4. In the Browser Support area, select the browsers that will be used to view your presentation. (Today, it's a safe bet that your visitors will be using IE4.0 or later.)

5. In the File Name field, confirm the path to your new folder and change the file-name if desired.

6. Change other settings, if necessary.

7. Click Web Options and select the General tab (**Figure 20.16**).

Uncheck this box to remove the notes pane

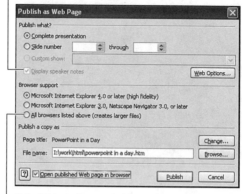

Select this option to enable any browser to view the Web page

Figure 20.15 Select your options in the Publish as Web Page dialog box.

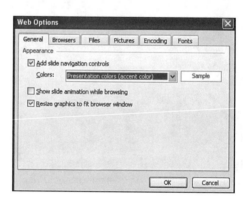

Figure 20.16 The General tab is one of six tabs used for setting Web options.

Hyperlinks in navigation pane *Current slide*

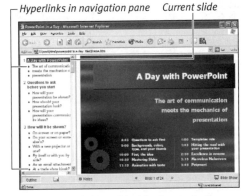

Figure 20.17 Clicking slide titles in a navigation pane helps the user to navigate your presentation.

Uncheck to place supporting files and Web page in a single folder. If you do this, however, you'll want to create a folder for all the files.

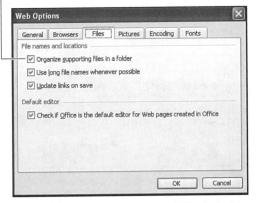

Figure 20.18 On the Files tab, you can indicate whether you want to place all supporting files in the same folder as the Web page or separate them in a subfolder.

Create New Folder tool

Figure 20.19 Create a new folder for your HTML files.

8. If your show requires the viewer to manually advance the slides, make sure the Add Slide Navigation Controls check box is selected. This gives the user a navigation pane on the left side of the window (**Figure 20.17**). If your presentation is self-running, remove the check mark from this box.

If you use the navigation pane, try to give every slide a title so that it will show up without a blank line next to the number. Remember, if you have a slide that uses a blank slide layout, it will appear with no text in the navigation pane. To correct this, change the Blank layout to a Title Only layout, then drag the title placeholder off the edge of the slide so it doesn't show on the slide itself.

9. Select the Files tab (**Figure 20.18**).

10. To place the Web page and its supporting files in a single folder, remove the check mark from the Organize Supporting Files in a Folder box.

or

To place the image files (such as bullets, background textures, graphics, and navigational buttons) in a subfolder, select the Organize Supporting Files check box.

Very important: If you uncheck the Organize the Supporting Files check box, you will want to use the Create New Folder tool (**Figure 20.19**) to create a folder for the Web page and its supporting files when you save your Web page. The Save As Web Page operation often creates many files, and it is helpful to keep them in one place. It is also important to be able to create the same folder hierarchy on your Web site so that paths to images and links will work properly.

continues on next page

345

11. Select the Pictures tab (**Figure 20.20**).

12. In the Screen Size field, select the desired resolution (800 x 600 is a safe bet for most systems).

13. Select the Browsers tab (**Figure 20.21**).

14. Make sure the Rely on VML for Displaying Graphics in Browsers check box is selected.

15. If you want the Web page to save as MHT (an one-page HTML file), save new Web pages as Single File Web Pages. If you want the Web page to save as HTM/HTML, deselect this option.

This setting can also be reached from PowerPoint's Tools > Options. On the General Tab, press the Web Options button. This brings up the same dialog as clicking Web Options from the Save As Web > Publish button. Changing this default setting in PowerPoint also changes the default behavior in both Word and Excel.

16. Change other settings on the other tabs, if desired, and then click OK.

17. In the Publish as Web Page dialog box, to see the Web page in your default browser, select the Open Published Web Page in Browser check box. This is not a preview option, it's a "postview." This opens the page in your browser after it's been published.

18. To create the Web page, click Publish.

After the file is created, the first slide in the show will appear in your default browser (**Figure 20.17**).

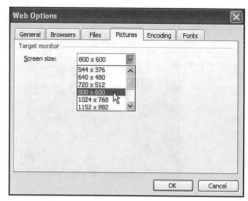

Figure 20.20 On the Pictures tab, select the screen size for the target monitor.

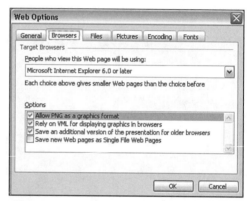

Figure 20.21 In the Browsers tab, select Rely on VML for Displaying Graphics in Browsers.

✔ Tips

■ There are two options for Web page creation: standard Web page and single file Web page. The latter creates one large file (with an .mht extension) with all of the elements needed. It is handy for organizational purposes, but it could make for a gigantic download. Therefore, it is popular for local and intranet situations.

■ To get an idea of what your presentation looks like as a Web page before you actually create the page, use the File > Web Page Preview command. This command is actually identical to the real thing, except it creates the file in a temp folder and then deletes it when you are done viewing it.

■ View your Web page in a variety of browsers (and different versions of each browser) to make sure it looks and functions as you intended.

■ There is an important difference between using File > Save as Web Page and using File > Save As and choosing Web Page as the file type. Using the Save as Web Page command is like an export command–it doesn't change the format of your open presentation. But using File > Save As > Web Page converts your open presentation into HTML format. Probably not what you want....

■ Creating a Web page from your presentation file does result in some noticeable loss of fidelity. Graphics are compressed, not all animations run as smoothly, and slides do not transition as seamlessly. If this is an issue, you are advised to post a PowerPoint Show (*.pps) file as well as the Web page, giving visitors their choice.

■ No matter what you choose to post on your Web site, watch file sizes carefully. Robust PowerPoint presentations, whether saved as .pps or .htm, can become very big in a hurry.

Previewing a Slide Show in a Web Browser

After you save your PowerPoint presentation as a Web page, you can view it as a slide show in any browser to see what it will look like on the Web. (At this point, you don't need to be connected to the Internet because your Web page is stored on your hard disk.)

To view a slide show in your default Web browser:

1. Choose View > Toolbars > Web to display the Web toolbar (**Figure 20.22**).

2. In the Address field on the Web toolbar, type the complete pathname and filename of the Web page and then press Enter.

   or

   Choose Go > Hyperlink and browse to the Web page file (**Figure 20.23**).

   The presentation's first slide appears in your browser window (**Figure 20.24**).

3. Use the navigation pane on the left to jump to other slides. (You can also provide navigation buttons if you enable them in the publishing options.)

   or

   If the slide show is self-running, your browser will automatically advance the slides in your presentation.

   If the slide show animates "on mouse click," the slides and animations will remain this way in the HTML version. Your viewers will need to know to click somewhere other than the Next Slide button in order to see the animation.

Go button ⌐ *Address field* ⌐

Figure 20.22 You can use the Web toolbar to open Web pages.

⌐ *Click Browse to find a file*

Figure 20.23 Use the Go button on the Web toolbar to browse to a Web page.

Slide titles

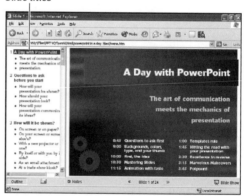

Figure 20.24 Click a slide title to display the slide in the browser window.

To view a show in other browsers:

1. Launch the browser.

2. Choose File > Open, navigate to the folder in which you saved the Web page, and select the filename.

3. To view other slides, click the slide title in the navigation pane on the left.

✔ Tip

■ When you use the Web toolbar to open a Web page, you are essentially opening the page in Internet Explorer. However, Windows manages the relationship between IE and PowerPoint so that clicking Back closes IE and returns you to PowerPoint.

PREVIEWING A SLIDE SHOW IN A WEB BROWSER

INDEX

Numbers

3-D Chart command (Chart menu), 111
3-D View command (Chart menu), 94
3-D View dialog box, 94, 111
3D effects
  charts, adjusting effects, 93-94
  graphical objects, 177-178
  pie charts, 110-111

A

abbreviated menu systems, 6
Acrobat Distiller, 334
Acrobat toolbars, 334
Action Button command (Slide Show menu), 260
  Custom option, 261
  Return option, 262
action buttons
  creating, 260-261
  customizing, 261
  Web site links, 339
Action Settings dialog box, 260
Add Clips to Organizer command (File menu), 181, 186
Add Custom Chart Type dialog box, 97
Add Effect menu commands, Entrance Effect, 286
Add/Modify FTP Locations dialog box, 341
Adobe Acrobat, creating PDF file, 334
agenda slides, 265-266
align left (Ctrl+L), 150
Align or Distribute command (Draw menu), 199-200
align right (Ctrl+R), 150
aligning graphical objects, 199
Alignment command (Format menu), 53
All Borders border buttons, 145
All Connecting Lines command (Select menu), 130
Always Show Full Menus command (Tools menu), 6
animation
  bulleted list, 279-281, 285
  charts, 288-289
  enhancements, 282-284
  schemes, 276-278
  Slide Master, 290-292

transitions, 274-275
triggers, 286-287
utilizing, 30
annotations, slide show, 267-268
anti-aliasing text fonts, xvii
Apply Slide Layout pane, 34
Arrange All command (Windows menu), 251
arrows, graphical objects
  drawing, 163
  formatting, 164
Assistance page, Help menu, 10
attributes
  copying format, 57
  graphical objects, copying, 202
Audio Video Interleave (AVI), 294
AutoCorrect command (Tools menu), 41
AutoCorrect dialog box, 41
AutoCorrect Options command (Tools menu), Smart Tags option, 42
autoformatting, removing, 129
Automatic Layout, xvii
Autoshape command (Format menu), 166
  Basic Shapes option, 169
  Size tab, 204
AutoShapes
  graphical objects, 169
  customizing, 170
AutoSum buttons, 157
AVI (Audio Video Interleave), 294
axis
  formatting numbers, 91
  scaling, 89-90

B

Background command (Format menu), 214
Background dialog box, 214
Backspace key, 35
Basic Shapes command (AutoShape menu), 169
bitmap images, scaling, 205
blended colors
  creating, 214-215
  two colors, 216-217

borders
  button description, 145
  tables, 144-147
Bottom Border border buttons, 145
bulleted lists
  animation, 279-281, 285
  charts, 288-289
  creating, 18
  enhancements, 282-284
  Outline view, 232
  placement, 49
  schemes, 276-278
  shape selection, 47-48
  Slide Master, 290-292
  transitions, 274-275
  triggers, 286-287
  utilizing, 30
Bullets and Numbering command (Format menu),
    18, 46-47
Bullets and Numbering dialog box, 46

C

Cancel Printing command (Document menu), 328
category axis (x-axis), 61
  formatting numbers, 91
  scaling, 89-90
CD Audio Options dialog box, 300
CDs
  packaging presentation, 314-315
  playing sound tracks, 300-301
cells, tables
  aligning text, 150-151
  selection, 137
  shading, 148-149
centering (Ctrl+E) shortcut key, 150
Change AutoShape command (Draw menu), 129
Change Case command (Format menu), 43
Change Case dialog box, 43
Change Source option (Link dialog box), 66
chart boxes, formatting, 128-129
Chart menu commands
  3-D View, 94, 111
  Chart Options, 69, 104
    Data Labels option, 103
    Gridlines tab, 86
  Chart Type, 21, 67, 96-97
    Doughnut option, 113
    Pie option, 101
  Selected Axis Title, 69
Chart Options command (Chart menu), 69, 104
    Data Labels option, 103
    Gridlines option, 86
  Format menu, Legend, 72
Chart Options dialog box, 86
  Data Labels tab, 70, 103-104
  Titles tab, 69
Chart Type command (Chart menu), 21, 67, 96-97
  Doughnut, 113
  Pie, 101
Chart Type dialog box, 21, 67, 96-97

charts
  animation, 288-289
  creating, 19-20, 62-63
  data entry, 64
  data labels, 70-71
  formatting. See formatting, charts
  Graph, 60
  importing data, 65
  inserting title, 69
  legends, formatting, 22
  linking data, 66
  organization. See organization charts
  pie. See pie charts
  revisions, 72
  selecting type, 21
  terminology, 61
  two charts on one slide, 73
  type selection, 67-68
Check Style command (Tools menu), 44
Clip Art command (Insert menu), 183
Clip Art task pane, 302
Clip Organizer, xx, 180-182, 302-303
Close and Return to command (File menu), 153
close buttons, 5
Close command (File menu), 25
Collapse All tool, 235
collapsing outlines, 233-234
Color/Grayscale command (View menu), 323
colors
  adding, 51-52
  defaults, changing, 212-213
  gradient fills
    creating, 214-215
    two colors, 216-217
  graphical objects, 171
  preview in grayscale, 323
  shadow adjustment, 175-176
Colors dialog box, 171, 203
columns
  sum formulas, 157
  table
    deleting, 141
    inserting, 140
    width adjustment, 138
commands
  Add Effect menu, Entrance Effect, 286
  AutoShape menu, Basic Shapes, 169
  Chart menu. See Chart menu commands
  Data menu. See Data menu commands
  Document menu, Cancel Printing, 328
  Draw menu. See Draw menu commands
  Edit menu. See Edit menu commands
  File menu. See File menu commands
  Format menu. See Format menu commands
  Help menu, Show the Office Assistant, 10, 44
  Insert menu. See Insert menu commands
  Pointer Options menu. See Pointer Options
    menu commands
  Screen menu, Speaker Notes, 271
  Select menu, All Connecting Lines, 130
  Slide Show menu. See Slide Show menu commands

Start menu, Control Panel, 312, 322
Table menu. *See* Table menu commands
Tools menu. *See* Tools menu commands
View menu. *See* View meu commands
Windows menu, Arrange All, 251
computers, matching resolution, 306
connector lines
    formatting, 130
    graphical objects, 165
Content area, xx
Control Panel command (Start menu), 312
    Printers and Faxes option, 322
Copy command (Edit menu), 66
copying
    graphical object attributes, 202
    slides, Slide Sorter view, 248-252
    text placeholders, 37
creating
    bulleted list, 18
    charts, 19-20
    text slides
        AutoCorrect, 41
        bullet placement, 49
        bullet shape selection, 47-48
        Change Case command, 43
        color, 51-52
        copying formatting attributes, 57
        cutting text, 38
        dragging and dropping text, 39
        effects, 51-52
        font, 50
        formatting placeholder, 54
        layout selection, 34
        line spacing, 55-56
        numbering list automatically, 46
        paragraph alignment, 53
        paragraph spacing, 55-56
        pasting text, 38
        placeholders, 35-37
        smart tag, 42
        spell checker, 40
        style inconsistencies, 44
        style preferences, 45
        text boxes, 36
Crop tool, 206
cropping, pictures, 206-207
current slide indicator, 5
Curved connector lines, 165
Custom Animation command (Slide Show menu), 280
Custom Animation task pane, 9, 278-280
customizing
    animation schemes, 278
    buttons, creating, 261
    charts, 96-98
    shows, 263-264
Custom Shows command (Slide Show menu), 263
Custom Shows dialog box, 263
Customize command
    Format menu, 47
    Tools menu , 6-7
Cut command (Edit menu), 38

cutting, text, 38
cycle diagrams, 124

D

data
    charts
        entering, 64
        importing, 65
        labels, 70-71
        linking, 66
    markers, formatting, 84-85
    pie charts
        entering data, 102
        labels, 103-106
        linked pies, 115
    points, 61
    series, 61
        color change, 79
        graphics file, 82-83
        patterns, 80-81
        textures, 80-81
Data labels
    formatting, 105
    tab, 104
    text, 106
Data menu commands
    Exclude Row/Col, 64, 102
    Series in Columns, 64, 102, 115
datasheet, chart
    entering data, 64
    importing data, 65
    linking data, 66
Define Custom Show dialog box, 263
Delete Columns command (Table menu), 141
Delete key, 35
Delete Rows command (Table menu), 141
Delete Slide command (Edit menu), 236, 250
deleting
    columns, 141
    rows, 141
    slides, 235-236
    Slide Sorter view, 250
    table borders, 145-146
Diagonal Down Border buttons, 145
Diagonal Up Border border buttons, 145
Diagram Gallery, xx, 120
Diagram objects, 120
    editing, 121-125
    type selection, 124
Diagram toolbar, 124
diagrams, 118-119
    chart boxes
        box formatting, 129
        text formatting, 128
    connecting lines, formatting, 130
    customizing, 126-127
    editing diagram objects, 120-125
    Zoom option, 131
Distribute Horizontally command (Draw menu), 200
Distribute Vertically command (Draw menu), 200

Document menu commands, Cancel Printing, 328
doughnut charts, 113
"drag and dupe" slides, 248
dragging, text, 39
Draw menu commands
    Align or Distribute, 199
        Relative to Slide option, 200
    Change AutoShape, 129
    Distribute Horizontally, 200
    Distribute Vertically, 200
    Flip, 210
    Group, 201
    Order, 208
    Regroup, 201
    Rotate, 210
    Ungroup, 201
Draw Table tool, 147
drawing table borders, 147
Drawing command (View menu), 36, 126
Drawing tool, graphical objects, 194
Drawing toolbar, 5, 73
    Clip Art
        inserting, 183-184
        online search, 187
        searching, 185-186
    embedding graphics, 190
    graphical objects. See graphical objects
    Text Box tool, 36
dropping text, 39
Duplicate command (Edit menu), 249
dynamic toolbars, utilizing, 7

E

Edit Color Scheme dialog box, 212
Edit menu commands
    Copy, 66
    Cut, 38
    Delete Slide, 236, 250
    Duplicate, 249
    Import File, 65
    Links, 66
    Movie Object, 309
    Paste, 38
    Paste Link, 66
    Paste Special, 190
    Redo, 11
    Sound Object, 309
    Undo, 11, 141
editing
    Diagram objects, 121-125
    Notes Master, 332
    Slide Master, 219
effects, adding, 51-52
ellipses, graphical objects, 166
embedding graphics, 190
Emphasis effect, 280
End key, 35
Entrance effect, 280
Entrance Effect command (Add Effect menu), 286
Eraser tool, 147
erasing table borders, 147

Excel spreadsheets, formulas, 158
Exclude Row/Col command (Data menu), 64, 102
Exit effect, 280
expanding outlines, 233-234

F

faxes, send to, xvi
File menu commands
    Add Clips to Organizer, 181, 186
    Close, 25
    Close and Return to, 153
    Open, 25
    Package for CD, 313
    Print, 26, 322-324
    Print Preview, 26
    Properties, Statistics, 309
    Save As, 24, 310
        Presentation for Review option, 316
        Web Page option, 347
    Save as Web Page, 344
    Send To
        Mail Recipient option, 316
        Microsoft Word option, 326
    Web Page Preview, 347
files
    Clip Organizer, 181-182
    copying linked files, 309
    graphics
        data series, 82-83
        inserting, 188-189
    HTML, creating, 344-347
    PDF, creating, 334
    .pps show file, opening without starting
        PowerPoint, 311-312
Fill Color tool, 171, 174
Fill Effects dialog box, 80
    Gradient tab, 172, 214
    Picture tab, 174
Flip command (Draw menu), 210
Flip Horizontal command, 210
Flip Vertical command, 210
flipping graphical objects, 210
flowcharts
    chart boxes
        box formatting, 129
        text formatting, 128
    connecting lines, formatting, 130
    customizing, 126-127
    Zoom option, 131
Font command (Format menu), 50-51, 70, 92, 128
Font dialog box, 50-51, 128
Font tab, 106
fonts
    changing, 50
    global changes, replacing, 218
    managing, 310
    text, anti-aliasing, xvii
footers, global change, inserting, 224-225
Format AutoShape dialog box, 54, 161, 204

INDEX

Format Axis dialog box, 88
    Number tab, 91
    Scale tab, 89
Format Axis Title dialog box, 69
Format Data Labels dialog box, 70
    Alignment tab, 71
    Number tab, 105
Format Data Point dialog box, Patterns tab, 108
Format Data Series dialog box
    Options tab, 93, 109
    Patterns tab, 79
Format dialog box, 22, 92
Format Gridlines dialog box, 87
Format Legend dialog box, 22
    Patterns tab, 77
    Placement tab, 78
Format menu commands
    Alignment, 53
    Autoshape, 166
        Size tab, 204
    Background, 214
    Bullets and Numbering, 18, 46-47
    Change Case, 43
    Chart Options, 72
    Font, 50-51, 70, 92, 128
    Line Spacing, 55
    Master Layout, 225
    Picture, 203
    Placeholder, 54
    Replace Font, 218
    Selected Axis, 88
        Number tab, 91
        Scale tab, 89
    Selected Data Labels, 70
        Font tab, 106
        Number tab, 105
    Selected Data Point
        Options tab, 109
        Patterns tab, 108
    Selected Data Series, 68, 79-80, 93
    Selected Gridlines, 87
    Selected Legend, 77
    Selected Plot Area, 95
    Slide Design, 212, 226, 276
    Slide Layout, 34
    Table, 146
Format Painter tool, 57, 202
Format Picture dialog box, Picture tab, 203
Format Plot Area dialog box, 95
Format Table dialog box, 146
formatting
    arrows, graphical objects, 164
    charts, 22, 76
        3D effects, 93-94
        axis numbers, 91
        axis scaling, 89-90
        boxes, 128-129
        custom chart types, 96-98
        data markers, 84-85
        data series, 79-83
        gridlines, 86-87

        legend, 77-78
        plot area, 95
        text, 92
        tick marks, 88
    connecting lines, 130
    copying attributes, 57
    data labels, 105-106
    handout pages, 326
    lines, graphical objects, 161-162
    table borders, 144
    text
        placeholder, 54
        tables, 142-143
Formatting command (View menu), 57
Formatting toolbars, 7
Formula command (Table menu), 158
Formula dialog box, 158
formulas, Word tables, 157-158
Freeform tool, 167
freehand drawings, graphical objects, 167-168
FTP sites, saving presentation, 341-342

G

global changes
    default colors, changing, 212-213
    font, replacing, 21,
    footers, inserting, 224-225
    gradient fills
        creating, 214-215
        two colors, 216-217
    graphics, adding, 223
    Slide Master, 211
        editing, 219
        multiple, 221
    templates, 226-227
    text, changing default, 222
    Title Master, inserting, 220
gradient fills, 172-173
    creating, 214-215
    two colors, 216-217
Graph charts, 60
graphical objects. See also graphics; images
    3D effects, 177-178
    aligning, 199
    arrows
        drawing, 163
        formatting, 164
    attributes, copying, 202
    AutoShapes, 169-170
    color filling, 171
    connector lines, 165
    Drawing toolbar, 159
    flipping, 210
    freehand drawings, 167-168
    graphics file, 174
    grid snap, 195
    grouping, 201
    guides, 194
    lines
        drawing, 160
        formatting, 161-162

ovals, 166
pattern filling, 172-173
picture, cropping, 206-207
polygons, 167-168
recoloring picture, 203
rectangles, 166
rotating, 209
rulers, 194
scaling, 204-205
shadow, 175-176
slide miniature, 198
snap-to-shape, 196
spacing, 200
stacking order, 208
zoom in and out, 197
graphics. *See also* graphical objects; images
clip art
inserting, 183-184
online search, 187
searching, 185-186
Clip Organizer, 180
adding files, 181-182
design enhancements, xviii
embedding, 190
files
data series, 82-83
filling an object, 174
global change
adding, 223
inserting files, 188
multiple graphics, 189
grayscale, previewing slides, 323
Grayscale View toolbar, 323
Grid and Guides dialog box, 194
grid snaps, graphical objects, 195
gridlines, 61
formatting, 87
inserting, 86
removing, 86
visible, xviii
Grids and Guides command (View menu), 194
Group command (Draw menu), 201
groups, graphical objects, 201
guides, graphical objects, 194

H

Handout Master View toolbar, 326
handout pages
formatting, 326
printing, 327
Header and Footer command (View menu), 224, 326
Header and Footer dialog box, 224
Help menu commands
Show the Office Assistant, 10, 44
utilizing, 10
hidden slides, 256-257
Hide Slide command (Slide Show menu), 257
hiding toolbars, 7
Home key, 35
HTML files, creating, 344-347

Hyperlink command (Insert menu), 337
Hyperlink to URL dialog box, 339
hyperlinks, 337-340

I

images. *See also* graphical objects; graphics
clip art
inserting, 183-184
online search, 187
searching, 185-186
graphics files, 188-189
Import Data Options dialog box, 65
Import File command (Edit menu), 65
Import File dialog box, 65
importing outlines, 238-239
Ink Color command (Pointer Options menu), 268
Insert Clip Art task pane, 185
Insert command (Table menu), 152
Insert Hyperlink dialog box, 337
Insert menu commands
Hyperlink, 337
Movies and Sounds, 294
Movie from Clip Organizer option, 302
Play CD Audio Track option, 300
Sound from File option, 298
New Slide, 18, 34
New Slide Master, 221
New Title Master, 220
Object
Excel Spreadsheet option, 158
Microsoft Word Picture option, 152
Picture
Clip Art option, 183
From File option, 188
New Photo Album option, 189
Slides from Files, 253
Slides from Outline, 238
Table, 135
Insert Movie dialog box, 294
Insert Outline dialog box, 238
Insert Picture dialog box, 188
Insert Rows Above command (Table menu), 140
Insert Rows Below command (Table menu), 140
Insert Sound dialog box, 298
Insert Table dialog box, 153
inserting
clip art, 183-184
columns, 140
presentation, Slide Sorter view, 253-254
rows, 140
Slide Master, multiple, 221
table slide, 134-135
Title Master, 220
Inside Borders border buttons, 145
Inside Horizontal border buttons, 145
Inside Vertical border buttons, 145
interfaces, 5
Internet
designing Web page, 343
FTP site, saving presentation, 341-342

INDEX

improvements, xviii
linking presentation to Web site, 337-340
previewing slide show in Web Browser, 348-349
saving presentation as Web page, 344-347

J-K

JawsPDF Creator, 334
justify (Ctrl+J), 150

Keep Source Formatting, 252
keyboard shortcuts, 6
 Ctrl+A (Select All command), 6, 137
 Ctrl+E (center), 150
 Ctrl+F4 (Close command), 25
 Ctrl+Home key, 23
 Ctrl+J (justify), 150
 Ctrl+L (align left), 150
 Ctrl+left arrow, 35
 Ctrl+M (New Slide command), 18, 34
 Ctrl+P (Print command), 26
 Ctrl+R (align right), 150
 Ctrl+right arrow, 35
 Ctrl+S (Save As command), 24
 Ctrl+V (Paste command), 38
 Ctrl+X (Cut command), 38
 Ctrl+Y (Bullets and Numbering command), 46
 Ctrl+Y (Redo command), 11
 Ctrl+Z (Undo command), 11
 Shift+F5 (slide show from current slide), xvi, 258

L

launching, 14
layers, graphical objects, 208
layouts, 5, 17
LCD projectors, 306
leader lines, pie charts, 104
Left Border border buttons, 145
Legend command (Chart Options menu), 72
legends, 61
 formatting, 22, 77
 positioning, 78
Line Spacing command (Format menu), 55
Line Spacing dialog box, 55
lines
 graphical objects
  drawing, 160
  formatting, 161-162
 leader, pie charts, 104
 organization charts, formatting, 130
 spacing, 55-56
Link dialog box
 Change Source option, 66
 Open Source option, 66
Link to Custom Show dialog box, 266
links
 creating to Web site, 337-340
 files, copying, 309
 pie charts, 114-115
Links command (Edit menu), 66

lists
 bulleted
  animation, 279-281, 285
  Outline view, 232
 text slides, numbering automatically, 46

M

Master command (View menu)
 Handout Master, 326
 Notes Master, 332
 Slide Master, 219
Master Layout command (Format menu), 225
masters
 Handout Master, 326
 multiple, xvii
 Notes Master, 332
 Slide Master. *See* Slide Master
 Title Master, inserting global changes, 220
menus.
 bar, 5
 shortcut, utilizing, 6-8
Microsoft Graph, 60
 charts. *See* charts
 formatting charts, 21
 pie charts. *See* pie charts
Microsoft Web site, 187, 336
Microsoft Word, sending file to, 326
miniatures, slide, 198
minimize buttons, 5
misspelled words, spell checker, 40
mistakes
 AutoCorrect, 41
 utilizing undo, 11
Modify Style dialog box, 156
monitors, multiple, xvii
monochrome printers, grayscale previewing, 323
Movie Object command (Edit menu), 309
movies
 Clip Organizer, 302-303
 clips
  adding sound, 298-299
  inserting, 294-295
  playback, 296-297
Movies and Sounds command (Insert menu), 294
Movie from Clip Organizer, 302
 Play CD Audio Track, 300
 Sound from File, 298
Moving Picture Experts Group (MPEG), 294
MPEG (Moving Picture Experts Group), 294
multimedia
 CDs, 300-301
 Clip Organizer, 302-303
 movie clips
  adding sound, 298-299
  inserting, 294-295
  playback, 296-297
multimedia clips, 309
multiple masters, xvii

N

navigation
    presentations, 23
    slide show, 258-259
new features, xv
New Photo Album command (Insert menu), 189
New Slide command (Insert menu), 18, 34, 62
New Slide Master command (Insert menu), 221
New Title Master command (Insert menu), 220
next slide buttons, 5
No Border border buttons, 145
Normal command (View menu), 27, 198, 230
Normal view, xv
    adding speaker notes, 330-331
    hyperlinks, 338
    Outline pane, 28
    utilizing, 27
normal view buttons, 5
notes
    area, 5
    global changes with Notes Master, 332
    slide show, 271
    speaker
        adding to slides, 330-331
        printing, 333
Notes Master, editing notes, 332
Notes Page command (View menu), 271, 330
Notes Page view, adding speaker notes, 330-331
Number tab, 105
numbering
    data labels, formatting, 105
    text slides, 46

O

Object command (Insert menu)
    Excel Spreadsheet option, 158
    Microsoft Word Picture option, 152
Office Run Time plug-in, installing, 336
Office XP, Compress Pictures technology, xviii
Open command (File menu), 25
Open dialog box, 25
Open Source option (Link dialog box), 66
opening presentations, 25
Options command (Tools menu)
    General option, 309
    Save option, 308
    Security option, 319
    Spelling and Style option, 40
    Spelling and Style option (Check Style), 44
    Spelling and Style option (Style Options), 45
Options tab, 109
Order command (Draw menu), 208
organization, slides, 256-257
Organization Chart Style Gallery, 122-123
organization charts
    chart boxes
        box formatting, 129
        text formatting, 128
    connecting lines, formatting, 130
    customizing, 126-127

    Diagram objects, 120-125
    uses, 118-119
    Zoom option, 131
Organize the Supporting Files check box, 345
Outline pane, 28
Outline view, xv, 229
    bulleted lists, 232
    collapsing outline, 233-234
    expanding outline, 233-234
    importing outline, 238-239
    presentation outlining, 231
    printing outline, 329
    slides
        deleting, 235-236
        rearranging, 235-236
    summary slide, 240-241
    text formatting, 237
    utilizing, 230
outlines
    importing, 238-239
    printing, 329
Outlining command (View menu), 28
Outlining toolbar, 233
Outside Borders border buttons, 145
Oval tool, 166
ovals, graphical objects, 166
overlap, graphical objects, 208

P

Pack and Go, xvi
Package for CD command (File menu), xvi, 313
Page Down key, 23
Page Up key, 23
paragraphs
    alignment, 53
    spacing, 55-56
passwords, creating, 319
Paste command (Edit menu), 38
Paste Link command (Edit menu), 66
Paste Smart Tag, 252
Paste Special command (Edit menu), 190
Paste Special dialog box, 190
pasting text, 38
patterns
    data series, 80-81
    graphical objects, 172-173
Patterns tab, 108
Pause Movie dialog box, 297
PDF files, creating, 334
Pen Color command (Pointer Options menu), 268
pen options, 267-268
Photo Album
    dialog box, 189
    inserting multiple graphics, 189
Picture Bullet dialog box, 48
Picture command
    Format menu, 203
    Insert menu
        Clip Art option, 183
        From File option, 188
        New Photo Album option, 189

Picture option (Bullets and Numbering dialog box), 48
Picture toolbar, 206
pictures
    cropping, 206-207
    recoloring, 203
pie charts
    3D effects, 110-111
    data labels, 103
        formatting, 105-106
        leader lines, 104
    doughnut chart, 113
    entering data, 102
    inserting slide, 100-101
    linked pies, 114-115
    pie slices
        coloring, 108
        exploding, 107
        rotating, 109
    repositioning, 112
    resizing, 112
Pinwheel dialog box, 286
Placeholder command (Format menu), 54
placeholders
    copying, 37
    entering text, 35
    formatting text, 54
    moving, 37
    resizing, 37
    title, summary slide, 246
Play Sound dialog box, 299
playback, movie clips, 296-297
plot area, formatting, 95
Pointer Options menu commands
    Ink Color, 268
    Pen Color, 268
polygons, graphical objects, 167-168
Portable Document Format files (PDF files),
        creating, 334
PowerPoint 2002
    creativity, 2-3
    new features, xv-xvi
.pps show file
    opening without starting PowerPoint, 311-312
    versus .ppt file, 312
.ppt file versus .pps show file, 312
presentations
    closing, 25
    fonts, managing, 310
    importing outline, 238-239
    Internet, linking to Web site, 337-340
    navigation, 23
    opening, 25
    outline, 231, 329
    packaging on CD, 314-315
    passwords, creating, 319
    .pps show files, 311-312
    printing, 26, 324-325
        handout pages, 326-327
        stopping job, 328

review, 316-317
    merging, 317
    revising reviews, 317-318
    sending, 316
saving, 24
    FTP site, 341-342
    as Web page, 344-347
saving in earlier version of PowerPoint, 308
showing on another computer, 306-310
Slide Sorter view
    copying slides, 248-249
    copying slides between two presentations, 251-252
    deleting slides, 250
    inserting, 253-254
    reordering slides, 247
    summary slide, 246
    utilizing, 244
    zoom, 245
spell checker, 40
summary slide, 240-241
title, 5
Viewer, 313
viewing with PDF file, 334
preset animations
    modification, 278
    utilizing, 276-277
preview
    in grayscale, 323
    slide show in Web Browser, 348-349
Preview/Properties dialog box, 302
previous slide buttons, 5
Print command (File menu), 26, 322-324
Print dialog box, 26, 321-322
Print Preview command (File menu), xvii, 26, 321
Printer and Faxes command (Start menu), 322
printers
    preview in grayscale, 323
    selection, 322
printing
    handout pages
        formatting, 326
        printing, 327
    outline, 329
    presentations, 26
    preview slides in grayscale, 323
    printer selection, 322
    slides, 324-325
    speaker notes, 333
    stopping job, 328
projectors, 306
    multiple, xvii
Properties command (File menu), Statistics, 309
Properties dialog box, 322
protection, creating password, 319
Publish as Web Page dialog box, 344
pyramid diagrams, 124

INDEX

Q-R

radial diagrams, 124
Recolor Picture dialog box, 203
recoloring pictures, 203
Rectangle tool, 166
rectangles, graphical objects, 166
Redo command (Edit menu), 11
Regroup command (Draw menu), 201
Rehearsal dialog box, 270
Rehearse Timings command (Slide Show menu), 270
Replace Font command (Format menu), 218
Replace Font dialog box, 218
Research Task pane, xvi
resizing
    graphical objects, 204-205
    pie charts, 112
    text placeholders, 37
resolutions, matching, 306
restore/maximize buttons, 5
return buttons, creating, 262
review, presentations, 316-317
    merging, 317
    revising reviews, 317-318
    sending, 316
revisions, presentation review, 317-318
Right Border border buttons, 145
Rotate command (Draw menu), 210
rotation, xviii
    graphical objects, 209
    pie slices, 109
rows
    sum formulas, 157
    table
        deleting, 141
        height adjustment, 139
        inserting, 140
Ruler command (View menu), 49, 194
rulers, graphical objects, 194

S

Save As command (File menu), 24, 310
    Presentation for Review option, 316
    Web Page option, 347
Save As dialog box, 24
Save as Web Page command (File menu), 344
saving
    in earlier versions PowerPoint, 308
    presentation, 24
        as Web page, 344-347
scaling, graphical objects, 204-205
schemes, animation
    modification, 278
    utilizing, 276-277
Screen menu command, Speaker Notes, 271
Scribble tool, 167
scroll bars
    slide, 5
    task pane, 5
Search command (Tools menu), 174
security, creating password, 319

Select menu commands, All Connecting Lines, 130
Select Picture dialog box, 82, 174
Selected Axis command (Format menu), 88
    Number tab, 91
    Scale tab, 89
Selected Axis Title command (Chart menu), 69
Selected Data Labels command (Format menu), 70
    Font tab, 106
    Number tab, 105
Selected Data Point command (Format menu)
    Options tab, 109
    Patterns tab, 108
Selected Data Series command (Format menu),
    68, 79-80, 93
Selected Gridlines command (Format menu), 87
Selected Legend command (Format menu), 77
Selected Plot Area command (Format menu), 95
self-running slide shows, 269
Send Backward command, 208
Send Forward command, 208
Send To command (File menu)
    Mail Recipient option, 316
    Microsoft Word option, 326
series axis, 61
Series in Columns command (Data menu), 64, 102, 115
Set Up Show command (Slide Show menu), 269-270
    Browsed option, 287
    Show Presenter View option, 330
Set Up Show dialog box, 270
shadow, graphical objects, 175-176
Shadow Settings toolbar, 176
shadows, color adjustment, 175-176
shapes, snap-to-shape feature, 196
shortcuts
    keyboard. *See* keyboard shortcuts
    menus, utilizing, 8
Show Office Assistant command (Help menu), 10
Show popup menu buttons, 259
Show the Office Assistant command (Help menu), 44
single file Web page, creating, 347
slices (pie charts)
    coloring, 108
    exploding, 107
    rotating, 109
slide area, 5
Slide Color Scheme, hyperlinks, 338
Slide Design command (Format menu), 212, 226, 276
Slide Design task pane, 212, 226, 276
Slide Finder dialog box, 253
Slide Layout command (View menu), 134
Slide Layout command (Format menu), 34
Slide Layout task pane, 17, 62-63
Slide Master, 211
    animation, 290-292
    default colors, changing, 212-213
    editing, 219
    font, replacing, 218
    footers, inserting, 224-225
    gradient fills
        creating, 214-215
        two colors, 216-217

graphics, adding, 223
  multiple, 221
  templates, 226-227
  text, changing default, 222
  Title Master, inserting, 220
  view, 219
slide miniature, 198
slide scroll bar, 5
slide short view buttons, 5
Slide Show buttons, 5, 258
Slide Show command (View menu), 31, 258
Slide Show menu commands
  Action Button, 260
    Custom option, 261
    Return option, 262
  Custom Animation, 280
  Custom Shows, 263
  Hide Slide, 257
  Rehearse Timings, 270
  Set Up Show, 269-270
    Browsed option, 287
    Show Presenter View option, 330
  Slide Transition, 269, 274
slide shows
  action buttons, 260-261
  agenda slide, 265-266
  annotating slide, 267-268
  custom shows
    creating, 263
    viewing, 264
  displaying, 258
  navigating to slide, 259
  navigation, 258
  organizing, 256-257
  previewing in Web Browser, 348-349
  rehearsing, 270
  return buttons, 262
  showing on another computer, 306-310
  speaker notes, 271
  Viewer, 313
  viewing, 31
Slide Sorter command (View menu), 29, 244, 251
Slide Sorter toolbar, 246
Slide Sorter view, 29
  presentation, inserting, 253-254
  slide range, 325
  slides
    copying, 248-249
    copying between presentations, 251-252
    deleting, 250
    reordering, 247
  summary slides, 241, 246
  utilizing, 244
  zoom, 245
Slide Thumbnail view, xv
slide thumbnails, 5
Slide Transition command (Slide Show menu), 269, 274
Slide Transition task pane, 274
slides
  agenda, 265-266
  annotating, 267-268

charts. *See* charts
copying, Slide Sorter view, 248-252
deleting, 235-236, 250
displaying slide show, 258
global changes. *See* global changes
graphical objects. *See* graphical objects
hiding, 250, 256-257
inserting presentations, 253-254
navigating to slides, 259
pie charts. *See* pie charts
placeholders, 35-37
preview in grayscale, 323
printing, 324-325
rearranging, 235-236, 256-257
reordering, Slide Sorter view, 247
summary, Slide Sorter view, 246
tables. *See* tables
text. *See* text
transitions, 274-275
Slides from Files command (Insert menu), 253
Slides from Outline command (Insert menu), 238
smart tags, xviii, 42
Smart Tags command (Tools menu), 42
snap-to-shape, graphical objects, 196
sound
  CDs, 300-301
  icon, hiding, 299
  movie clips
    adding, 298-299
    inserting, 294-295
    playback, 296-297
Sound Object command (Edit menu), 309
sounds, Clip Organizer, 302-303
spacing, graphical objects, 200
speaker notes
  adding to slides, 330-331
  printing, 333
Speaker Notes command (Screen menu), 271
Speaker Notes dialog box, 271
special effects, animation
  bulleted list, 279-281
  charts, 288-289
  enhancements, 282-285
  modification, 278
  Slide Master, 290-292
  transitions, 274-275
  triggers, 286-287
  utilizing, 276-277
spell checker
  misspelled words, 40
  presentation check, 40
Spelling and Style command (Tools menu), 40
  Check Style option, 44
  Style Options option, 45
Spelling command (Tools menu), 40
Spelling dialog box, 40-41
stacking, graphical objects, 208
Standard toolbars, 7
Start menu commands, Control Panel, 312, 322

INDEX

style, text slides
   inconsistencies, 44
   preferences, 45
Style Checker, 43
Style Options (Tools menu), 45
Style Options dialog box, 45
sub-types, chart, 67-68
summary slides
   creating, 240-241
   Slide Sorter view, 246
Symbol dialog box, 47

T

Table AutoFormat command (Table menu), 155
Table AutoFormat dialog box, 155
Table command
   Format menu, 146
   Insert menu, 135
Table menu commands
   Delete Columns, 141
   Delete Rows, 141
   Formula, 158
   Insert, 152
   Insert Rows Above, 140
   Insert Rows Below, 140
   Table AutoFormat, 155
tables
   borders
      deleting, 145-146
      drawing, 147
      erasing, 147
      formatting, 144
   cells
      aligning text, 150-151
      selection, 137
      shading, 148-149
   columns
      deleting, 141
      inserting, 140
      width adjustment, 138
   inserting slide, 134-135
   rows
      deleting, 141
      height adjustment, 139
      inserting, 140
   text
      entering, 136
      formatting, 142-143
   word tables
      autoformatting, 155-156
      formulas, 157-158
      inserting, 152-154
Tables and Borders command (View menu), 135
target diagrams, 124
Task Pane command (View menu), 14, 62
   Slide Layout option, 17, 134
task panes, xix, 5
   Clip Art task pane, 302
   Custom Animation task pane, 9, 278-280
   Insert Clip Art task pane, 185

options, 5
Research Task pane, xvi
scroll bar, 5
Slide Design task pane, 212, 226, 276
Slide Layout task pane, 17, 62-63
Slide Transition task pane, 274
utilizing, 9
templates
   global change, 226-227
   names, 5
   selection, 16
text
   AutoCorrect, 41
   boxes, 36
   bullets
      placement, 49
      shape selection, 47-48
   Change Case command, 43
   charts
      boxes, 128
      formatting, 92
   color, 51-52
   copying format attributes, 57
   cutting, 38
   data label, formatting, 106
   drag and drop, 39
   effects, 51-52
   fonts
      anti-aliasing, xvii
      changing, 50
   formatting
      displaying, 237
      hiding, 237
      placeholder, 54
   global change, default change, 222
   layout selection, 34
   line spacing, 55-56
   numbering list automatically, 46
   paragraph
      alignment, 53
      spacing, 55-56
   pasting, 38
   placeholders, 35
      copying, 37
      moving, 37
      resizing, 37
   smart tag, 42
   spell checker, 40
   style
      inconsistencies, 44
      preferences, 45
   tables
      aligning, 150-151
      entering, 136
      formatting, 142-143
Text Box tool (Drawing toolbar), 36
textures
   data series, 80-81
   fills, 172-173
three-dimensional charts, z-axis, 61

thumbnails, slide, 5
tick marks, 61, 88
Title Case option, 43
titles
    bars, 5
    chart, inserting, 69
    placeholders, summary slide, 246
Toggle Case option, 43
toggle tab/outline view, 5
toolbars, 5
    Diagram, 124
    displaying, 7
    drawing, 5
    Grayscale View, 323
    Handout Master View, 326
    utilizing, 7
    Web, 348
Toolbars command (View menu), 7
    Drawing option, 36, 126, 159
    Drawing Toolbar option, 73
    Formatting option, 57
    Outlining option, 28, 233
        Collapse All, 235
        Summary Slide, 240
    Picture option, 207
    Tables and Borders option, 135
    Web option, 348
Tools menu commands
    AutoCorrect Options, 42
    Customize (Options), 7
    Options
        General option, 309
        Save option, 308
        Security option, 319
        Spelling and Style option, 44
    Spelling, 40
    Search, 174
Top Border border buttons, 145
Transitions, 30 274-275
triggers, animation, 286-287

U-V

undo, utilizing, 11
Undo command (Edit menu), 11, 141
Ungroup command (Draw menu), 201
URLs, creating hyperlinks, 338
user-defined charts, applying, 98

value axis (y-axis), 61
    formatting numbers, 91
    scaling, 89-90
Venn diagrams, 124
videos
    Clip Organizer, 302-303
    movie clips
        adding sound, 298-299
        inserting, 294-295
        playback, 296-297

View menu commands
    Color/Grayscale, 323
    Grids and Guides, 194
    Header and Footer, 224, 326
    Master
        Handout Master option, 326
        Notes Master option, 332
        Slide Master option, 219
    Normal, 27, 198, 230
    Notes Page, 271, 330
    Ruler, 49, 194
    Slide Show, 31, 258
    Slide Sorter, 29, 244, 251
    Task Pane, 14, 17, 62, 134
    Toolbars, 7, 135
        Drawing option, 126, 159
        Drawing Toolbar option, 73
        Formatting option, 57
        Outlining option, 28, 233
        Picture option, 207
        Web option, 348
    Zoom, 197, 245
Viewer utility, xvi, 313
viewing slide shows, 31
views. *See* Normal view; Outline view; Slide Sorter view
visible grid, xviii

W

WAV files, embedding, 303
Web
    browsers, previewing slide show, 348-349
    designing Web page, 343
    linking presentations to Web site, 337-340
    saving presentations, 341-342, 344-347
    toolbar, 348
Web Page Preview command (File menu), 347
Web sites, Microsoft, 336
Windows Clipboard, xvii
Windows Media Player, support, xvi
Windows menu command, Arrange All, 251
Wingdings, 48
Word tables
    autoformatting, 155-156
    formulas, 157-158
    inserting, 152-154

X-Z

x-axis (category axis), 61
y-axis (value axis), 61
z-axis, 61
Zapf Dingbats, 48
zoom
    graphical objects, 197
    Slide Sorter view, 245
Zoom command (View menu), 197, 245
Zoom dialog box, 197
Zoom option (View menu), 131